Frontispiece: Lépicié's engraving (Bibliothèque Nationale, Paris) of a painting by ...rdin (Louvre). The painting, when originally exhibited in 1737, was entitled "Un ...miste dans son laboratoire," but in 1753, when it was again exhibited, the title was ...nged to "Un philosophe occupé de sa lecture."

Between the Library
and the Laboratory

THE LANGUAGE OF CHEMISTRY
IN EIGHTEENTH-CENTURY FRANCE

Wilda C. Anderson

The Johns Hopkins University Press
BALTIMORE AND LONDON

This book has been brought to publication with
the generous assistance of the
Andrew W. Mellon Foundation.

The Johns Hopkins University Press, Baltimore, Maryland 21218
The Johns Hopkins Press Ltd., London

*The paper in this book is acid-free and meets the guidelines for
permanence and durability of the Committee on Production
Guidelines for Book Longevity of the Council on Library Resources.*

Library of Congress Cataloging in Publication Data

Anderson, Wilda C.
Between the library and the laboratory.

Bibliography: pp. 183–88
Includes index.
1. French prose literature—18th century—History and
criticism. 2. Lavoisier, Antoine Laurent, 1743–1794.
3. Macquer, Pierre Joseph, 1718–1784. 4. Enlightenment.
5. Chemistry—Philosophy. 6. Chemistry—France—History
—18th century. 7. Literature and science—France.
8. France—Intellectual life—18th century. I. Title.
PQ618.A5   1984   194   84-47942
ISBN 0-8018-3229-2 (alk. paper)

CONTENTS

ACKNOWLEDGMENTS

I would like to thank my Hopkins colleagues Josué Harari, Gary Hatfield, Horace Judson, and Ruth Leys for their generous willingness to read various stages of this manuscript and to provide many helpful suggestions. I would also like to thank Hayden White and Jean-Claude Guédon whose feedback was essential to the project.

I have benefited from the resources of the Rare Books Library at Cornell University and the Archives de l'Institut de France at the Bibliothèque Mazarine in Paris. Much of the time for rewriting the draft was made possible by a grant from the American Council of Learned Societies.

I would like to acknowledge a special debt to Carol Weinreich, Jim Jones, and above all, to William Winn of the Johns Hopkins University Computing Center for their tireless effort to develop and modify text editing programs that made the production of this manuscript so much simpler and faster, and for their cheerful willingness to spend the time necessary to teach and advise a novice computer user.

William Sisler, my editor at the Johns Hopkins University Press, was unstinting in his support and encouragement, and the manuscript is greatly improved thanks to the patient efforts of copy editors Caroline Moser and Mary Louise Kenney, to whom I express my appreciation.

Between the Library and the Laboratory

CHAPTER 1

Introduction:
Speaking about Science

ALTHOUGH ANTOINE-LAURENT LAVOISIER IS THOUGHT OF PRIMARILY as a chemist, he was also a philosopher, specifically a philosopher in the French Enlightenment. French philosophy from the time of the Port-Royal *Logique* had been preoccupied with the relationship between "language and the world," that is, between the symbols of a language and the objects they signify. Whether writing about logic, literature, or chemistry, they persistently returned to this problem. Lavoisier not only was no exception to this bent, but he was among the most ardent to embody it. It is within this development that Lavoisier's works must be read.

A good deal of the philosophers' debates concerned the nature of language, of rhetoric, and of literary invention, and their role in the production of knowledge of all types. Lavoisier was necessarily a writer as well as an experimentalist. As a writer he ranged far beyond obviously chemical subjects. By combining experimentation and writing, we shall see, he played a powerful role in the development of the Enlightenment epistemology. I shall not address such questions as whether or not Lavoisier was the one who discovered oxygen. The question cannot be resolved— not because the historical facts are unknown, but because the meanings of key terms, of *oxygen* and, at another level, of *discovery,* have changed too much. Furthermore, the changes were set in motion by Lavoisier's work—by the reform of chemical nomenclatures, and even more by his invention of norms, of standardized structures, for scientific argument. Curiously, though today he is celebrated for the revision of chemical terminology, others in fact initiated that reform: Lavoisier took control of their enterprise as a weapon in his larger campaign. Thus, even while working within the epistemological context, he displaced and reorganized it. His most fundamental innovations transformed how one presents, how one *argues,* scientific knowledge, and how, as a result, one develops and transmits it. The transformation of the terms and structures of scientific discussion had consequences beyond chemistry—consequences that Lavoisier himself did not foresee and that indeed led to his becoming estranged, toward the end of his life, from the type of scientific argument he himself had set in motion.[1]

Existing biographies and scientific interpretations of Lavoisier do not isolate the kinds of questions I wish to pose.[2] They approach his work from the point of view of the history of science, and see it in the context of the development of chemical thought. My special interest is not in the development of chemical thought *per se.* Rather, I would like to pursue something different: a literary analysis of a group of related texts, mostly about chemical subjects, from the last half of the eighteenth century in France. I will treat these writings as works from the heart of the French Enlightenment that not only debate, but which also attempt to test, theories about how language operates. Because they explicitly address problems about the structure of language, they are usually regarded as philosophical or scientific. However, they may also be approached as literary writings. This does not mean, of course, that I equate scientific writing with literature, in any of the commonly held meanings of the latter term. These texts are not fiction. Moreover, the introduction of literary procedures into a text does not undermine the attempt to develop and to transmit reliable knowledge. Nonetheless, their stated concern with the relationship between language and knowledge leads them to be more "literary" than is the case with modern scientific writing: much of the serious intellectual work in them is accomplished precisely through sophisticated rhetorical and literary maneuvers.

In order to dissect these procedures I have focused on describing the

1. Michel Foucault argues the practical distinction between the content of a discourse and its imposition of a style or procedure of thought in "Qu'est-ce qu'un auteur?" *Bulletin de la société française de philosophie,* July-September 1969, 73–104, and the later, extended version in English translation in *Textual Strategies,* ed. Josué Harari (Ithaca: Cornell University Press, 1979), 141–60. Foucault holds up Marx and Freud as "founders of discursivity." They are "fundamental" or indirect authors whose work defines the theoretical field rather than the historical knowledge in a discipline. Foucault specifically exempts the discourse of the natural sciences from the influence of such epistemologically organizing or revolutionizing figures, but cases like Lavoisier's seem to prove him to have been selective in his vision.

2. The canonical biographies are Marcellin Berthelot, *La Révolution chimique: Lavoisier* (Paris: Alcan, 1890); Maurice Daumas, *Lavoisier: Théoricien et expérimentateur* (Paris: PUF, 1955); and Henry Guerlac, *Antoine-Laurent Lavoisier: Chemist and Revolutionary* (New York: ACLS, 1975). Two other important works are Guerlac's *Lavoisier—The Crucial Year: The Background and Origin of His First Experiments on Combustion in 1772* (Ithaca: Cornell University Press, 1961), and François Dagognet's *Tableaux et langages de la chimie* (Paris: Seuil, 1969).

texts in terms of a number of literary and rhetorical dimensions. These include the following: the logical development of the arguments, the construction of semantic fields (that is, the introduction of key terms either through allusion and juxtaposition, or through chains of interrelated definitions), and the use of literary devices (such as analogy, metaphor, or imagery) and conventions (such as the adoption of the format of a particular literary genre to set up a desired relationship of the reader to the text).

The authors that I am studying use these tools in conjunction with each other to provide, to reinforce, sometimes even to undercut the stated intended effect on the reader. I reiterate that the type of analysis I am applying to these texts does not necessarily undermine the trustworthiness of the knowledge they present. In some extreme cases, in fact, the literary operations are the ones that actually deliver the useful knowledge to the reader.

This kind of analysis presents a different picture of the way the knowledge acquired by the reader of these texts is transmitted by and dependent on the verbal constructs that embody it. Rather than reading these texts "minimally"—rather than trying to extract the essence and paraphrase it (for example, by restating experimental findings in modern chemical notation)—I am trying to reestablish the weight of the contemporary intellectual context, which they draw on for clusters of terms, for tools, and for rhetorical procedures. It is then possible to begin distinguishing the ways that the different authors adopt what appears on the surface to be the same position in order to produce very different types of knowledge. In the French Enlightenment, this is particularly useful, because the explicit program of the *philosophes* is so tightly linked to a seemingly simplistic and banal theory of the relationship of language to knowledge, that it can be difficult to take the individual texts seriously on their own terms.

I shall discuss Lavoisier in comparison to Enlightenment figures both literary, particularly Diderot, and philosophical, particularly Condillac, who were pursuing the issues Lavoisier raised. The crucial figure, though, who reveals the nature of the generation of scientific knowledge as a result of discursive procedures (by *discursive* procedures I mean the tools of poetic innovation, of rhetoric in the largest sense, as well as the standard tools of logical exposition), is another chemist, contemporary with Lavoisier and then well known, Pierre-Joseph Macquer.

Such a choice is not without its difficulties. Macquer was a respected chemical theoretician whose work needs to be studied in depth on its own merits in the context of the chemical debates precipitated by the *Encyclopédie*. It would be interesting to elaborate the interconnections between his development of a theory of chemical epistemology and his battles with Rouelle and Venel over the place of Newtonianism in the theory of chemical affinities. But for two reasons, I shall not engage this subject beyond a strategic minimum.

First, in strictly scientific terms, Macquer and Lavoisier were unquestionably opponents concerning their chemical theories and professional alliances. But seen within the larger intellectual context, they have much more in common: they both embody that peculiar phenomenon known as the Enlightenment *philosophe*. For these philosophers, it is the founding fact of their program that the structure of knowledge is the only order that can be relied upon to reproduce the order inherent in Nature. Out of this global theory of knowledge can be generated many parallel disciplines such as metaphysics, chemistry, political theory, literature, and ethics. But none carries its full intellectual weight outside the context of the privileged and general symmetry between knowledge and nature. An Enlightenment philosopher is the person who recognizes this fact and who attempts to determine his actions in accordance with it, who therefore understands his specialized work as a subset of the larger field of Enlightenment philosophy. Because all disciplines derive from the same general structure of knowledge, they have similar epistemological configurations. Hence the Enlightenment philosopher sees work in his field as having resonances with or consequences for work in other disciplines. This is a predisciplinary attitude, not an interdisciplinary attitude. Even more, a refusal to separate the domains of thought and action underlies the notion of a philosopher's moral and social responsibilities. Whence, perhaps, the intensity of the Age of Reason's belief in its mandate for social change. A statement like Diderot's, in his article "Encyclopédie," that "the goal of every good dictionary is to change the common way of thinking," can allow a modern reader to assign a project like the *Encyclopédie,* or Macquer's *Dictionnaire de chymie,* its broad-ranging predisciplinary weight.

Secondly, I do not discuss Macquer more thoroughly in his chemical context because I do not use him to portray the historical development of the field of chemistry. I am focusing on the structure of Lavoisier's philosophical discourse. A chemical discussion would distract both from my focus on Lavoisier and from the type of problem I am trying to analyze in his work. Moreover, Macquer is probably neither the most central nor the most representative philosophical chemist of the period. However, he is a theoretician whom Lavoisier confronts directly and explicitly in his articles when he is struggling to work out the nature of scientific argument. Macquer is a worthy opponent for Lavoisier, and for my purposes is the very best example of the thought of his time, precisely because he represents a philosophical extreme for chemistry. He tries to push the implications of Enlightenment theories about the relationship of writing and knowledge to their logical limits in a field of study that we no longer define in terms of authorship or literary innovation. It is through Lavoisier's continuation of Macquer's efforts and through the unforeseen results that a paradoxical event takes place. From using its own philosophical tools, a subset of Enlightenment philosophy—the discipline we will eventually call chemistry—becomes conscious of no longer being a part of the overall philosophy, but as having developed into a self-constituting, independent branch of knowledge. Lavoisier's and Macquer's attempts to apply in good faith the underlying definition of philosophy as the unifying foundation of all ordered knowledge results in the dismantling of the very theory of language that made such a project comprehensible. The universal philosophy of the Enlightenment splits into a myriad of self-sufficient disciplines.

In order to demonstrate my hypothesis, I will ask the reader to follow a detailed textual analysis of the work of Macquer for the first half of this book. A discussion of his work allows me to set out the complex context in which the self-effacing statements of Lavoisier concerning scientific argument will once again be audible.

In order to place my argument in a light in which it will seem more natural, it is necessary to make a small introductory detour. The figure that long before had set the stage for the Enlightenment's discursive stance toward knowledge was, of course, Descartes. He was originally important for the early Enlightenment explicitly in terms of his theories of matter and motion. Although these were discarded in favor of Newton's, his influence nonetheless persisted in the epistemological ground rules that he had established for speaking within science and for speaking about science for a whole age. A short exposition of his most relevant work in this light, the *Discours de la méthode,* will provide both a preliminary lexicon of the epistemological terms that were the crucial ones for the Enlightenment philosophers and a first sketch of the semantic and logical relationships between these terms. Descartes is also useful in our terms because he allows us to shift our emphasis away from the chemistry itself, to focus on the relationships between rhetorical and epistemological strategies apart from chemical theories, to distinguish and define our own analytic terms, before taking on the interrelationships between chemical theory and epistemological development that become so intertwined in the Enlightenment. He will also help attune the reader to the different type of reading that I will be trying to perform on otherwise familiar texts; the elaboration of Descartes' rhetorical procedures and goals should help to demonstrate my own.

A caveat. The following reading of the *Discours* is biased towards and polarized by the fascination of the late-eighteenth-century French Enlightenment philosophers with language and words and with the project for a "natural" language or rhetorical procedure. It is likely that Descartes would have found this reading through eighteenth-century eyes to be missing the point, even to be antithetical to his ultimate goals. He certainly would have found the emphasis on language and words rather than on ideas and intuited certainties to be heavy-handed. But the reading of the *Discours* I want to present is the one that will eventually allow me to make sense and understand the weight of statements such as Condillac's when he expressed his desire to reconcile Descartes and Locke in a model of science that would be founded in the structure of language.

Even though the substance of the physical, chemical, and biological theories of Descartes was discarded long before the beginning of Lavoisier's chemical revolution, the effect of his scientific writing persisted in the model he provided for a scientific author. To speak about science, about organized knowledge, with any sort of authority at all, seems to have been a nearly impossible task after the skepticism of Montaigne and the late Renaissance. Absolute, fixed, or certain knowledge was not to be found in the domain of the always-suspect commonsense knowledge about the world, nor any longer in its accustomed domain, in the realm of divinely inspired, directly revealed truth.

For much later writers, this will be the resource offered by Descartes: an answer to the question, How can one speak at all about the nature of the physical world? How is knowledge constructed, and who has the authority to speak? Only then can the question be asked, What is the correct rhetorical procedure for speaking? The answer to any one of these questions requires that the other two be answered first; this is what Descartes sets himself up to accomplish in the *Discours de la méthode.*

The *Meditations* and the *Discours de la méthode* both tell the same story, but from a different perspective. The *Discours* presents itself as the simpler, purely autobiographical apology for the process of meditating to reach *certain* knowledge that the *Meditations* will walk the reader through. The two intersect through the tale of the *cogito* and the proofs of the existence of God. But the uses made of this same content are opposed if complementary. They tie together the process of finding truth and then of passing it on, of transmitting it to a reader or listener who accepts the authority of the speaker.

Let us begin first by explicating the title of the *Discours,* for it conveniently sets out most of the terms and implies most of the oppositions that we will be encountering. The full title is *Discours de la méthode pour bien conduire sa raison et chercher la vérité dans les sciences.* Every one of these terms—*discours, méthode, raison, vérité, sciences*—refers to a key idea in the body of the *Discours,* and each term forms part of the definition of the others. The order of terms in the title, moreover, follows the procession of the sections of the *Discours,* and provides us with a selective but penetrating device for probing the central discursive elements and stratagems of Descartes' text.

Discours. We are, as Descartes insists from the very beginning, not in the presence of a tightly structured logical proof nor of a dialectical construction. Descartes is discussing in a literary format, relatively informally, the events of his life that led to the mental experience that he will depict in the *Meditations.* He presents us, not with an argument explicitly aimed at persuading, but merely, so he tells us, with a "fable."[3] His goal is not to impose, but to suggest by entertaining, to carry on a conversation. Of course, on the one hand Descartes' motives for such a speaking position are purely rhetorical, as he gets behind his readers' defenses by establishing an ostensibly nonpedagogical, conversational format.[4] Second, as I will discuss later in more detail, this nondidactic attitude will not even allow him to suggest openly that his readers observe his past life and imitate it *if they so desire*—"si mon ouvrage m'ayant assez plu, je vous en fais voir ici le modèle, ce n'est pas pour cela que je veuille conseiller à personne de l'imiter" (II.15) [3]—but in fact, he is inviting them to read the *Meditations.* He is thus putting them in a position to discover true knowledge for themselves (the only way it can be obtained), rather than by having it explained to them (part II).

Méthode. Descartes' tactic here is a subtle move. By downplaying his direct role in the transmission of knowledge, he undermines his predecessors without having to meet them on their own grounds. As in the *Recherche de la vérité,* he does not need either to confront or to disprove the content of their theories at all, since he has abolished the authority of their very methods of arguing. They constantly justify their arguments by finding the same argument in the work of their own predecessors; for Descartes, nothing could be more irrelevant. Rather, his objective is to set a barrier between us and prior rhetorical methods in order to prepare the ground for a new beginning that will *"bien* conduire la raison." He will not define his own method until his discussion of reason.

La raison. "La raison," as presented in part II and defended in part III, is a natural and innate method which provides the ordered linking together

3. As he reminds the reader in part I, a fable is a story, more or less truthful in this case, intended to impart a moral; in other words, it is intended to be useful. "Mais ne proposant cet écrit que comme une histoire, ou si vous l'aimez mieux, que comme une fable en laquelle, parmi quelques exemples qu'on peut imiter, on en trouvera peut-être aussi plusieurs autres qu'on aura raison de ne pas suivre, j'espère qu'il sera utile à quelques-uns, sans être nuisible à personne, et que tous me sauront gré de ma franchise" [1]. Bracketed arabic numerals following French quotations both in the text and in the notes refer to their numbered English translations in Appendix D. René Descartes, *Discours de la méthode pour bien conduire sa raison et chercher la vérité dans les sciences* (1637), ed. Etienne Gilson (Paris: Vrin, 1925; reissued 1976) part I, p. 4. Hereafter cited in the text by part and page number.

4. "La lecture de tous les bons livres est comme une conversation avec les plus honnêtes gens des siècles passés qui en ont été les auteurs, et même une conversation étudiée, en laquelle ils ne nous découvrent que les meilleures de leurs pensées" (I.5) [2].

of the minimal truths derived from the analysis of complex problems into their smallest components.[5] The long chain of truths is so convincing that all that is visible is the staggering truth of the components, rather than the process of the original analysis and the choice or judgment that went into their ordering.

> Considérez que, n'y ayant qu'une vérité de chaque chose, quiconque la trouve en sait autant qu'on peut en savoir, et que, par exemple, un enfant instruit en arithmétique, ayant fait une addition suivant les règles, se peut assurer d'avoir trouvé, touchant la somme qu'il examinait, tout ce que l'esprit humain saurait trouver. Car enfin la méthode qui enseigne à suivre le vrai ordre et à dénombrer exactement toutes les circonstances de ce qu'on cherche, contient tout ce qui donne de la certitude aux règles d'arithmétique. (II.21) [5]

The method leads, invisibly, implacably, hiding its own efficacity and authority. But where did it come from? And where did Descartes get these truths; what does he mean by *true*?

La vérité. Here we find ourselves at the heart of the *Discours.* The first three sections can be seen as but a long preamble to part IV, in which truth is defined and therefore the authority for Descartes' method is established. The emplotment of part IV is dense and sophisticated. We have here a shorthand account of the genesis of the project that will later develop into the *Meditations.*[6] First Descartes evacuates his mind.[6] This, of course, is precisely the kind of search for a privileged and inspired knowledge that Montaigne had warned might, imprudently carried out, result in the unleashing of chimeras, illusions, and other uncontrolled figments of the imagination.[7] But Descartes, in several passages early on in the *Discours* and elsewhere, had already confessed that he found himself to be lacking in imagination (I.2)—so lacking that he had had to abandon his desire to be a poet and settle for being a philosopher!

Now, what drops into his receptive mind is not a blinding divine presence, but the perception of a unit of reason—more precisely, the first possible unit of reason, the *cogito.* The process is described as follows:

5. "Ceux qui ont le raisonnement le plus fort, et qui digèrent [élaborent] le mieux leurs pensées afin de les rendre claires et intelligibles, peuvent toujours le mieux persuader de ce qu'ils proposent, *encore* qu'ils ne parlassent que du bas-breton, et *qu'ils n'eussent jamais appris de rhétorique* et ceux qui ont les inventions les plus agréables et qui les savent exprimer avec le plus d'ornement et de douceur ne laisseraient pas d'être les meilleurs poètes, *encore que l'art poétique leur fût inconnu*" (I.7) [4].

6. Cf., on this point, Roland Barthes, *Sade, Fourier, Loyola* (Paris: Seuil, 1971), 45–80. According to Barthes, this is the well-known procedure of supplicant prayer that is supposed to lead the person praying to a total nullification of his own desires and identity in order to provide a passive, empty, and receptive space in which God will inscribe his message.

7. See the discussion of this topic in M. A. Screech's *Montaigne and Melancholy,* Susquehanna: Susquehanna University Press, 1984.

"*Je pris garde que,* pendant que je voulais ainsi penser que tout était faux, il fallait nécessairement que moi qui le pensais fusse quelquechose; et, remarquant que cette vérité: *je pense, donc je suis,* était si ferme et si assurée que toutes les plus extravagantes suppositions des sceptiques *n'étaient pas capables de l'ébranler,* je jugeais que je pouvais la recevoir sans scrupule pour le premier principe" (IV.32) [6]. This "self that is something" is only and necessarily an embodiment of the act of thinking. How was Descartes able to make this singular observation? He had already hinted in part III that "Dieu nous [a] donné à chacun quelque lumière pour discerner le vrai d'avec le faux" (III.27) [7]. But here the order of the argument is in fact reversed. To paraphrase Descartes in a schematic way: "I see clearly and distinctly this first truth, which is the fact that I think. Hence 'clear and distinct' will be the sign by which I will recognize other truths. Such recognition is more perfect than doubt, hence perfection exists. I am not perfect, therefore this idea does not come from my image of myself, but from that which only is perfect, which is God. Hence God exists. What I have that is perfect, like these clear and distinct ideas, must come from what is perfect, i.e. from God." What is striking here is that this God does not actively manifest himself to Descartes; his existence is derived. Descartes perceives a first truth that *already exists* in his mind; hence the first truth is not deduced from but is prior to the existence of God. Therefore, from an epistemological point of view, the first principle from which all else is derived cannot be the existence of God. Instead, God is derived from the existence of Descartes' mind.

The first, or Cartesian, proof of the existence of God is almost circular: the existence of Descartes' thinking proves the existence of God who made possible the existence of Descartes' thinking. But this restatement leaves out one component: Descartes perceives that he is thinking and then is able to see that act of perception as a fact. In the first proof the act of perception itself is an event, not a logical deduction; it is not derived from anything. Moreover, the clear and distinct idea that he perceived was already there, and therefore we assume at first that this is the originary link, the "premier principe," in the chain of deductive truths. But the object of the second proof is to show where this clear and distinct idea came from, from what it, also, can be in fact derived.

The second proof of the existence of God is a corollary to the first. Baldly stated, it is that God is perfect. The last then states that imperfection, being finite, depends for its continued existence on something else. Finite beings endure because God is continuously creating them. Descartes will use this argument to explain the possibility of the first proof: "Because God at every moment acts to maintain the existence and order of the rest of the objects in the world, all imperfect and hence incapable of existing without his continuous willed action, the first principle of truth which I found in my mind must indeed have been put there and was maintained there by God."

The last argument is necessary to establish the prior existence of this clear and distinct idea in Descartes' mind. He neutralizes in this way the singularity of the perception as an event and incorporates it into the body of the logical argument. Using the tools of the last proof, he can argue that the autobiographical event of the perception is a necessary consequence of the prior existence of the clear and distinct idea. Therefore the first proof can be seen as *effectively* circular, or unassailable on its own logical grounds, only when it is completed by the assertion that continuity results from the last "proof" of the existence of God. Rather than undermining the validity of Descartes' position, the assertion that the proofs are circular—*when put together*—constitutes their rhetorical strength.

Let us argue that this larger circular proof provides him with the only possible model of knowledge that can escape the vulnerability of positions based on experiential knowledge or on the illusion of having received divine revelation. For this circular construct is not merely logical. It is divided between two modes of argumentation: logical exposition and the description of an event. The first sounds like "this is, therefore that must be," whereas the second has connotations of "this is, therefore that must have been."[8]

The formation of this hybrid mode of discourse has allowed Descartes both to use logic to support experiential events and to use the description of those events to support the authority of logic. At the same time, and because of the way it has redefined the necessary conditions for "clear and distinct," absolute and transmissible (rather than ineffable) knowledge, this hybrid discourse has established a new mode of speaking in and about the world.

The consequences of this maneuver are multiple, and they give Descartes several rhetorical advantages:

(1) His system cannot be "disproved" by anyone's questioning the very possibility of an originary logical truth. Anyone attempting to analyze his way back up the chain of ordered truths to find the starting point will

8. Logic and autobiography are woven seamlessly together and support each other in an unbreakable circle. In terms of the autobiographical event being recounted, one perception in the circle must of course have taken place before the others, but not one of the terms can have *logical* precedence over the others. They define and support each other. Remove one term and the logical meaning of the others is also undermined. But although there is no way to get inside the circle to begin to describe it in purely logical terms, the autobiographical mode allows Descartes to narrativize his logical construct, to give a beginning and an end to what would otherwise be an insight as inaccessible as any divine revelation. The logical exposition allows him to perceive his insight himself, but, paradoxically, the transmission of knowledge—its explicability—is in this case linked not to the logical but to the personalized and chronologized mode of exposition made possible by autobiography.

arrive at the circular proof. But once inside it, there is no end point to be questioned. One can go around the circle forever but can never get beyond the confines set by the hybrid argument. One either accepts it on its own grounds or rejects it entirely—which Descartes leaves his reader perfectly free to do by presenting the *Discours* as a fable.

(2) This procedure will work only if the process of self-reeducation is carried out correctly by each reader by himself. The possibility of such an event can be demonstrated to the reader of the *Discours,* but only as an autobiographical, singular event that happened to one man. Hence the *Meditations:* the truth of the experience can be fully transmitted only if the reader goes on to perform the exercise himself, in his own time and place, by reading the *Meditations.*[9] Curiously, Descartes has developed what seems to be an antitutorial pedagogy, a "natural method," a "true logic"; all of these terms were oxymorons prior to the *Discours,* itself an autobiographical fable. Now they are fitting descriptions of an innovative epistemological speaking position.

(3) The circular argument gives Descartes an unassailable justification for claiming that the method he will propose is the *natural method.* In other words, he did not think it up himself. He claims no authorship for his method; he did not contrive it. He was only lucky enough to discover it. Its authority does not derive from his fallible, merely human statements. The relationship of authority to authorship has been dismantled. The author of any statement, from this point on, appears to be the method itself, and the authority that stands behind it is God. We no longer, therefore, have plausible arguments; we have true knowledge. Descartes' method is not only necessary, but it is also sufficient for thinking the truth into existence. We are finally in the domain of scientific rhetoric (another oxymoron). It is a rhetoric which cannot be seen as such because it makes no attempt to persuade: it seeks only to utter truths.

(4) We then confront a crucial point for understanding late Enlightenment scientific argumentation. Descartes has become invisible behind this new narrative procedure. In Part II he had only locally discredited the Renaissance rhetoricians. Here, he has cut his readers off from ever accepting his predecessors at their word because he has made it impossible ever to do so for anyone, including himself. He has used the discursive procedure just elaborated to reinforce the elimination of all other argument structures that might be used to present knowledge. The *Discours,* which began as a fable, ends as a small demonstration of scientific thinking (parts V and VI). Literature transforms itself into autobiography, which turns into science.

9. For a convincing recent reading of the *Meditations* from a similar point of view, see Gary C. Hatfield, "The Senses and the Fleshless Eye: the *Meditations* as Cognitive Exercises." Forthcoming in *Essays on Descartes' Meditations,* ed. Amelie Rorty.

Les sciences. Science is the *chaîne des vérités* (V.40) about any particular
subject matter that will be deducible from these first principles established
in part IV. The content may change from science to science, but the basic
structure of ordered knowledge—for that is what the word *science* means—
will remain the same: that of this natural method.

There is one further consequence that Descartes draws from the divine
authority given to the natural method: "J'ai cru que je ne pouvais tenir
cachées [quelques notions générales sur la physique], sans pécher grande-
ment contre la loi qui nous oblige à procurer autant qu'il est en nous le
bien général de tous les hommes: car elles m'ont fait voir qu'il est possible
de parvenir à des connaissances qui soient fort utiles à la vie" (VI.61) [8].
Scientific knowledge is not just any knowledge. It is useful and *necessary*
knowledge. God put this method into the minds of men in order to allow
them to know the things necessary for survival in the material world.[10]
There is a natural harmony between the processes of science and the
physical structure of the world. The one was designed in order to allow
us to perceive the other.

For Descartes, therefore, philosophers are not merely people who seek
out knowledge for its own sake. They are the chosen instruments of a
divine project. The scientific truths being discovered are not prophetic or
revealed messages from God; they are discovered by each researcher by
himself as he reasons through a problem. At this first level, philosophy
has been secularized. It is secularized at a second level, too: the divinely
designated object of study is no longer a theological issue, but the natural
world. But after designating the subjects to be studied and establishing
the authority of scientific procedure, the God of the *Discours,* like the God
who establishes the laws of motion in the *Principia,* disappears. He is no
longer a necessary component to every argument. Curiously enough, the
result is that, instead of dispensing with ethical questions by dispensing
with theological issues, this definition of a philosopher-scientist implies
the necessary interdependence of philosophy and ethics. Parts V and VI
are technological and medical discussions encoded in an apology for the
usefulness and necessity of Descartes' work. The philosopher replaces the
prophet as the voice of truth and the focus is shifted from an afterlife to
life in this world.

This argument will be amplified and elaborated by seventeenth- and
eighteenth-century thinkers. The French Enlightenment itself can be seen
as the attempt to embody on a larger scale the interdependence of science

10. See Richard B. Carter's argument in *Descartes' Medical Philosophy: The Organic
Solution to the Mind-Body Problem.* (Baltimore: Johns Hopkins University Press, 1983). He
argues that Descartes describes the mind itself as the servant of physical survival, beginning
with passages like VI.62 and ending in the *Traité des passions* (1645–46).

and ethics, and to see an ideal society, in fact, as patterned on the structure of knowledge. The result, as I suggested at the beginning of this introduction, is that epitome of Enlightenment social man, the optimistic, positivist rationalist philosophe.

The various Enlightenment authors to be discussed in the following chapters all work out the consequences—in both their scientific and their philosophical writings (when these can even be distinguished)—of the redefinitions of precisely the terms explicated here in Descartes. Often the results they arrive at are contradictory, but they are all working within basically the same overall epistemic structure. Discourse (rhetoric), method, truth, science—it is precisely these Cartesian terms that will haunt the ensuing discussion of the development of the languages and literature of chemistry from its position as a component of Enlightenment philosophy to its eventual status as a self-sufficient discipline. I shall try to show that the arguments around these concepts underlie what at first appear to be only local scientific questions in the sense that modern historians often use the term. But if one understands "science" as Descartes has generated it, one must immediately realize that for Macquer, Diderot, Condillac, and even Lavoisier, questions concerning the historical priority of specific discoveries, the existence of phlogiston, or the names of oxygen form only the smallest and most visible part of the complex edifice being constructed by Enlightenment philosophers. The stakes are not merely "chemical"; the overriding issues are epistemological, philosophical, and even literary. In the changes that occur between the philosophical chemistry of Macquer and the positivist chemistry of Lavoisier, more than a chemical revolution has been effected. In a curious way, the philosophical revolution begun by Descartes will have been both finally completed and, as a result, superseded.

Given that I will not be dealing with such information at any length later in this essay, it might be useful for the reader to have a few reference points regarding the choice of texts and some information about the two major figures that I shall be discussing.

The texts come from two kinds of sources. Except in very rare cases, I am working either with published treatises or with reports read to the Academy of Sciences. My choice has been guided by the following conditions:

1. They must be recognized as important in the overall scheme of the author's corpus.
2. They must include works that had an impact on the actual practice of chemistry, and not be limited to theoretical position-papers (whether substantive or merely programmatic).

In many cases it will be difficult to distinguish the two. But at any rate, Kuhn's warning that "the relation of prefaces and programmatic writings to substantive science is seldom literal and always problematic"[11] must be taken seriously and developed at length for such an analysis to yield trustworthy results.

A quick biographical excursus:

Pierre Joseph Macquer (1718–84) was a student of G. F. Rouelle and eventually succeeded to Bourdelin's chair in chemistry at the Jardin du roi, which was the major academic post in chemistry, in 1777. He is not known for great or innovative experimentation, but he established a solid reputation as a practical chemist through his developments in the techniques of dyeing and in the introduction of kaolin-based porcelains into France when he was the superintendent of the royal porcelain factory at Sèvres. But above all he is known for two complementary treatises on chemistry—one practical and one theoretical—and for his *Dictionnaire de chymie,* first published in 1766. The second and more important edition of this work, dated 1778, attempted in part to propose a theory which would be a compromise between the old phlogiston theory and the new discoveries of Lavoisier, but it was rapidly made obsolete by the work of the antiphlogistians. He is generally recognized as having been one of the last and most important spokesmen for the chemistry of affinities—the phlogiston theory—that dominated chemistry from around the time of Georg Stahl until the major changes brought about by the French chemists led by Lavoisier toward the end of the eighteenth century.[12] Macquer was not simply a technical chemist. He had ties to the group of chemists that produced the chemical articles for the *Encyclopédie* of Diderot and D'Alembert in the 1750s. He was heavily involved in the intellectual debates surrounding chemical theorizing through his directorship of the *Journal des savants,* which came out emphatically in support of the phlogiston theory. He was also very active in group research projects and in the administrative work of the Academy of Sciences. In his writing and in his polemics he has a clear investment in his literary reputation as well as in his reputation as a man of science, and he goes to some lengths to defend his own style and to argue that style is an important indication of the social and ideological sensitivity of a writer or thinker. The *Dictionnaire de chymie,* which may be seen by modern eyes as a lesser chemical achievement, was in fact the work to which Macquer was the most attached, and

11. Thomas S. Kuhn, "The Relations between History and the History of Science," in *The Essential Tension: Selected Studies in Scientific Tradition and Change.* (Chicago: University of Chicago Press, 1977), 133.

12. See Jean-Paul Contant, *L'Enseignement de la chimie au Jardin royal des plantes de Paris* (Cahors: Coneslant, 1952); Leslie J.-M. Coleby, *The Chemical Studies of P. J. Macquer* (London: n.p., 1938); and Douglas McKie, "Macquer, the First Lexicographer of Chemistry," *Endeavour* 16, no. 63 (July 1957): 133–36.

which he saw as being his real philosophical contribution to the *cité scientifique* of the Enlightenment. In it and through his other writing he develops a model of the chemist as the ideal citizen, whose attitude toward the rest of society is determined and prescribed by his identity as a philosopher.

Antoine-Laurent Lavoisier (1743–94) was among the first to argue the significance of quantifying experimental procedures and of reducing the importance of purely qualitative analysis; he refined the study of pneumatic chemistry, developed the rudiments of thermodynamics in his study of heat capacities with Laplace, arguably discovered several aeriform elements— most notably oxygen—and presented the first sketches for a general table of the chemical elements in his *Traité élémentaire de chimie* of 1789. He is traditionally hailed as the father of modern chemistry. Through his application of quantitative methods of analysis to very practical problems such as the analysis of the various mineral waters of France, the proposal of a system of lighting for Paris and the setting up of a series of tests to regulate the quality of tobacco being sold by the state monopoly, Lavoisier proved himself to be a gifted industrial chemist as well. He was for many years the head of the Salpétrière in Paris and one of the most influential members of the Academy of Sciences, including a period as the perpetual secretary, up until its dissolution in 1793. He was executed as a member of the General Tax Farm during the Reign of Terror in April 1794, but his chemical theories and discoveries served as the basis of the "New French Chemistry," as Fourcroy called it, until at least the advent of Dalton's work.

In an Enlightenment context, Lavoisier's biography is even more striking than Macquer's. He was an outspoken and fairly flamboyant public figure who took his social position as a man of knowledge with great seriousness. He invested the money that he had inherited from his mother in a share of a seat on the General Tax Farm and married the fourteen-year-old daughter of the tax farmer who held the majority interest. Miss Paulze, who was a student of the painter Jacques-Louis David, turned her social, artistic, and lucrative endowments to the single-minded service of her husband's none-too-minor ambitions, and together they kept a kind of *salon* and held famous dinners to which the most significant European and American men of science were eager to come. Their social lives jelled a kind of permanent active scientific conversation around them, a permanent intellectual ferment. Lavoisier made little distinction between his public and private life—all was cast in terms of his intellectual identity— and his many public works, such as running the tobacco and saltpeter bureaucracies, or his institution of agricultural experiments and public schools in the wardship of his tax farm seat were logical consequences of his definition of himself as an Enlightenment physiocrat. Lavoisier enriched himself through the tax farm to pay the salaries and support many of the public projects and expensive experiments of the Academy of Sciences, and in the hectic and chaotic days just before its dissolution, he was almost its sole financial support. Lavoisier was also a great polemicist both in person and in his writings, even the most technical of which show a constant concern for the wider philosophical and sometimes social implications of his innovations. One of the last projects that he was involved with was an attempt, with Condorcet and Lakanal, to revolutionize the educational system of France to reflect and institutionalize the overall structure of knowledge as the Enlightenment understood it, from the elementary schools up to the Institute of Sciences, which would replace the Academy of Sciences, at the top. In this way, society would eventually be incorporated into a *cité scientifique* with the Institute, a sort of living *Encyclopédie,* directing the intellectual development of the country.

PART I

THE LIBRARY
OF CHEMISTRY

CHAPTER 2

Rhetorical and
Chemical Figures

MACQUER PREFACES HIS DICTIONARY WITH THE TRADITIONAL SHORT history of chemistry. As do many of the other histories of chemistry of the time (those of Scheele, Rouelle, and especially Torbern Bergman), he makes use of standardized *topoi:* in the prehistory of modern science, there existed many figures whose names come down to us still through legend, but of their work nothing substantive is known. Certain practical chemical arts had been invented by craftsmen and artisans, but no philosopher appeared to weld the knowledge of the artisans into a science. The medieval alchemists, although ostensibly "philosophical" rather than practical, did not fulfill this role; on the contrary, it was only with the passing of alchemy that chemistry could become the great science that it had always had the potential to be.

This history was not intended to be a factual description of the history of chemistry, and one does not gain from it any understanding of the technical subject matter of chemical research. But it is far from being an irrelevant adjunct to a reference work. It has a carefully worked-out rhetorical structure, one that provides both an initial description of the field and a justification for the claims to be made in various places in the body of the *Dictionnaire.*

The past is presented as a long, slow development towards a utopian future in which chemistry will have attained the status of a science by combining disparate technical practices under a coherent philosophy. However, it would be a mistake to perceive this development as the continuous or irreversible evolution of a clearly reasoned discipline. Chemistry for Macquer is not yet a self-transforming philosophical tradition, becoming, as it progresses, more complex and efficient in its ability to answer the primary technical questions which create at the same time the foundations for and the goal of the research. On the contrary. Chemistry is unified only through the illusion produced by the existence of a *name* for a discipline which does not yet exist. The image Macquer uses to describe this evolution is not that of progress along a line, but that of a three-dimensional map of the subject matter in which the natural philosophers wander about. The sum of all of their paths should eventually circumscribe a hypothetical or potential field of inquiry—chemistry. "L'histoire des sciences est en même-temps celle des travaux, des succès & des écarts de ceux qui les ont cultivées; elle indique les obstacles qu'ils ont eu à surmonter, & les fausses-routes dans lesquelles ils se sont egarés. Notre objet est de mettre *sous les yeux* les différents états par lesquels cette science a passé, les révolutions qu'elle a eprouvées, les circonstances qui ont favorisé ou retardé ses progrès" [9].[1]

The dependence on spatial metaphors and multiple subjects implies simultaneous events and an overview of unifying events that seem to be unrelated by cause and effect. There may be many obstacles in the voyagers' way; they may take wrong paths and have to retrace their steps several times; other dangers on the way may threaten or even interrupt the journey. It is by using such an analytical space that simultaneous opposing or unrelated lines of development can be analyzed by the historian.

The idea of a spatial development is more profoundly linked to Macquer's concept of chemistry than this common eighteenth-century image may at first suggest. Later, I will examine the organization of the articles in the *Dictionnaire* in order to show that Macquer's concept of the "state of the art" can be presented and understood only in spatial terms. But before we examine the content of the science as he perceived it, it helps to understand how Macquer derived the existence of a science that even he said did not yet exist.

The main forces that created chemistry were originally social ones. At the beginning of the world mankind was faced with the necessity to survive; hence "les premiers hommes nécessiteux ont été, par cela même, les premiers artisans" *(Dict.,* xvi) [10]. To this end, they invented the arts; they used various "chemical" practices to create material objects. These objects had two functions. The first was simply to serve as a tool for its maker. The second, which surpassed in importance but depended on the first, was to serve as a commodity to be traded for other artisans' products. Thus these objects constituted the basis of an economic system and involved the artisans in a social network. Macquer very clearly makes the point, however, that these artisans were not scientists according to his definition.

1. Pierre Joseph Macquer, *Dictionnaire de chymie,* 2d ed. (Paris: Lacombe, 1778), 1:xiii; my emphasis. Hereafter cited as *Dict.* All references in this chapter are to volume 1. References in later chapters to the 1766 edition (Paris: Lacombe) have the year indicated.

They were practitioners of the chemical arts. By *arts,* Macquer means
something similar to *crafts.* Arts were applied for the sake of the product;[2]
they held no intellectual interest for the artisans. "Ils ont saisi les principes
des arts par un effort naturel, bien différent de ce raisonnement perfec-
tionné qui peut seul enfanter les sciences & qui ne s'est formé que dans
l'espace d'une longue suite de siècles" (xvi) [11]. Any thinking about the
process of creating a given product was the result of pure accident or a
freakish curiosity and was likely to be aimed only at the improvement of
the product's quality. In Macquer's eyes, a necessary consequence of this
attitude was that the artisans neglected to write down their empirical
knowledge. In fact, the apprenticeship system was based on a *lack* of books,
as the knowledge existed unsystematized (and thus by Macquer's definition
"naturally") in the mind of the artisan and could be transmitted to his
apprentice only through direct example as each problem presented itself.
"Avant l'invention de l'écriture, l'apprentis ne pratiquoit que ce qu'il apprenoit
de son maître par une tradition orale & transmettoit de même ses connoissances à celui qui lui succédoit; comme le font encore nos ouvriers, qui
n'écrivent rien, quoique vivant tant de siècles après l'invention de l'écriture" (xvii) [12].

Macquer here breaks from considering the strictly chemical arts and
moves to the general case of all of the practical arts and professions, for
the next step, although it had taken place in other fields, had not occurred
in chemistry. Macquer has to describe it by analogy.

The invention of writing did not automatically lead to the systematization
of the arts, as Macquer demonstrates by pointing to the continued existence
of illiterate artisans. But in the legends, he tells us, we find those other
persons who, using the tools provided by language, and especially written
language, operated on the "silent" knowledge of the artisans. By virtue of
their wisdom and knowledge, a privileged class of people came into being:
the priests and kings who, as a result, could have an overview of the
"connoissances humaines" developed by the artisans. They participated
by way of language products rather than by way of economic products in
the social organization.

C'est à cette heureuse époque qu'on peut véritablement rapporter celle de
l'accroissement des connoissances humaines, & la naissance des sciences ...
[ils] recueillirent avec soin toutes les connoissances qui pouvoient étendre &
orner l'esprit humain, en firent l'objet de leurs recherches, les accrurent en
les méditant & en les comparant, les rédigerent par écrit, se les communi-

2. This traditional distinction and its origins in Greek medicine are discussed at length
in Owsei Temkin's "Greek Medicine as Science and Craft," in his *Double Face of Janus and
Other Essays in the History of Medicine* (Baltimore: Johns Hopkins University Press, 1978),
137–53.

querent; en un mot, jetterent vraiment les fondemens de la philosophie. Ces hommes précieux furent les Prêtres et les Rois d'un peuple assez sage pour leur accorder ses respects. (xviii) [13]

A systematizing overview was turned onto the heretofore "silent" arts. Their organization took place from the starting point of an amorphous collection of facts, contiguous in their existence but not related to each other. He who had the overview, who was able to see and thus to compare all of the elements at once, who had "[le génie d'appercevoir] d'un même coup d'oeil la multitude immense des phénomènes chymiques" (xxxiii) [14], was able to unify them into a coherent system: "Il est certain que ce que nous appelons *science,* est l'étude & la connoissance des rapports que peuvent avoir ensemble un certain nombre de faits" (xv) [15].[3]

Macquer has used this structure before, at the beginning of the preface: it is the image he uses to describe the history of chemistry, and the similarity is not gratuitous. The spatial metaphor of the map or territory, obviously a visual figure, is homologous with the common eighteenth-century formulation of systematic knowledge as resulting from a unifying overview turned onto a "countryside" or a "field" of knowledge. The components or elements of a scene, as they are simultaneously available to perception, are the figure for the prerequisite object of *analysis.* As I shall discuss in greater detail later, analysis was commonly accepted as the first and most natural procedure for the human mind to follow in coming to grips with its environment. The abbé de Condillac's definition is the most succinct: "Analyser n'est donc autre chose qu'observer, dans un ordre successif, les qualités d'un objet, afin de leur donner dans l'esprit l'ordre simultané dans lequel elles existent. C'est ce que la nature nous fait faire à tous" [17].[4] By extension, analysis was the privileged procedure to follow in investigating the material world. It was also both the proper

3. An even more precise description of this process is found in the article "Phlogistique": "Tous ceux qui connoissent en détail les phénomènes des opérations de la Chymie, & qui ont le génie de cette science, c'est-à-dire, la faculté d'appercevoir & de comparer les rapports que ces phénomènes ont entr'eux" *(Dict.,* 3:121) [16].

4. Etienne Bonnot de Condillac, *La Logique; ou, Les premiers développemens de l'Art de Penser, ouvrage élémentaire, que le Conseil préposé aux Ecoles palatines avoit demandé et qu'il a honoré de son approbation* (Geneva: n.p., 1785), 19. Hereafter cited in the text. The "object" that Condillac is describing, in a highly imaginative passage, is the view of a countryside from the window of a castle on a hill.

In general, I will use definitions from the *Logique.* It would also have been possible, in terms of Macquer, to refer back to the *Essay Concerning Human Understanding* of Locke or to the *Encyclopédie* of Diderot and D'Alembert for definitions of such major terms as *idea, perception, generalizations, abstraction,* and even for descriptions of the *scène de l'analyse,* as the basic concepts are part of a long and widespread tradition. Macquer had read Locke and the other philosophers who make use of the concept of analysis. The work I am using here, Condillac's *Logique,* was not printed until after the second edition of the

format to follow in attempting to comprehend one's own thinking and in communicating the results to others. Again, in Condillac's words:

> Il en est de même de la vue de l'esprit. J'ai à la fois présentes un grand nombre de connoissances qui me sont devenues familières; je les vois toutes, mais je ne les démêle pas également. Pour voir d'une manière distincte tout ce qui s'offre à la fois dans mon esprit, il faut que je decompose comme j'ai décomposé ce qui s'offrait à mes yeux; il faut que j'analyse ma pensée.
>
> Cette analyse ne se fait pas autrement que celle des objets extérieurs ... *Dans l'un et l'autre cas, il faut tout voir à la fois. (La Logique,* 19; my emphasis) [18]

Further on, he adds: "Pour parler d'une manière à se faire entendre, il faut concevoir & rendre ses idées dans l'ordre analytique, qui décompose et recompose chaque pensée. Cet ordre est le seul qui puisse leur donner toute la clarté & toute la précision dont elles sont susceptibles; & comme nous n'avons pas d'autre moyen pour nous instruire nous-mêmes, nous n'en avons pas d'autres pour communiquer nos connoissances" (22) [19]. The view, the scene of analysis, must first be analyzed: it must be decomposed into elements which are then organized according to their relationships to each other in such a way that the scene is reproduced in the mind. It is then set into language.

Inversely, thought, perceived as a procedure of analysis, is possible only through the medium of language, for language itself is an analytical system. The most important qualities of language are that it is a collection of elements (words) plus the understood but unspoken system of their relationships to each other (grammar) and to their referents (objects and facts). One can immediately see that there is a similarity in the structure of the analysis of the elements of a visual object and the structure of language. Perhaps one can go so far as to say that the structures are not merely similar but identical, since to use language is to apply analysis for

---

Dictionnaire de chymie, although Macquer was certainly aware of Condillac's critique of Locke in the *Essai sur l'origine des connoissances humaines.* My reasons for using Condillac, however, are several. His are the simplest or at least the most schematic descriptions of the mental procedures under discussion. Since I am talking here about analysis as a commonplace of Enlightenment thought, or rather, as one of the major organizing principles of the classical *épistémè,* there is perhaps no reason to privilege chronological priority over clarity in choosing the basic model. More importantly, while the distinctions between Locke and Condillac do not seem crucial for my discussion of Macquer, Lavoisier, in the *Méthode de nomenclature chimique* and in the *Traité élémentaire de chimie,* refers specifically to the *Logique* of Condillac as the philosophical authority for his work. Hence, I prefer for the sake of consistency to use Condillac as the background reading for both chemists; in this way, the differences inherent in their concepts of chemistry and of the role of the scientist may be brought into relief more clearly. (Cf. Michel Foucault's *Les Mots et les choses* for a general discussion of the classical *épistémè.)*

all intents and purposes. "Tout confirme donc que nous devons consiuérer les langages comme autant de méthodes analytiques; méthodes qui d'abord ont toute l'imperfection des langages qui commencent et qui, dans la suite, font des progrès à mesure que les langues en font elles-mêmes" [20].[5] The perfected language is the ultimate science, in that it is the ultimate analytical tool for the mind to use to cope with the "natural" but unstructured and infinite world of perceptions. But language—and by extension science, as a perfect language—exists only as a mental framework. It may be well-ordered, but it does not reproduce the material world. "Les idées exactes que l'on acquiert par l'analyse, ne sont pas toujours des idées complettes: elles ne peuvent même jamais l'être, lorsque nous nous occupons des objets sensibles. Alors nous ne découvrons que quelques qualités, & nous ne pouvons connoître qu'en partie" *(La Logique,* 36–37) [21]. But to say that science exists only in the mind does not preclude two very important limitations. Chemical science, as structured inside a language, is the ordering of named facts, but the facts which it orders exist in the material world. The relationships between these facts have nothing to do with any material order: they are a product of the perception of the philosopher; they are "idées *incomplettes.*" Order is not a quality to be sought for in itself to reproduce some real hierarchy inherent in the material world. The relationships exist between the words, the idées incomplettes, and not necessarily between the essentially unknowable things. Degérando, later on in the century, underlines a similar distinction in his *Histoire comparée des systèmes de philosophie,* in which he criticizes the typical scientist for believing himself to have "given the *facts* a simplicity which he had introduced only into the *terms.*"[6]

Later scientists like Fermi may be seen to be reductionists in that they attempt to fit the greatest number of facts into the smallest number of relationships or categories or rules. Truth for a modern scientist might be seen in terms of the elegance of his reductionist system, and this elegance is defined by its simplicity. The philosopher described by Macquer, on the other hand, would try to know the greatest number of facts and all of the relationships that linked them together. He would try to maintain their specificity, to preserve their individuality. This brings us to the second point which Macquer develops later both implicitly and explicitly in the organization of the body of the dictionary. For Macquer, the analytic tool *carries no element of truth, only utility.* The order developed by the philosopher is artificial and arbitrary, for the only truth that exists lies in

5. Etienne Bonnot de Condillac, "De l'analyse du discours," extrait du *Cours d'étude pour l'instruction du prince de Parme* (1775), in *Varia Linguistica,* ed. Charles Porset (Bordeaux: Ducros, 1970), 75.

6. Quoted in H B. Acton, "The Philosophy of Language in Revolutionary France," in *Studies in Philosophy,* ed. J. N. Findlay (London: Oxford University Press, 1966), 156.

the irreducible multiplicity of the facts or perceptions and cannot ever be totally comprehended by anyone's mind. Utility results from a synthesis performed after the decomposition effected by the primary analysis. Generalization, the creation of a system of classification, although not *true,* is a tool to help the finite human mind take shortcuts, to enable it to operate in the world without having to perceive the totality *(La Logique,* 30–31, and *Dict.,* xv-xvi).

As we saw earlier, the "vrais savans" who create this tool, who build artificial systems in a coherent body of language, are called the *philosophers (Dict.,* xviii). But this is just one half of the philosopher's functions. He has another, without which, for Macquer, his system would remain only in his poetic imagination and would not be a part of philosophy. It is not enough to perceive order through analysis; the results must be exchanged with others. Through the act of writing his philosopy, the philosopher takes on a role analogous to that of the artisan, but not reducible to it. From the starting point of the same "connoissances humaines," the artisan and the philosopher produce very different products—one a material object, the other a written body of organized knowledge—but both products result in the integration of the producer into a social system through a system of exchange.

The philosophers that Macquer describes in his preface are identified primarily according to the number and quality of the books they wrote, rather than through reference to their experimental discoveries or procedures, "car pour figurer parmi les Savans, il faut bien faire des livres" *(Dict.,* s.v. "affinité") [22]. From this point of view, we can perhaps explain Macquer's seemingly indistinguishable usage, in both the preface and the body of the *Dictionnaire,* of the titles "philosophe," "savant," and "auteur." The philosopher is an "auteur savant," i.e. a person whose primary task of *knowing* is balanced by and defined in terms of his *teaching* as much or more than in terms of his experimental discoveries, and whose teaching is carried out through written language. To be an author is not to be concerned with aesthetics, therefore, but with pedagogy; hence the qualities that are prized by Macquer are precision and clarity. Macquer explicitly condemns complexity and unrestricted imaginative or metaphorical manipulations used for their own sake, seeing such work as an abuse that does not reveal any useful knowledge to either readers or writers. These standards are presented mainly through criticisms of the work of other chemists or through polemical discussions of chemists of whose work he does approve:

> Qui croirait qu'un Auteur, d'ailleurs très estimable, ait voulu renouveller de nos jours le goût que l'on avoit dans les siècles d'ignorance, pour écrire d'une manière obscure sur les Sciences, & en particulier sur la Chymie; que, pour accréditer cette prétention, il ait loué *Stahl* d'une obscurité qu'on ne

trouvera jamais dans cet Auteur, à moins qu'on ne soit encore bien novice en Chymie; qu'il ait presque fait un crime à ceux qui tâchent de dissiper les ténèbres naturelles de cette Science! *(Dict.,* xxxiv) [23]

The primary fault of obscure writing is that it breaks down communication and hence withdraws its author from the mechanism of social exchange: "On peut juger du degré de considération que s'acquirent dans la société ces personnages [les chymistes obscurantistes] qui n'y faisoient rien et dont on n'apprenoit rien!" *(Dict.,* xxiii) [24].

It is important to underline that clarity in an author's writings is the mark not only of a good chemist, but also of a "good citizen." Moreover, Macquer goes to great pains, not only in the *Dictionnaire,* but also elsewhere in his work, to "justifier la réputation littéraire des chymistes."[7] He is trying to fit his discipline into the "goût philosophique du siècle" *(Dict.,* xxxv); he is trying to make his definition of the scientific philosopher coincide with the overlapping of the moral and philosophical stances that define the social nature of the philosopher for many of the writers of the French Enlightenment.

The equation of the social system with systems of economic and linguistic exchange is very much of a piece with the "bourgeois moral philosophy" of Diderot and the other philosophers. The primary human function is to be a *good citizen:* the moral and enlightened man takes his place in society through a process of, literally, give-and-take with his fellow man on all levels. Just as in any analytic system, each element is defined by its position and relationship to other elements in the network. Arbitrary social distinctions and personal pride are to be minimized, while the "sensibilité naturelle" and spontaneous virtue are emphasized. In direct opposition to Rousseau's view of civilization as the corruption of the natural state of man, the philosophes believed that man's very nature was social, and therefore that the person who separated himself from the processes of exchange or who created for himself a privileged position with respect to them was in the truest sense perverted. [8]

Macquer's artisan fits into this structure quite well. But more importantly, his abstracting philosopher is unlike the scientist that Venel's *sansculottes* will ridicule in the *Encyclopédie* article on chemistry for being

7. *Eléméns de Chymie-Pratique* (Paris: Jean-Thomas Hérissant, 1756), 1:xx.

8. See, for example, the writings of the Earl of Shaftsbury, of Diderot *(Le Fils naturel* and the *Eloge de Richardson),* Voltaire's description of the Quakers in the *Lettres philosophiques,* and many of the articles in the *Encyclopédie,* notably "Genève," "Citoyen," "Commerce," "Encyclopédie," "Patrie," and "Tolérance," and the view of the artisan implied in the plates of the *Encyclopédie.* A discussion of this last is found in Roland Barthes, "Les Planches de l'Encyclopédie," in his *Degré zéro de l'écriture, suivi de nouveaux essais critiques* (Paris: Seuil-Points, 1972), 89–105.

out of touch with the world.[9] Neither is he the thanatocratic scientist that Diderot will accuse of destroying the world as he analyzes it without ever understanding that its nature lies in its dynamism.[10] No matter whether the subject matter is political science or chemistry, Macquer's philosopher is doubly valuable because his abstract analytical verifications lead to two complementary syntheses: the philosopher and the artisans work together to form a whole society only because the analysis of the philosopher-king allows him to comprehend *at the same time* both the interrelationships of the artisan-citizens and of their knowledge. He is the motor without which both would remain static, disorganized; he is the equivalent that Macquer presents of the Great Clockmaker.

Now, against the background of his social and epistemological definition of the artisan and the philosopher, and in the context of his general formulation of a science as a systematization of knowledge, Macquer presents what he considers to be the most significant failures (the "fausses-routes" or "écarts") in the history of chemistry. Up to this point, what was originally proposed as a history of the chemical arts has in fact been the description of two hypothetical components of a social organization rather than a factual recounting of historical events. It is the form of Macquer's description rather than the factual data that we expect that actually reveals, to a great extent, the arguments he is presenting. This "history" of chemistry is less a history than a well-constructed story, tale, or myth. Macquer has so far only presented the character descriptions of the protagonists in a literary epic: the main characters, the heroes, the artisan, and especially the philosopher, the "good citizens" who produce, organize, and exchange, have been described for the reader. Now the opposing character, the antagonist, must be introduced on the several levels corresponding to the multiple functions of the artisan and philosopher.

It is significant that the antagonist in this epic of chemistry is introduced indirectly through a figurative representation, not as a character, but as an epistemological perversion that develops in the protagonists. "Une singulière manie ... attaqua la tête de tous les Chymistes ... Ce fut une sorte d'épidémie générale dont les symptômes prouvent jusqu'où peut aller la folie de l'esprit humain, lorsqu'il est vivement préoccupé de quelque objet, qui fit faire aux Chymistes des efforts surprenans, des découvertes admirables & mit néanmoins de grands obstacles à l'avancement de la Chymie" *(Dict.,* xxv) [25]. A plague or madness has singled out the practitioners of

9. *Encyclopédie,* 8:12–62, s.v. "Chymie." Cf. Charles Coulton Gillispie, "The Encyclopédie and the Jacobin Philosophy of Science: A Study in Ideas and Consequences," in *Critical Problems in the History of Science,* ed. Marshall Clagett (Madison: University of Wisconsin Press, 1959), 255–89.

10. Denis Diderot, "Pensées sur l'interprétation de la nature," *Oeuvres philosophiques,* ed. Paul Vernière (Paris: Garnier, 1965), 175–245.

chemistry. The plague as a literary symbol has many traditional connotations or associations for the reader, and Macquer exploits them to provide
a ready-made framework for his argument, one which creates expectations
in the reader, one which leads the reader to look for particular developments in the story that will fit in with his image of the functioning of
the plague myth. The allegory suggests roles or positions which impose
a pattern on isolated events in the development of chemistry, events that
otherwise would have had no relation to each other. This rhetorical strategy
has its basis in the very philosophy which Macquer has just derived: the
world is made up of disordered events from which a philosopher constructs
an artificial and arbitrary system. Hence, he will take an artificial structure,
that supplied by the plague myth, and read the events in the history of
chemistry through an analogous emplotment. His plague myth predisposes
the reader to see the history of chemistry the way Macquer wishes; it
provides an outline to be filled in.

As a consequence of this allegorical structure, an opposition has already
been set up: that between the healthy chemical artisans and the "diseased"
ones. A negative impression of the antagonists has been created in the
mind of the reader only by the choice of the plague metaphor. The characteristic attributes of the antagonist are not drawn from the factual description of a known historical figure, but are derived from the myth precisely
in order to be put into opposition with the rationality and moderation of
the artisans and philosophers. The antagonist attacks and takes over the
mind of the ersatz chemist, instilling a disease whose main symptom is
immoderation, or passion. "Par malheur ce nouvel objet de leurs recherches
n'étoit que trop capable d'exciter dans leur âme des mouvemens bien
opposés aux dispositions philosophiques" (xxii) [26].

But these "mouvemens" define the alchemist. He will be the opposite
of both the artisan and the philosopher: he is recognized by his *lack* of
contribution—either through product or philosophy—to his society or
to the development of chemistry. By now, the reader is not surprised to
find that the peculiarity of the alchemist is not to be found in the few
chemical practices that he shares with the artisan and the philosopher-
author. It is to be found in the *aim* of his practice.

Society, as implicitly defined by Macquer in his evocation of the artisan
and the philosopher, is constituted by the operation of some variant of a
system of exchange. The variants presented are twofold: that of the market-
place and that of language. In the mania of the alchemists, these two systems
become one. The disease that attacks is greed, and it has certain very
particular properties: its object is absolute; the alchemist is not interested
in collecting and enjoying material goods. He wants to be able to produce
that which, in itself, as an object, is not particularly useful and enjoyable,
but which, through its definition as "le prix de tous les biens" (xxii) [27],

represents, or leads to, every other commodity.[11] The goal of the artisan
is a material product; that of the philosopher is a coherent, written body
of knowledge; but that of the alchemist is of another order: it is power.
He seeks the knowledge of how to make gold, rather than the gold itself.
By knowing how to create directly the medium of exchange rather than
objects which pass through it, the alchemist puts himself in a privileged
position with respect to the economic system. The consequences of this
fascination with power are significant. Both the artisan and the philosopher
are involved in pursuits that must preserve the essential differences between
products, people, and ideas for the process of exchange to have any meaning, and in effect the process of exchange reaffirms these identities at every
interaction. Macquer's alchemist, however, translates every problem in his
chemistry and his philosophy—in fact, every event in the natural world—
in terms of its relationship to the problem of making gold.

> On voit bien sans doute que je veux parler du désir de faire de l'or. Dès que
> ce métal fut devenu, par une convention unanime, le prix de tous les biens,
> ... il s'empara tellement de leur attention, qu'il leur fit perdre de vue les
> autres objets; ils crurent voir la perfection de toute la Chymie dans ce qui
> n'étoit que la solution d'un problème particulier de Chymie; la sphère de
> leur science, au lieu de s'étendre, se trouva par-là concentrée autour d'un
> point unique. (xxii) [28]

For the alchemist, any type of analogy or similarity will suffice to prove
a link between the object of his obsession and the world outside his
fixation. The writing of the alchemists is highly metaphorical precisely in
order to bring about the reduction of the world to this "point unique";
in the best of cases, the result is that the alchemist creates only confusion,
and Macquer dismisses his work as not being philosophical. Macquer even
denies alchemists the status of authors, even though they write books:
"Pour soutenir leur nom, ils firent des livres comme les Philosophes, ils
écrivirent les principes de leur prétendue science; mais comme le carac-
tère ne se dément point, ils le firent d'une manière si obscure & si peu
intelligible, qu'ils ne donnerent pas plus de lumière sur leur art prétendu,
que n'en donnent, sur les métiers qu'ils exercent, les ouvriers qui n'écrivent rien" (xxiii) [29].

The confusion engendered is so great that they cannot even be distinguished one from another: "Aussi leur histoire n'est-elle pas moins obscure
& moins embrouillée que leurs écrits. On ne sait au-juste le vrai nom de
la plupart d'entre eux ... en un mot, tout ce qui les concerne est une
énigme perpétuelle" (xxiii) [30]. Those who undermine the differences

---

11. A few years later, Degérando will make this distinction very clear: "Money does not
show us objects, but only the road that must be followed to discover them." *Des Signes et
de l'art de penser* (Paris: n.p., An VII), quoted in Acton, "Language in Revolutionary France,"
158.

on which linguistic exchanges are based will find themselves without even names to be distinguished from each other.

But Macquer, instead of merely explaining why the alchemist's thought processes are incorrect, wishes to use this to prove the moral and social defect resulting from his fixation. He returns to the disease figure: "La manie alchymique étoit [une] lèpre qui ... défigurait [la chymie] et s'op-posait à ses progrès" (xxxii) [31]. A mania at this time was defined as a malady that disfigured, not the physical appearance of the person, but his thinking. As Foucault describes the insane in *Les Mots et les choses,* the madman was he for whom all concepts were related to each other by the unchecked process of analogy: "[Le fou] est celui qui s'est aliéné dans l'analogie ... il n'est le Différent que dans la mesure où il ne connaît pas la Différence; tous les signes pour lui se ressemblent, et toutes les ressemblances valent comme des signes. Le fou assure la fonction de *l'homosémantisme:* il rassemble tous les signes, et les comble d'une ressemblance qui ne cesse de proliférer" [32].[12]

For Macquer, the rampant *homosémantisme* of the alchemist is the proof of his mania. It destroys the network of relative differences and relation-ships by which thinking functions and makes every idea analogous to and ultimately indistinguishable from the others. But this mania is also a leprosy. The disfiguring effects of leprosy both destroy the distinguishing charac-teristics of the person afflicted and cause him to be excluded from his society. His soul may be read on his face.

Throughout the preface, Macquer is in the process of building up a semantic field based on the idea of the alchemists as minds attacked by disease. The afflicted are described in increasingly negative and finally in openly ironic terms, until Macquer ceases even pretending to justify his use of particular adjectives. The alchemists are described many times as "obscurs, sots, contre la raison, indéchiffrables, inintelligibles, inutiles, outrés, ineptes" [33]. He speaks of their "foiblesses, extravagance, manie, aveuglement, folie, enthousiasme, sotte vanité, frénésie, exagération," and on and on (xxxiii-xxxv) [34]. Any reference to a variant of these derogatory adjectives immediately evokes the general term "alchemist," and "alche-mist" immediately refers not to a concrete or historical set of persons or procedures, but to the negative connotations already present in the mind of the reader.

In this first part of Macquer's "history," the figure that is developed out of the plague myth is the logically weaker though poetically more effective of two characterizations, those of the "good citizen" and of the alchemist. Although often supported—after the fact—by examples taken from histor-ical accounts, the impact on the reader nonetheless comes largely from

12. Michel Foucault, *Les Mots et les choses* (Paris: Gallimard, 1966), 63; my emphasis.

the way in which the figure was built in opposition to the systems of philosophical and economic exchange. But this relationship between the rhetorically derived picture of a social ideal shifts in the second section of the history. Macquer comes to rely increasingly on the figurative disease vocabulary that he has developed out of the plague myth and less on historical description, to show the evolution of the field. The associations that the disease allegory has already acquired for the reader are carried over into a description in which rhetoric, instead of serving merely as stylistic support, is substituted for logical or factual explanation.

Macquer describes another group of alchemists, the philosopher-doctors of the Renaissance. He does not show the philosopher-doctors as having evolved from the gold-making alchemists in either procedure or philosophy; in fact, no historical link is presented between the two groups at all. They have in common only a certain extravagance and unintelligibility which does not result in any particular antisocial behavior on their part. The philosopher-doctors tried to discover a universal medicine—a very utilitarian goal as opposed to that of the alchemists' search for gold. But from their immoderation, their passion, their single-mindedness, and especially from their obstinacy in searching for *one* philosophical cure for a *multiplicity* of diseases—"[ils] s'imaginerent que toutes ces merveilles pouvaient s'opérer par un seul et même procédé" (xxvi) [35], Macquer derives their similarity to the previous alchemists. He then singles out a specific historical figure to be at the center of this philosophical disorder: Paracelsus. Paracelsus will serve as a figurehead for the alchemists, as the "negative pole" against which the positive pole of the modern chemist is to be described.

> Ce fut dans ce tems qu'un fameux Alchymiste nommé Paracelse, homme d'un esprit *vif, extravagant & impétueux,* ajouta une nouvelle folie à celle de tous ses prédécesseurs. Comme il étoit fils d'un Médecin, & Médecin lui-même, il imagina que, par le moyen de l'Alchymie, on devoit trouver aussi la Médecine universelle, & mourut à quarante-huit ans, en publiant qu'il avoit des secrets capables de prolonger la vie jusqu'à l'âge de Mathusalem. Cette prétention, toute insensée qu'elle étoit, trouva néanmoins beaucoup de partisans, & occasionna un *violent redoublement dans la manie* des Alchymistes. (xxv; my emphasis) [36]

The key terms of the semantic field Macquer has generated are here displayed at their densest. The growing extravagance and irony of Macquer's style underlines the description of the extravagance and failure of Paracelsus, makes of him the example of the insane alchemist, and prepares the reader for the swing to the opposite but corresponding pole.

For now Macquer has come to the point in his argument for which he has carefully conditioned the reader: he will evoke, out of the metaphorical system he has painstakingly devised, the new science of chemistry. The

traditional disease metaphor has one last consequence, and Macquer uses
it to provide a bridge to his new and better chemists. "Il est vrai qu'une
maladie opiniâtre & invétérée ne disparoît jamais subitement & sans laisser
aucune trace" (xxxi) [37]. This mark is reminiscent of the concept of
vaccination; the same substance is potentially both disease (uncontrolled)
or immunization (controlled). This concept parallels Macquer's opposition
between the passion (immoderation) of the alchemists versus the sang-
froid (moderation) of the philosophers. It is not the traces that are left,
the ideas of the alchemists that are in themselves dangerous, but simply
the quantity of control that the practitioner does or does not have over
them. The alchemists were not totally counterproductive.

> La Médecine Universelle, quoique la plus folle sans doute de toutes les idées
> qui étoient entrées dans la tête des Alchymistes, fut cependant ce qui
> commença à établir la Chymie raisonnable, & à l'élever sur les ruines de
> l'alchymie. (xxvii) [38]
>
>   Le service le plus essentiel que [les alchymistes] pouvaient rendre à la
> Chymie, c'étoit d'exposer aussi clairement les expériences qui leur ont
> manqué, qu'ils ont décrit obscurément celles qui, selon eux, leur avoient
> réussi. (xxv) [39]

Having the data left from the failed experiments of the alchemists, the
artisans have the trace of the disease, the vaccination and its signature: the
awareness of the disease and its dangers provides a sort of immunity to
the immoderation, and they are still able to use the data that their predecessors unknowingly provided. As alchemy was a disease, chemistry will
be the cured state, a return to health and sanity.

The new artisans, and ultimately the "chemists," are described using a
careful point-by-point reversal of the system of derogatory adjectives built
up to define the alchemists. The definition of the new chemists also includes
those qualities that defined the artisan/philosopher; the result is again a
general or abstract description: "Ces vrais citoyens [de] la Chymie pouvoient
fournir d'excellens remèdes . . . par un travail digne des plus grands éloges,
puisqu'il avoit pour objet le bien de l'humanité. Ils furent, à proprement
parler, les inventeurs d'un nouvel art Chymique . . . ils écrivirent leur art
parcequ'ils n'étoient point artisans, et l'écrivirent clairement, *parce qu'ils
n'étoient point Alchymistes*" (xxvii) [40]. The new chemists are, not surpris-
ingly, primarily qualified as *good citizens.* But oddly enough, they are good
citizens only because they are not alchemists. And merely because they
are not alchemists, they must write clearly. Obviously, they exist only
because Macquer can reverse his definition of what is bad to set up a
definition of what is good. Thus it is again through a rhetorical device as
opposed to a recounting of factual events that Macquer finally describes
the birth of the real science of chemistry.

Nous arrivons enfin à une des plus brillantes époques de la Chymie, je veux parler du tems où ses différentes parties commencerent à être recueillies, examinées, comparées par des hommes d'un génie assez étendu et assez profond pour les rassembler toutes, en découvrir les principes, en saisir les rapports, les réunir en un corps de doctrine raisonné, et poser véritablement les fondemens de la Chymie, considérée comme science. (xxxii) [41] Macquer has simply restated his own carefully worked-out general definition of an analytic science, and by using the series of words opposing those he used to describe the alchemists (who did exist, although they did not necessarily behave in the way that Macquer's plague myth implies they did), he suggests that their opposites also exist. Just as in the case of the alchemists, an excess of rhetoric replaces historical data. The final parallel is then created: the counterpart to Paracelsus, the opposite figurehead, the "positive pole," is described in terms which again refer only to other terms already systematized, to reactions already programmed into the reader.

The German chemist Stahl, who has an "imagination aussi vive, aussi brillante, & aussi active que celle de son prédécesseur," has nevertheless, Macquer tells us, "l'avantage inestimable d'être réglé par cette sagesse & ce sang-froid philosophiques" (xxxi) [42]. Macquer then enumerates several other chemists of Stahl's generation, among them Beccher, "[qui] mérita l'honneur d'avoir pour partisan & pour commentateur le plus grand & le plus sublime de tous les Chymistes Physiciens ... On doit reconnoître à ces titres glorieux et si bien mérités l'illustre Stahl, premier Médecin du feu roi de Prusse" (xxxiii) [43]. To the blindness, folly, and immoderation, and especially to the obscurity of their writings and the antisocial attitudes of the alchemists, we find opposed the vision that spreads light (presumably on the *scène de l'analyse)*, the humanitarian intent, and the clarity of the most beautiful and methodical analysis: "C'est à côté de Stahl, ... qu'on doit placer l'immortel Boerhaave. Ce puissant génie, l'honneur de son pays, de sa profession, & de son siècle, a répandu la lumière sur toutes les sciences dont il s'est occupé. Nous devons à un regard dont il a favorisé la Chymie, la plus belle et la plus méthodique analyse du règne végétal ... il semble laisser l'esprit humain dans l'impuissance d'y rien ajouter" (xxxv) [44]. The reader doesn't know much more about Boerhaave and Stahl than their names, but they have already been described in terms of more grandeur, honors, and well-earned and glorious titles than could ever be factually supported in Macquer's few remaining pages. The powerful attitude-directing mechanism works on the reader through a circular, self-referential system of adjectives. It creates a positive image of "la belle science" that Macquer can see may perhaps exist in the future, but which for the moment exists only in the tenuous space created in and held by his rhetorical imagination. The rhetorical machine eliminates the necessity for, and short-circuits any reference to, concrete or historical objects and events. It is not at all the impartial, factual, and concretely supported logical exposition that we call "scientific" or "historical" and that one would have normally expected to find at the beginning of a *Dictionnaire de chymie,* if one expected to find anything at all.

One is immediately tempted to ask what possible difference it makes to have the preface of the *Dictionnaire* organized in such a fashion. But the *Dictionnaire de chymie* was a major chemical reference-work of the time, and in some ways a most sophisticated pedagogical "treatise" of pre-Lavoisien chemistry. The body of the *Dictionnaire,* which holds a peda-gogical system, relies heavily on the preface; many of the theoretical articles refer back to the oppositions so carefully spelled out in it in order to justify using constantly the writings of the "immortal Boerhaave" and the "illustrious Stahl."

And yet, it is significant that this preface never speaks about the subject matter of chemistry. It makes no attempt to provide, as one would have expected at the beginning of a major work on a field of study, a definition of either the technical goals or the experimental procedures of the science. On the contrary, it is a myth. It provides an ethical model of a society through symbols and archetypes. What it does define is the proper *behavior* of the student of chemistry himself: his temperament, his ideal attitude towards his work, and his place in society are the subjects that are time and again emphasized.

What Macquer is trying to show his reader is not a body of knowledge, but a posture *towards* knowledge. The ethical makeup of a philosopher is congruent to his scientific understanding. Neither is derived from nor privileged over the other; each one implies and necessitates the other. After Descartes, philosophy is secularized, and secularized it becomes Janus-like: not directly from God, but from the underlying epistemological structure, two complementary identities are constructed, that of the social man and that of the intellectual man. For Macquer, one does not exist without the other.

The attitude that Macquer has developed in his reader will be crucial to the functioning of the body of the *Dictionnaire* as a pedagogical treatise. Its operation is more complex than might at first appear; I will discuss the epistemological basis of Macquer's philosophy in Chapter 3 and the struc-ture of his science in Chapter 4. As we shall see, the question of ethical attitude, because it implies the notion of scientific comportment, is one that must constantly be reinforced by Macquer. It is precisely in this ques-tion of "attitude" that one of the pivotal differences between the philo-sophical chemistry of Macquer and the scientific chemistry of Lavoisier lies.

What Is a Dictionary?

I HAVE JUST DISCUSSED WHAT AT FIRST GLANCE WOULD SEEM TO BE a literary anomaly in a scientific work: the preface to a dictionary of chemical terms. This preface may seem at once trivial and out of place, as the ordinary reason for a specialized dictionary is to provide a reference tool for a reader already acquainted with the field. That reader would have his own assumptions about what the subject matter is, what its goals and parameters are, how its knowledge is organized, and which methods constitute work in the discipline and which do not. In other words, he would already be an educated chemist, interested primarily in checking the meaning of an isolated word here and there. His way of using the dictionary would make the preface superfluous: he would refer to a particular article in the book, easily accessible because of the alphabetic format, in order to find as quickly as possible the specific information needed to continue his technical work. But Macquer's preface to the *Dictionnaire de chymie* is not related to this type of use, for it does not give the reader any directions for using the dictionary and would most likely not even be noticed by a working chemist, who need not read from beginning to end to find the information he is searching for. A historical preface like this one, concerned with a nonscientific or nonreferential subject, would be read only by the uninitiated in search of a general overview of chemistry. The preface I have already discussed is not the only indication of this double purpose of the *Dictionnaire de chymie:* the book's first edition has *two* prefaces, and the second edition has two prefaces and two long postscripts, one discussing alternate sequences in which one may read the dictionary, and the other a table of contents—to an alphabetical work!

Macquer is aware of the seeming paradox presented by the contrast between the traditional use of a dictionary and those different uses made possible by his own. The "Avertissement de l'auteur" in the first edition discusses this problem specifically:

> Depuis que la Chymie, ramenée à son véritable objet, a été cultivée comme
> une partie fondamentale & essentielle de la Physique, on a publié un assez
> grand nombre de bons Traités de cette Science; mais aucun de ces Traités
> n'est sous la forme de Dictionnaire. Plusieurs Savans & Amateurs sembloient
> cependant désirer un Ouvrage de cette nature, & l'on m'a proposé de l'en-
> treprendre. J'avoue que j'ai eu d'abord quelque peine à me prêter à l'exécu-
> tion de ce projet, parce qu'il me sembloit que toutes les parties de la
> Chymie étant liées entr'elles & dépendantes les unes des autres, cette
> Science étoit peu propre à être traitée dans l'ordre alphabétique. Mais à
> mesure que j'ai travaillé à l'Ouvrage que je présente aujourd'hui au Public,
> j'ai reconnu que la forme de Dictionnaire étoit moins imparfaite, & même
> beaucoup plus avantageuse que ne le pensent un certain nombre de Savans
> & de Gens de Lettres.
>
> A la vérité, la disposition alphabétique paroît interrompre & déranger
> toute espèce de plan & de système dans une Science, mais on peut remédier
> à ce défaut par des renvois qui établissent la liaison nécessaire entre tous les
> articles correspondans, comme on l'a fait dans cet Ouvrage, & dans plusieurs
> bons Dictionnaires de Sciences qui sont entre les mains du Public; d'ailleurs
> ce désordre apparent laisse au lecteur la liberté de se former tel plan qu'il
> juge à propos, & qu'il est très possible qu'il fasse à cet égard un meilleur
> choix que l'Auteur même.
>
> Au reste, ceux qui prendront la peine de lire ou de consulter cet
> Ouvrage, reconnoîtront facilement qu'il n'est point un simple vocabulaire ni
> un Dictionnaire de définitions, mais plutôt une suite de Dissertations, la
> plupart même fort étendues, sur tous les objets importans de la Chymie,
> dans lesquelles on a taché de remplir exactement tout ce qui est annoncé
> dans le titre. *(Dict.* [1766], 1:ii) [45]

Macquer himself has set up the opposition: one can either read *or* consult
this work. It is at the same time a reference work and, more importantly,
a "treatise" in the form of a dictionary. It therefore serves both as a learning
tool and as a reference work for the accomplished scientist. It provides
instruction for the student who as yet has no chemical philosophy of his
own in which to situate the disparate facts. This paradox is underlined by
the distinction Macquer makes: there is only a "désordre apparent," not
a real one. The disorder is balanced by the all-important system of cross-
references that ties the articles together. He also emphasizes that this work
is not a dictionary in the simple sense of the word: "Il n'est point un
simple vocabulaire ni un Dictionnaire de définitions, mais plutôt une suite
de Dissertations." We easily recognize the format in question. This dual
organization was well-known in the eighteenth century, the most explicit

example being the *Encyclopédie; ou, Dictionnaire raisonné des sciences, des arts, et des métiers* of Diderot and D'Alembert.[1]

The problems and possibilities of alphabetical ordering are carefully considered by Diderot in his article "Encyclopédie" *(Enc.,* vol. 13), and we will examine his presentation of the theoretical and general case later in this chapter.[2] In many ways, his is the most radical and original discussion of a structure which, although perhaps without inherent interest for a modern writer, was the epistemologically privileged one for the philosophes of the Enlightenment: it is the format of a *language analyzed*. I shall attempt, by taking a detour through several of the authors who discuss the concept of analysis, to make clear the consequences that would have been implicit for Macquer in his choice of the format of his *Dictionnaire de chymie*.

Analysis

As we saw in the discussion of his history of chemistry, Macquer's concept of the ideal chemical perception—the one that he praises at the end of his preface and in several other places—is that of an instantaneous vision which includes at once all of the elements and their interrelationships *(Dict.,* 1:xxxviii and 3:121, s.v. "Phlogistique"). It is difficult, however, to go from a simultaneous visual perception (ordered in space) to a description ordered in time (linearly or successively). And yet this is basically the problem set by those philosophes who accept analysis as the model for human perception.

Here again is Condillac, one of the most persistent advocates of analytical thinking, describing the process of analysis and the attempt to speak about what has been analyzed. The object being described is the countryside as seen from the window of a castle on a high hill.

> Si dans la suite nous voulons parler de cette campagne, on remarquera que nous ne la connoissons pas tous également bien. Quelques uns *feront des tableaux* plus ou moins vrais . . . .

1. Denis Diderot, Jean le Rond D'Alembert, et al., *L'Encyclopédie; ou, Dictionnaire raisonné des sciences, des arts, et des métiers,* 2d ed. (Berne: Sociétés Typographiques, 1781). Hereafter cited as *Enc.*

2. This article (hereafter cited as "Enc") has been discussed by Jean Starobinski in "Remarques sur *l'Encyclopédie,*" *Revue de métaphysique et de morale,* no. 75 (1970): 284–91, which deals with the subversive structure made possible by the alphabetical ordering of the *Encyclopédie.* Starobinski concentrates on the mechanism of social subversion, which I present only in outline here, and goes on to show how this philosophy is presented by other means, notably through the organization of the plates and the use of metaphors of trees, maps, and machines, all of which were commonly used by Diderot to demonstrate his concepts of man, society, and language and his view of the project of the *Encyclopédie.*

(Et pour les concevoir *telles qu'elles* [*les choses*] *sont,* il faut que l'ordre successif dans lequel on les observe les rassemble dans *l'ordre simultané* qui est entr'elles.)

Or, quel est cet ordre? La nature l'indique elle-même; c'est celui dans lequel elle offre les objets. Il y en a qui appellent plus particulièrement les regards; ils sont plus frappans; ils dominent; & tous les autres *semblent* s'arranger *autour* d'eux pour eux. Voilà ce qu'on observe d'abord: & quand on a remarqué leurs situations respectives, les autres se mettent dans les intervalles, *chacun à leur place.* On commence donc par les objets principaux: on les observe successivement, & on les compare, pour juger des rapports où ils sont. Quand, par ce moyen, on a leurs situations respectives, on observe successivement tous ceux qui remplissent les intervalles, on les compare chacun avec l'objet principal le plus prochain, & on en détermine la position.

Alors, on démêle tous les objets dont on a saisi la forme & la situation, & on les embrasse d'un seul regard. L'ordre qui est entr'eux dans notre esprit, n'est donc plus successif, il est simultané. C'est celui-là même dans lequel ils existent, & nous les voyons tous à la fois d'une manière distincte. *(La Logique,* 16–17) [46]

Analysis proceeds from the global impression provided by the "coup d'oeil," to successive observations of each major object in the field (a linear procedure), to the establishment of relationships between them (no longer linear), and from there returns to the global view (analyzed), which is organized, understood, and comprehensive; once again, it is spatial.

The relationships perceived are artificial but not arbitrary mental constructs. They have a real existence, though not in the material world outside of perception. They exist as a necessary analogue to the organization of the body that makes perception possible.[3]

Je vois donc dans la sphère de mes connoissances un système qui correspond à celui que l'Auteur de ma nature a suivi en me formant: & cela n'est pas étonnant; car mes besoins & mes facultés étant donnés, mes recherches & mes connoissances sont données elles-mêmes.

Tout est lié également dans l'un et l'autre système. Mes organes, les sensations que j'éprouve, les jugemens que je porte, l'expérience qui les confirme ou les corrige, forment l'un & l'autre système pour ma conservation . . . voilà le système qu'il faudroit étudier pour apprendre à raisonner. *(La Logique,* 77) [47]

Facts are not perceptions of the nature of things in themselves. They are perceptions of the relationships material objects have to human beings, and investigations carried out to discover more facts (experiments) have an essential place in scientific work. But an experiment has value only if

---

3. The concept of the organizational determinism of perception comes from Descartes. He saw the senses as the body's means of survival; one perceived what it was necessary to sense in order to survive physically. Psychic survival, moreover, had as a goal physical survival.

it leads to the creation of a system. Or rather, a system is true only insofar as it is useful; science cannot be distinguished from technology nor philosophy from ethics.

> L'Auteur de notre nature veut seulement que nous jugions des rapports que les choses ont à nous, & de ceux qu'elles ont entr'elles, *lorsque la connoissance de ces derniers peut nous être de quelque utilité* . . . Nous avons un moyen pour juger de ces rapports, & il est unique; c'est d'observer les sensations que les objets font sur nous. Autant nos sensations peuvent s'étendre, autant la sphère de nos connoissances peut s'étendre elle-même: au delà, toute découverte nous est interdite. (77–78) [48]

Each man sees what he needs to see; therefore there may be a multiplicity of different systems. The savant cannot know the essential nature of the things he is describing; he knows only his perceptions of them, which he calls *ideas.*

> Les sensations, considérées comme *représentant les objets sensibles,* se nomment *idées;* expression figurée, qui au propre signifie la même chose *qu'images.*
>
> Autant nous distinguons de sensations différentes, autant nous distinguons d'espèces d'idées; & ces idées sont ou des sensations actuelles, ou elles ne sont qu'un souvenir des sensations que nous avons eues. (21) [49]

Each idea is given a word to index it, to make it available for communication or for later thinking. The "truth" factor of a nomenclature comes from the care with which the facts are named. The relationships between the precisely denoted, hence "true," words are not true themselves; they are simply useful constructions. But if the proper analytic procedure is followed in the creation of a vocabulary from the very first perception, the result will be an error-free system of language, one which will be, unlike the alchemists' uncontrollably metaphoric theories, free from ambiguity, vagueness, or meaningless terms.

> Nous venons de voir que la cause de nos erreurs est dans l'habitude de juger d'après les mots dont nous n'avons pas déterminé le sens: nous avons vu . . . que les mots nous sont absolument nécessaires pour nous faire des idées de toutes espèces; & nous verrons bientôt que les idées abstraites & générales ne sont que des délimitations. Tout confirme donc que nous ne pensons qu'avec le secours des mots. C'en est assez pour faire comprendre que l'art de raisonner a commencé avec les langues; qu'elle n'a pu faire des progrès qu'autant qu'elles en ont fait elles-mêmes; & que par conséquent elles doivent renfermer tous les moyens que nous pouvons avoir pour analyser bien ou mal. Il faut donc observer les langues. (86–87) [50]

Condillac has brought in a new and crucial point. Words are not merely passive signifiers of sensations. They also structure the possibility of later perception. Moreover, it is words rather than ideas that are manipulated

in abstract thought. The crux of Condillac's theory, which has important
and profound implications for Macquer's chemical analyses, lies in his
statement that "l'analyse ne se fait et ne peut se faire qu'avec des signes"
(93) [51].

The *Encyclopédie*

Diderot, as editor of the *Encyclopédie,* proceeds to put into action the
same language-dominated theory of analytic perception and knowledge.
His starting point is that "la langue d'un peuple donne son vocabulaire,
& le vocabulaire est une table assez fidèle de toutes les connaissances de
ce peuple" ("Enc.," 189) [52]. Knowledge is understood nominalistically,
as ideas representing things; these ideas are made accessible by the use
of signs to mark them. "La langue est un symbole de cette multitude de
choses hétérogènes" (190) [53], whether they are in the world (objects)
or in the mind (judgments of the relationships of objects to each other).
Whence Diderot's immediate assertion that the first consideration for the
encyclopédiste must be to work on the perfecting of his language: "Mais
la connaissance de la langue est le fondement de toutes ces grandes
espérances; elles resteront incertaines, si la langue n'est fixée & transmise
à la postérité dans toute sa perfection; & cet objet est le premier de ceux
dont il convenait à des encyclopédistes de s'occuper profondément" (188)
[54]. Complementarily, the analytic process itself establishes as homologous to each other these three networks or systems of comparison (things
and their relations to each other, ideas and their relations to each other,
words and their relations to each other). Language is the most abstract of
the three systems; it embodies both the vocabulary (the elements of knowledge) and the abstract judgments that link and order the elements. Diderot
defines the process of generating these links as philosophy: "La comparaison des phénomènes s'appelle la philosophie" (190) [55].

But Bachelard had claimed in turn that the quality distinguishing "pre-
science," or science as an amateur pastime, from a true science, is that a
true science has reached a state of epistemological autonomy. It is at the
same time a body of organized knowledge and the methodology used to
reflect on the nature of this knowledge.[4] In other words, modern physics
embodies its own metaphysics.[5] Bachelard uses this definition to characterize the philosophical barriers between scientific disciplines as both
inevitable and effectively permanent. Diderot, however, is writing precisely

4. Gaston Bachelard, *La Formation de l'esprit scientifique* (Paris: Vrin; 1926, reprinted,
1975), "Discours préliminaire."
5. Michel Serres, "L'Histoire des sciences," in *Hermès V: Le Passage du Nord-Ouest* (Paris:
Minuit, 1980), 131–64.

during the period that Bachelard dismisses as being still pre- or unscientific for chemistry, and yet we find that he has derived the same model as Bachelard. It is worth recalling that Condillac had pushed the model to one higher level of generality and had come to the opposite conclusion: language is the combination of organized knowledge and analysis, including—and in fact privileging—its own self-analysis. For Condillac there is and can be only one science in the Enlightenment that will fulfill Bachelard's conditions, a science which by its very definition will include all the other sciences that the nineteenth century will separate by subject matter. This science is the analysis of language. The proposition is tautological, for language is analysis of the world and of itself. Ideally, general grammar and logic become one and the same, leading eventually to the hall of mirrors constituted by Condillac's *Traité des sensations, Grammaire, Logique,* and the *Langue des calculs.*[6]

For the nominalist analytic epistemologist of the Enlightenment, therefore, the ideal, the most natural, the most effective format to use to present the encyclopedia, the "science universelle, recueil ou enchaînement de toutes les sciences ensemble," [56][7] is the network formed by the alphabetically organized dictionary. In this format, the rhetorical structure is based in the philosophical structure being valorized. Furthermore, each article, by itself a semi-independent treatise, should also attempt to follow an analytic format; the result is a veritable *mise-en-abîme* of analytic networks. From this perspective, Macquer's *Dictionnaire de chymie,* for instance, would form merely a subsection of an ideal, perfect *Encyclopédie.* The science of chemistry, with all other sciences, is subsumed into the more general science of language.[8]

Diderot is aware of the possibilities presented by the dictionary format. Just as for Macquer, the principal and defining quality of a dictionary is, for Diderot, its alphabetical format. Yet it is not by the alphabetical order alone, but in conjunction with its necessary counterpart, the system of cross-references, that the dictionary becomes a subtle, multifaceted tool. This format makes possible many uses of the book that a purely linear work could not afford. Concerning this point, Diderot and Macquer are in agreement. The uses that Diderot suggests are necessitated by a particular social philosophy which is similar to the one that Macquer refers to

6. The *Langue des calculs* in effect defines philosophy tautologically. All meditation becomes a mirrorlike process of reflection: one translates the questions successively until the question becomes itself the answer. As all knowledge is potentially already coded into a well-analyzed analytic language, it suffices to manipulate the *same* until the answer comes into focus.

7. Diderot refers (174) to this definition, taken from the *Dictionnaire de Trévoux,* 1752 ed., s.v. "Encyclopédie."

8. For an in-depth discussion of the arguments on the theories of language in the *Encyclopédie,* see Sylvain Auroux, *La Sémiotique des Encyclopédistes* (Paris: Payot, 1979).

in the preface of his dictionary. They are both derived from the same underlying epistemology, but the full-scale demonstration is worked out only in the *Encyclopédie.* This social philosophy, which is the major undertaking of the *Encyclopédie,* is embedded in the cross-references.

> Les renvois de choses éclaircissent l'objet, indiquent ses liaisons prochaines avec ceux qui le touchent immédiatement, & ses liaisons éloignées avec d'autres qu'on en croirait isolés, rappellent les notions communes & les principes analogues, fortifient les conséquences, entrelacent la branche au tronc, & donnent au tout cette unité si favorable à l'établissement de la vérité & à la persuasion. Mais quand il le faudra, ils produiront aussi un effet tout contraire; ils opposeront les notions; ils feront contraster les principes; ils attaqueront, ébranleront, renverseront secrètement quelques opinions ridicules qu'on n'oserait insulter ouvertement. *Si l'auteur est impartial, ils auront toujours la double fonction de confirmer & de réfuter, de troubler & de concilier* . . . Si ces renvois de confirmation & de réfutation sont prévus de loin, & préparés avec adresse, ils donneront à une Encyclopédie le caractère que doit avoir un bon dictionnaire; ce caractère est *de changer la façon commune de penser.* ("Enc.," 367; my emphasis) [57]

The good dictionary is a subversive work. It presents at least two systems of judgment:

1. The institutionalized or accepted way of viewing the world is presented explicitly in each dissertation, but the totality is fragmented by the arbitrary structure of the alphabetical ordering.
2. The system of cross-references provides at least one other implicit judgment on the explicit world-view: the network of connections and oppositions brings into contact ideas which would never before have been considered in terms of each other.

The dominant metaphors in the article for the cross-reference system are all spatial as opposed to linear—trees, maps, terrains—and this fact underlines the great distinction that Diderot is making between his work and the ordinary linear treatises. It is important to notice here that Diderot's most important tactical decision has been to put into opposition two rhetorical structures:

1. *The linear treatise format* typical of a mathematical model (associated more generally with other forms of explicit argumentation, for example, with inductive proofs). The process of reasoning in the treatise is dominant over the content. Perhaps it is more precise to say that it makes no sense to separate the content from its rhetorical framework in this case. No real distinction can be made between the "facts" (as content) and the rhetorical system (that which determines the order and form the argumentation takes) that communicates it. There is no freedom for the reader to judge by himself, to make his own connections between various pieces of data;

he has no choice but to acquiesce when confronted by a logical proof, whether he likes the consequences or not. The implication is that there is something necessary about the conclusions of a proof, simply because "it follows." Because the data are linked together one after another in a supposed cause-and-effect relationship, they produce the illusion of being merely the representation of a naturally (or divinely) preordained order, which it would be absurd and irrelevant to challenge. Hence both the knowledge and those who use it or who are privileged by it are in a position of mastery with respect to the reader.

2. *The spatial format* (associated with implicit persuasion). The distinction between the content and its rhetorical context is signalled to the reader by the arbitrary format of the alphabetical dictionary. This first operation has two direct results: first the alphabetical format fragments the context; hence the persuasive power of the linear treatise, dependent on its continuity, is annulled. The "facts" are left isolated, pinned down in a seemingly arbitrary order, ready to be scrutinized in any order, or none, as the reader sees fit. As a consequence, it is revealed to the reader that content and rhetorical framework are *not* one and the same. By extrapolation, he deduces that the order and therefore the philosophical, social, or theological conclusions reached in traditional linear treatises are also dependent only on the rhetorical programming. The philosophical implications are no longer seen as natural or necessary, but as having been imposed by the person (or institution) that produced the treatise. The arbitrarily (alphabetically) organized dictionary leaves (at first glance) each reader free to develop whatever connections he feels are useful between the facts put at his disposal. The reader has an apparent mastery over his knowledge; it cannot be used to master him.

But the alphabetical organization is only one of two components that make up the dictionary format. It eliminates the privilege accorded to demonstrative modes of argumentation. Diderot replaces the rhetorical form of the treatise and its particular "metaphysics," as he calls it, with another: the one embodied in the system of cross-references. This system is implicit, however; it works by placing units of knowledge in communication with each other, and not by openly telling the reader what he is supposed to deduce. "Des renvois forment un tableau dont les vides ou les intervalles *suggèrent* les suppositions philosophiques" (371; my emphasis) [58]. The space is provided for the reader to exercise his own judgment; actually a new and less visible philosophy is being created. Where one persuasive framework is being destroyed, another one is created, but only through suggestion. However, this new framework is much less evidently constraining to the liberty of the reader. The equally artificial rhetorical maneuver of the author of the dictionary is masked by Diderot in three ways:

1. by being implicit instead of explicit;
2. by being described in figures which *suggest* a natural order (trees, terrains, gardens); and
3. by being spatial: implying a multitude of possible paths and goals proper to attain the particular concrete knowledge desired, but all leading to the same social and political conclusions.[9]

Emphasis is put, significantly, on the critical powers of the reader rather than on the rhetorical skill of the writer. This emphasis also serves to hide from the reader what the writer is doing. But there are two quite distinct readers of the *Encyclopédie,* who correspond to its dual aim, as presented by its two editors and their complementary expositions of the potential of the cross-reference system. For D'Alembert, the Tree of Knowledge that he describes in the "Discours préliminaire" *(Enc.,* vol. 1) gives, not an arbitrary, but a true picture of the structure of knowledge. It therefore necessarily provides a simplified map to the system of the cross-references. The *Encyclopédie* is the only possible format in which to present the result of an analysis of all knowledge that will allow an unassisted reader to generate both a true and a general view of the world. It thus serves as a self-programming education for those who for social or other reasons had limited access to schools.[10] But Diderot's "Encyclopédie" article focuses on the subtle philosophical and political conversion of the "elect," of the (presumably well-educated) readers who are interested in understanding not so much the *sciences* (the content) as in taking advantage of the *dictionnaire* (the format) in the *Dictionnaire raisonné des sciences, des arts, et des métiers.* For in the *Encyclopédie,* the spatial format provides for the intersection of ideas, from which new ideas are suggested. However, a new idea, although only suggested, is nonetheless carefully determined: every "intelligent" or "enlightened" reader should come to the same conclusions by following the same leads. The editor knows what is being

9. As is well known, the butt of the philosophers' attack in the *Encyclopédie* was the political and social monolith formed by the church and the aristocracy. The central attack is provided not so much by the political and social content of the articles, however, as by the very existence of the *Encyclopédie* as an alternate rhetorical structure and hence as an alternate system of logic. It is the *plurality* of logics thus demonstrated that threatens not only particular institutions, practices, and beliefs, but also the entire scholastic tradition by which these beliefs were constituted as natural and justified.

10. The *tiers état* did not, in fact, form a significant part of the readership of the *Encyclopédie* once it was published; neither did the commercially oriented bourgeoisie, as one might have expected. For a surprising discussion of the actual readership, see Robert Darnton's exhaustive study, *The Business of the Enlightenment: A Publishing History of the Encyclopédie, 1775–1800* (Cambridge: Harvard University Press, Belknap, 1979).

implied; he is leading the reader along. The process is similar to that of a Socratic dialogue, except that only the student is present. The reader-student must be forced to ask the correct questions *and* to give the correct answers.

To make this sophisticated tool functional, it is necessary to have a complete system of cross-references, to leave no gaps. For the dictionary to be a properly subversive tool, it must be complete, and to be complete, it must be finite, it must close on itself. The articles may be as numerous as necessary, but they must form a unity with the cross-references to effectively create a network that will enclose the philosophically oriented reader. It must be an "ensemble très-serré, très-lié, & très-continu" (369) [59]. If the network is too diffuse, the reader will never be able to cover enough of the articles and cross-references to perceive the network at all. In practical terms, this is a very real danger. Given the scope of the project, it threatens to make the encyclopedia obsolete before it ever comes into existence.

D'Alembert looks at the organization of the ideal encyclopedia as structurally related to the most natural organization of knowledge. He and Diderot both consider it from the point of view of the reader: D'Alembert is concerned with a pedagogical system (facilitating the use of the work), Diderot with the training of ideological perceptions. But Diderot alone also insists on the practical social organization of men of knowledge implied by a multiauthorial project like the production of a *real,* not an *ideal,* encyclopedia. It would be a sort of superacademy which

> devrait avoir pour but de rassembler tout ce qui s'est publié sur chaque matière, de le digérer, de l'éclaircir, de le serrer, de l'ordonner et d'en publier des traités où chaque chose n'occupât que l'espace qu'elle mérite d'occuper ... C'est à l'exécution de ce projet étendu, non seulement aux différents objets de nos académies, mais à toutes les branches de la connaissance humaine, qu'une *encyclopédie* doit suppléer; ouvrage qui ne s'exécutera que par une société de gens de lettres et d'artistes, épars, occupés chacun de sa partie, & liés seulement par l'intérêt général du genre humain, & par un sentiment de bienveillance réciproque. (179–80) [60]

The model is striking in its similarity to the picture of social organization painted by Macquer. The authors will be kept quite separate from each other; the *editor,* a businessman like Zadig, will fill the place of the philosopher-king who alone has the right to regulate the multitude of relations between the isolated bodies of specialized expertise. All conversations pass through him; he selects and facilitates all dialogues. The monads talk to each other only through the intercession of the Great Editor, the philosopher-king, who has replaced the Great Clockmaker.

The results of these contacts are then incorporated into the final work as the cross-references, but more importantly, Diderot brings to our notice the real, living *Encyclopédie* that lies behind the dead or unchanging books that are finally published. The conversation and organization thus established live far beyond the (always already out-of-date) work whose creation was the pretext for the bringing together of the various philosophers. In fact, it often seems as though for Diderot, the *Encyclopédie* itself is merely the symbol of this other more natural, more perfect social order.

In the "great chain of being" that links the lowest level of inanimate matter to God in preclassical cosmology, the next step up the scale after man was occupied by angels.[11] In Diderot's updated Enlightenment version, the levels are ranked in terms of increasing *ordered dynamic complexity*. The stage after man is therefore no longer a move into the divine, but into this encyclopedic organized mind which also embodies a perfect social order. Its structure is in homology with the structure of the material world, and its understanding of the universe exceeds that possible for any one man. To form part of this group is what it really means to be a philosopher, for "la philosophie ne connaît que les règles fondées dans la nature des êtres, qui est immuable et éternelle" (185) [61]. A true philosopher is inescapably the good citizen of Macquer's preface: he is a philosopher because he understands the natural and inevitable relationship between the structure of knowledge and that of the ideal social order, and he works to realize it in the society of his day and place.[12] But the article "Encyclopédie" implies no social contract. Neither does it call for violent revolution. The meritocracy proposed in the encyclopedia embodies a *dynamic* order. The *cité scientifique* that is brought into existence by the writing of the various articles of the work to be published is itself the real goal of the work. Each person that writes finds himself drawn into discussion with the others of the group who are working on related subjects; their conversations are the living embodiment of the cross-references, while their own continued meditations on their assigned topics are the living "articles." Thus the published *Encyclopédie* can never be finished, but precisely because it can never be perfected, it keeps the living encyclopedia, the *cité scientifique,* engaged in producing changes in the social order and in perfecting language. This development can be followed by matching the changes in the successive editions of the *Encyclopédie.* The finished ency-

11. See especially A. O. Lovejoy, *The Great Chain of Being* (Cambridge: Harvard University Press, 1936).

12. The same hierarchy structures many of Diderot's speculative essays. In terms of explicit dogma, both *Le Neveu de Rameau* and *Le Rêve de D'Alembert* discuss and even demonstrate the dissolution of separate individuals into an organic hyperindividual. The humor of the anecdote of the statue in the *Rêve* depends on D'Alembert's slowness in catching on to Diderot's replacement of evolution as perfection of the individual, with evolution defined as the growth of ordered dynamic complexity. Even the structure of the *Rêve* itself demonstrates such an evolution. See my "Diderot's Laboratory of Sensibility," *Yale French Studies.* 67 (1984).

clopedia of the "Discours préliminaire" is for Diderot only a utopian goal. The real encyclopedia, although of necessity imperfect, provides through its very structure the means to remedy its imperfection. "Il y a une 3e sorte de renvoi à laquelle il ne faut ni s'abandonner, ni se refuser entière- ment; ce sont ceux qui en rapprochant dans les sciences certains rapports, dans des substances naturelles des qualités analogues, dans les arts des manoeuvres semblables, conduiroient ou à de nouvelles vérités spécula- tives, ou à la perfection des arts connus, ou à l'invention de nouveaux arts, ou à la restitution d'anciens arts perdus" (367) [62]. Diderot defines these *vérités spéculatives* (the oxymoron provides in itself an interesting insight into the makeup of scientific truth for Diderot) as the primary aim of work in the sciences. Progress is arrived at primarily through introspection, rather than by experimentation. It is a result of thinking around, or against, or in spite of, the prevailing "metaphysics," just as the social message of the *Encyclopédie* is supposed to be arrived at against the institutionalized views. The end product is the same: the overturning of a metaphysics leads to a revolution in thinking which in turn transforms the field of study. "La révolution est le moyen de progrès dans les sciences comme dans les arts" (345) [63]. In the case of the sciences, two kinds of revolution are suggested by Diderot.

The first occurs at the level of the metaphysics: the context built by the cross-references suggests to the reader precisely the new way of looking at the science that the author wishes him to accept. For Diderot, the encyclopedia is a philosophical or social weapon. It changes the ideas of the reader from those supporting a particular philosophy or social insti- tution to the very specific and contrary ideas suggested by the author. The scientific dictionary would be only a subset of the total encyclopedia, and the subversion it attempts would be defined as what constitutes "scientific progress."

On the level of the explicit knowledge, we find that the second kind of revolution, which results from the reader's careful use of his imagination to make unforeseen analogies, is not built into the dictionary format the way the subversion of social systems in the *Encyclopédie* is, but happens only by chance, and is dependent not on the constraints imposed by the cross-references, but on the freedom created for the reader by the frag- mentation of the rhetorical emplotment.

The *Dictionnaire de chymie*

As we shall see in discussing Lavoisier, revolution through a carefully worked-out nomenclature, whose terms and cross-references determine the conclusions of the reader in advance, will be at the heart of his reor- ganization of chemistry. But at this early stage of chemistry, Macquer is not attempting to reduce this science to a completely predetermined and defined terminology. Creative thinking, while possible only up to a certain, highly problematic point, is also the goal of the *Dictionnaire de chymie* as Macquer states it: "D'ailleurs ce désordre apparent laisse au lecteur la liberté de se former tel plan qu'il juge à propos, & il est très-possible qu'il fasse à cet égard un meilleur choix que l'Auteur même" *(Dict.* [1766], 1:ii) [64]. Macquer is not just repeating the traditional prefatory expressions of authorial humility. The reader's liberty is fundamental to his definition of scientific philosophy and is a necessary result of his general definition of science and of chemistry.

As we have seen, for Macquer the first criterion of a science is that it constitute a discourse, especially in written form. There must be a systematization of a "philosophy," as Macquer calls it in the preface, and that system can exist only as a function of language. However, one must not forget that it does not represent any system or order hidden in nature itself. It is an artificial and arbitrary creation which serves to marshall many separate facts into a coherent, manageable, and useful tool: "La perfection des Arts, la découverte de nouveaux objets de manufacture & de commerce sont, sans contredit, ce qu'il y a de plus beau, de plus intéressant dans la Chymie, & ce qui la rend vraiment estimable" *(Dict.,* 3:488, s.v. "Laboratoire")* [65]. Just as there can be no distinction between science and philosophy, so, too, any distinction between science and its application, technology, is a Rousseau-like misunderstanding of the inseparability of knowledge from social duty.

Another necessary part of Macquer's concept of chemical systematization is its spatial quality. He specifically wishes to distinguish the *Dictionnaire de chymie* from the traditional Cartesian philosophical treatises (including the two that he wrote ten years before the publication of the *Dictionnaire),* which are linear and persuasive presentations. He also insists on distinguishing his new work from any reliance on the scholastic tradition, which, given its associations and the body of philosophers on which it draws, is anathema to Macquer.

Tout le monde sait en effet que ce terme de scholastique n'a été imaginé que depuis Descartes, dans le tems du renouvellement des Sciences, & pour désigner d'une manière méprisante, ce que l'on appelloit la *Philosophie de l'Ecole?* Or, quelle étoit cette Philosophie de l'Ecole? c'étoit celle d'Aristote, de ses nombreux Sectateurs ... Tous ceux qui ont quelques notions sur l'histoire des études & des connoissances humaines, savent jusqu'à quel point on avoit porté dans les Ecoles péripatéticiennes l'abus de ce que l'on nomme l'autorité du maître ... un jargon composé de mots barbares, qui n'avoient point de sens, ou qui ne servoient qu'à exprimer des idées abstraites & vagues, formoit la Logique & la Métaphysique de l'Ecole, & les subtilités de ces deux dernières faisoient même tout le fond d'une Physique aussi remplie de chimères que dénuée d'expérience. *(Dict.,* 1:67–68, s.v. "affinité") [66]

The most efficient format for Macquer's formulation of his conception of chemistry—a system which is the ordering of analyzed chemical phenomena—would be a spatial one. This format should force the reader to follow the backtracking or branching path necessary to cover the territory. The first postface to the second edition contains an attempt at making a "traité suivi," or a "traité estimable de Chymie raisonné" (1:xxxiii), out of the elements of his *Dictionnaire.* "Tous les articles essentiels de cet ouvrage ayant une étendue assez considérable, ils auraient pu former un Traité ordinaire de Chymie, s'ils n'avoient pas été assujettis à l'ordre alphabétique. [Il faut] déranger cet ordre qui ne comporte aucun enchaîne-ment, liaison, & en indiquer un *autre* qui fût exempt de cet inconvénient: [le résultat est] la *Table* suivante" (4:305) [67]. Upon reading the description of this treatise, one discovers that it cannot be written out linearly, for to write a true treatise, Macquer would have had to be able to write a coherent, linear argument. The "treatise" we are presented actually shares only one characteristic of the treatise: it is limited and definitive, leaving no option in the work for either the judgment or the imagination of the reader. It is actually what Macquer calls it at the end of his description: not a treatise at all, but a table. It operates in a way similar to the instantaneous planar vision: it attempts to be a guide, giving a certain order in which to read the articles, but ends up by being a subset of cross-references taken out of the dictionary's context and gathered into one place. The reader is instructed several times to reread groups of articles that he has already read, or to refer to several other articles at a time for comparison. The map of the reader's trajectory would not be a straight line, as it would be when reading a treatise, but a wandering, backtracking, and sometimes multiple or splintered path, as would be the path of Diderot's reader of the *Encyclopédie.* The image is limited and finite and thus leaves no choice to the reader as to the overview of chemistry he will reach. In this formu-lation, the table, rather than the *Dictionnaire* itself, seems to be Macquer's equivalent to the encyclopedic format of Diderot, to that which imposes answers or ways of thinking. But this is not Macquer's plan for the *Diction-naire* as a whole. He does not wish to force any particular chemical philosophy on the reader of his work.

Avec cette seule préparation, je ne doute point que quiconque a quelque goût & quelque disposition pour la chymie ne puisse lire avec beaucoup de fruit les Traités de cette science dans quelque ordre qu'ils soient disposés, parce qu'on sera en état de les entendre, de saisir les rapports & les *liaisons que l'Auteur aura mis entre les faits, ou bien de s'en former à soi-même un autre ensemble plus analogue à sa manière propre de considérer la Nature:*

ensemble qui pourra être très différent du système de l'Auteur dont on
étudie l'Ouvrage. *(Dict.,* 4:306–7; my emphasis) [68]

No one system satisfies Macquer completely as yet; theories have their
uses (incuding the one that he defends so well in several of the key
articles),[13] but "il faut avouer aussi qu'elles peuvent produire un effet tout
contraire, lorsqu'on s'y livre avec trop de confiance, & qu'on étend leur
usage au-delà de ses limites" (1:xxxv) [69]. But what is it that determines
the limits of a system or of a theory? This seems to be the key question
for understanding exactly what it is that Macquer is attempting to provide
in his dictionary.

What is the status of a system or theory in its relationship to the "real"
world if one can choose "un *autre* ensemble plus analogue à *sa manière
propre* de considérer la Nature"? It implies that an absolute or general
truth that would be independent of the reasoning process of the researcher
is impossible. Evidently, one cannot know the essence of the real world.
But then, how does Macquer justify his, or any, scientific system; how does
he distinguish it from the scholastic theories which were "un jargon composé
de mots barbares, qui n'avoient point de sens, ou qui ne servoient qu'à
exprimer des idées abstraites et vagues" (1:67–68, s.v. "affinité") [70]? As
he suggested in his prefatory history of chemistry, the answer to these
questions lies in his concept of language as a whole, and of the way that
theory and experiment relate to each other inside the context established
by language.

This is particularly relevant for the science of chemistry, as the one
common denominator in all eighteenth-century definitions of chemistry
is the description of the fundamental laboratory or experimental procedure as being that of *analysis.*

> ANALYSE, est aussi en usage *dans la Chymie* pour dissoudre un corps
> composé ou en diviser les différens principes . . . .
>   Analyser les corps, ou les résoudre en leurs parties composantes, est le
> principal objet de l'art chymique. *(Enc.,* 2:488) [71]

> ANALYSE. Les Chymistes entendent par le mot d'analyse, la décomposition
> d'un corps, ou la séparation des principes & parties constituantes d'un
> composé . . . On ne dira ici rien de plus sur l'analyse en général; ce sujet est
> si étendu, qu'il faudroit passer en revue tous les objets de la Chymie, si l'on
> vouloit faire des applications particulières. *(Dict.,* 1:169, 173) [72]

Now, as Macquer has so carefully discussed in his preface, a science is
made up of a philosophy and a practice. In chemistry, the philosophy
(analysis) and the practice (analysis) have the same structure. This same

---

13. The phlogiston theory (of Stahl, primarily) is explained in the article "Phlogistique";
it is defended against the "new chemistry" of Lavoisier in the articles "gas," "gas inflammable,"
"gas phlogistique," "causticité," "feu," and especially in the article "gas nitreux."

structure is also that of language and of the proper pedagogical method: "Parler, éclairer et savoir sont, au sens strict du terme, *du même ordre*" [73].[14]

Degérando will say, twenty-five years later, that "the elements of chemistry are of comparable type with one another."[15] For Macquer, this is true in a very profound sense: the elements of his science are not of a physical type at all. They are, on the contrary, the elements that make up the system derived from and making possible further analysis. They are ideas that represent both judgments and objects; in practice, they are words. In spite of his insistence on the necessity for laboratory data, in the end, the privileged analysis, the one that counts, is not the decomposition of matter into its principal parts, but the creation of the system. It is through the transformation of physical phenomena into words that Macquer can attempt to deal with the chaotic universe of material objects. The things words represent may be inexorably different from each other, but if one collapses the analysis of chemistry onto the analysis of grammar, then they can be manipulated as words all subject to the same operations in the mind of the philosopher and related in ways that nullify or neutralize or simply ignore these differences.

Now, perhaps, we can characterize the nonreferential use of Macquer's dictionary and explain his numerous references to his wish to leave his reader the "liberté de se former tel plan qu'il juge à propos." We have seen that the table, or spatially oriented but finite treatise, is not what the *Dictionnaire* is. Given that the words, as elements in his dictionary, cover the material world that has been analyzed, Macquer's project becomes that of creating, by his arbitrarily ordered listing of all the "elements" of chemistry, a philosophical laboratory. By experimenting in the only partly ordered and hence nonpersuasive space set up by his alphabetical system with its cross-references, the student or scientist can simulate the analysis of the physical laboratory. Macquer has provided the overview of all of the territory of chemistry, and it is up to the reader not merely to choose but to construct his own map, to pick his own individual way of ordering chemical phenomena, the one that best suits his particular experimental purposes.

If the substances are all named or defined correctly, then Macquer's *Dictionnaire de chymie* should be the ideal of the scientific tool for a reader from the classical *épistémè*. The equation *word = world* can be established only at the level of the initial process of assigning words to name direct sense perceptions, but if this process is carried out with great care and precision, then the dictionary that contains all of these word-perception units also contains (unfortunately only *ideally*) all of the

14. Foucault, *Les Mots et les choses,* 103.

15. Joseph Degérando, *Des Signes et de l'art de penser* (Paris: n.p., An VIII). Cited in Acton, "Language in Revolutionary France," 158.

"elements" out of which the reader can construct his theories. If the division of the material into articles has been done well, then the chemist should be able to carry out his task—the comparing of and organizing of data into artificial systems—in the "laboratory" formed by the *Dictionnaire*. In the preface, science was, for Macquer, collapsible to an artificial written system, and the chemist, therefore, inevitably played the role of an author. This relationship between chemical and linguistic analyses brings support from another direction to Macquer's insistence, previously noted, on calling his natural philosophers "authors" and never "scientists," and to his defense of the *literary* as well as *professional* reputations of the practitioners of "la belle science." For Macquer, the workshop of science—analysis—is always figured inside its language, and the major function of the chemist is to write and exchange his findings.

In his article "Encyclopédie," Diderot suggested two schemas in the alphabetically organized work: the philosophically predetermined encyclopedia versus the philosophically undetermined series of cross-references. It is clear which of these fits Macquer's concept of his *Dictionnaire*. The unforeseen and unplanned analogies between structures, procedures, or qualities which result in possible scientific breakthroughs are not a secondary result of the dictionary format. On the contrary, Macquer is attempting, in at least as radical a way as Diderot, to emphasize precisely this potential that the analysis/dictionary format provides for original or creative thinking. Macquer is not writing his dictionary in order to facilitate an implicit revolution of scientific theory like the well-programmed ideological subversion that is of major interest to Diderot. His "philosophical laboratory," if the words are defined correctly, if the nomenclature is perfected, would provide the ultimate remedy for the primary flaw he deplores in all bad scientific thinking, especially as he described it both in the alchemists' and scholastics' writings: that of enthusiasm, immoderate use of the metaphoric imagination to make meaningless unfounded analogies and judgments. For if the "elements" available are precisely defined, then the "moderation" is built into the system. No matter what analogies or suppositions the imagination may suggest, the particular combinations or relationships between the words are limited, by their definitions, to what should have a foundation in direct perceptions of the real world, what should be readily understood, communicated, and verified.

Instead of being merely a reference work to be used occasionally, the *Dictionnaire de chymie* that Macquer has constructed should be the very heart of chemical research, the place in which physical, philosophical, and linguistic analysis can take place using the very same elements, justifying most dramatically Condillac's statement that "l'analyse ne se fait et ne peut se faire qu'avec des signes" *(La Logique,* 93) [74].

CHAPTER 4

Affinity

*Classer, oui; nommer, certes—mais nous sommes
persuadés que ces efforts dépassent le génie et
supposent les dieux.* [75]
—François Dagognet

IN THE FIRST EDITION, THE RELATIONSHIP OF THE *DICTIONNAIRE DE chymie's* goals to its content is not problematic. However, by the second edition, these goals reveal themselves as having been impractical. For although Macquer's dictionary *cum* philosophical laboratory can be imagined, it cannot really exist; it is based on the paradox of having to enumerate the elements of a field while at the same time denying the possibility of previously established criteria for selection. The impossibility of resolving this paradox is what makes the second version of the *Dictionnaire* inevitable.

The many differences between the first and second editions betray the problems Macquer was having with his project, which, as implied by the first edition's "Avertissement," was to give a complete nomenclature of chemistry's separate parts, from which each student could construct his own practical or technical working system. Macquer wished to describe the whole spectrum of chemistry, to leave out nothing, while keeping open for his reader the possibility of constructing his own particular theory. These theories were to constitute coexisting functional systems, none of which claimed to be true, and which were to exist side by side as useful.

But is this project realizable? Let us look for a moment at some of the changes to be found in the second edition.

The first, optimistic "Avertissement de l'Auteur" has disappeared, and in its place is a self-doubting apology for the format of the book—that same format Macquer was so proud of in the first edition: "Je conviens donc que celui-ci n'est point un vrai dictionnaire ou que, si l'on veut le considérer comme tel, c'en est un mauvais, parce que, dans l'état où j'ai pu le mettre, il a tous les défauts attachés à cette forme, sans en avoir les avantages, qui consistent principalement en une nomenclature très complette, jointe à une entière exactitude pour les renvois" (*Dict.,* 1:v) [76]. Macquer feels that his book is not what he had originally hoped it would be; it does not follow the general definition of a proper dictionary given either by Diderot or by Macquer in the first edition of his own *Dictionnaire.* There is a great increase in the number of articles, and many articles which had already been included in the book have been significantly expanded. A third change is the addition of two long postscripts. The first is the table treatise already discussed. The second postscript, in theory unnecessary in a dictionary with an alphabetic ordering system, is a table of contents. Owing to the expansion, the material contained in each article has become impossible to locate. Hence there is a real need for this table of contents, which actually serves as an index. It is a cross-reference system at a glance, an attempt to remedy the disorder created by the proliferation of words in the revised edition. The generally pessimistic tone of the second edition's "Avertissement" is exemplified by an apology for the "désordre que je n'ai pu éviter" (1:vi) [77]. Macquer has lost control of his work; his main criticism of it demonstrates a feeling of helplessness in the face of a too-complex, rapidly expanding field. He talks about a plan for the new edition, but he explains neither what it is nor how it operates on the selection of his subject matter. The major criterion seems to be a negative one, based almost on chance: subjects are left out merely because the dictionary has gotten too large. He apologizes for the resulting change in the comprehensiveness of the book: "Je prie donc qu'on ne considère cet Ouvrage que comme un Recueil de définitions & de dissertations sur les principaux objets de la Chymie, distribuées à peu près suivant le rang des lettres de l'alphabet" (1:vi) [78]. In many cases, the definitions have indeed become dissertations, not at all limited to defining the word in question, but expanding into free-associative digressions on other subjects.

These digressions are not arbitrary, however. They follow a predictable pattern revealing time and again the paradoxical insufficiency at the heart of Macquer's concept of his science and of the tool that he has invented to activate it. This insufficiency is a crucial one for the development of chemistry; it demonstrates the ultimate workability of the concept of "natural philosophy," that harmonious integration of the classical theories of language, social man, and the physical universe.[1] We recall that Macquer's

1. In *La Formation de l'esprit scientifique,* Bachelard underlines the distinction between "natural philosophy" and contemporary science: "En fait, la science contemporaine s'instruit

project had its origin in the assumption that the analytical model of thought or of language is the general format not only of chemical research, but of chemical theories. By following this format, most elegantly embodied in the *Dictionnaire,* Macquer had hoped that proper chemical theories would be "naturally" generated. But they are not. Instead of the highly complex and "active" order that he had hoped for, the result is a confusing accumulation of unrelated pieces of technical advice. The dictionary may still be (and was) used for reference, but it is inoperative as a generative theoretical or pedagogical tool.

How did this breakdown come about? Why do the three analytical systems—philosophical, linguistic, and chemical—"disconnect" from each other?

There are two especially striking examples in the dictionary that demonstrate the faults in Macquer's edifice. The first is the article "affinité." It is only in this article or in the context of articles related to it that Macquer gives a specifically chemical conceptual definition of several of the most important terms in his chemistry: *analysis, affinity,* and *principle.* The second is a group of cross-referenced articles that do support a particular theory of chemical elements, the phlogiston theory, which Macquer attributes to Stahl. A simple definition of chemical substances is at stake in Macquer's attempt to rework the phlogiston theory to bring it into alignment with recent discoveries. But in this reworking, Macquer is forced to call into question the entire system of representation that maintains it.

The organization of the article "affinité" is simple but eloquent. For the first ten pages, Macquer outlines a theory of the scalar combinations and compositions of chemical principles or simple substances derived from the one that Geoffroy had instituted in his "Tables of Affinities" in 1717.[2] The basic assumption of this theory was as follows: matter can be analyzed into smaller components, either quantitatively or qualitatively. Carrying out either of these two very different kinds of composition requires overcoming the affinity that the parts have for each other. Macquer defines affinity as both a tendency and a force:

---

sur des *systèmes isolés,* sur des *unités parcellaires.* Elle sait maintenir ses systèmes isolés" (90) [79].

2. Etienne-François Geoffroy published his "Tables of Affinities" in the *Mémoires de l'Académie royale des sciences* of 1718 (202–12). This version of the affinity theory was explained in Macquer's *Dictionnaire* of 1766; the revised edition of 1778, although it does not discuss the fact, is actually a recapitulation of Torbern Bergman's refinements to the theory of Geoffroy (in *N. Actes d'Upsal* 3:1775). François Dagognet credits Macquer with having introduced the scalar composition of compounds, see Chapter 5 at n. 6. The concept of the scalar composition of compounds is actually necessary for the drawing up of tables of affinity; it is hence not in this concept alone that either Macquer's or Lavoisier's revolutionary reformulations of chemical methodologies can be situated.

AFFINITE. On doit entendre par affinité, la tendance qu'ont les parties, soit constituantes [heterogeneous], soit intégrantes [homogeneous] des corps, les unes vers les autres, & la force qui les fait adhérer ensemble lorsqu'elles sont unies. (*Dict.*, 1:57, s.v. "affinité") [80]

The concept of affinity is clearly an application, into the domain of chemistry, of the image associated with Newton's universal attraction.[3] It is a sort of microcosmic gravity. It is important to notice that for Macquer, the empirical or primary observation that leads to the postulation of this force is the affinity that operates between two bodies of the same substance, especially liquids:

[L'affinité] est d'ailleurs démontrée par une infinité d'expériences, comme, par exemple, par l'adhérence qu'ont ensemble deux corps appliqués l'un sur l'autre par des surfaces très polies; la tendance qu'ont l'une vers l'autre deux gouttes d'eau, d'huile, de mercure ou de quelqu'autre fluide, placées l'une auprès de l'autre, qui se confondent aussitôt ensemble, & se réunissent en une seule masse; la forme convexe ou sphérique qu'affectent les gouttes des différens fluides, quand elles sont isolées ou supportées par un corps avec lequel elles ne sont point disposées à s'unir: effets qui ont lieu même dans le vide, & qui démontrent l'affinité qu'ont entre elles les parties intégrantes des corps, tant solides que fluides. (57) [81]

The empirically observed and verifiable attraction of like for like is explained by analogy with gravity as the force inherent in things that causes them to move towards each other.

The postulation of this new force, the affinity of aggregation, is already an interpretation of the data, a generalization that implies a judgment (to use the terminology of Condillac) on the part of the experimenter. Therefore, even this generalization from the simplest discrete perceptions such as the coagulation of two drops of the same liquid, is already in the domain of what Macquer in his preface has distinctly labelled as theory.

However, Macquer does not consider affinity to be a theoretical force. It is an essential property of matter, a factual given not requiring justification and not open to question: "[Ce grand effet] est peut-être une propriété aussi essentielle de la matière que son étendue & son impénétrabilité, & dont on ne peut pas dire autre chose, sinon, qu'elle est ainsi" (57) [82]. In the case of the two drops of water, Macquer's acceptance of the concept of affinity as a *fact* is in itself not very interesting. It becomes crucial, however, as it is from this point that Macquer jumps off into a general description of all chemical reactions, whether between identical substances (mechanical affinities of aggregation) or heterogeneous substances (chemical affinities):

3. The general idea was suggested in the *Queries* to Newton's *Opticks* (1704). As we shall see, this was only one of two images closely associated with the term, however.

L'affinité des parties principes ou constituantes, est démontrée par le détail de tous les phénomènes de la Chymie.

On ne recherche point ici la cause de ce grand effet, qui est si général qu'il peut être regardé lui-même comme cause de toutes les combinaisons, & servir à en rendre raison. (57) [83]

The *abstraction* of the idea of affinity (again, to use Condillac's hierarchy of mental processes) from a generalization about the behavior of like substances to the behavior of all substances in contact with each other is not justified in the same way that the first generalization was. Macquer extrapolates logically from the behavior of like substances to posit the analogical behavior of heterogeneous substances. Only then, after having presented the theory, does he support it experimentally, and then in the form of *definitions* rather than of observations of the composites:

Je crois qu'on peut distinguer plusieurs sortes d'affinités: *non, que je pense qu'il y en a réellement de plusieurs espèces; car il est bien certain que ce n'est toujours qu'une seule & même propriété de la matière qui se modifie diversement, suivant les diverses circonstances* ...

La seconde espèce d'affinité simple produisant l'union et l'adhérence des parties hétérogènes ... se nomme *Affinité* de composition ... Si, par exemple, les molécules primitives intégrantes de l'acide vitriolique s'unissent avec celles du fer, il résulte de cette union un nouveau corps qui n'est ni de l'acide vitriolique, ni du fer, mais un composé des deux, qu'on nomme Vitriol martial. (58–59; my emphasis) [84]

From this point, he abstracts even further to complex affinity, the various combinations of three or more elements:

On peut nommer *Affinité compliquée* celle dans laquelle il y a plus de deux corps, qui agissent l'un sur l'autre ... Lorsque deux principes sont unis ensemble, s'il en survient un troisième, on voit paroître des phénomènes de composition ou de décomposition, qui diffèrent suivant les affinités qu'ont ensemble les trois corps.

3e Quelquefois un troisième principe, qui se joint à un composé de deux principes, ne s'unit qu'avec un de ces deux principes, & oblige l'autre à se séparer entièrement de celui avec lequel il s'étoit d'abord uni. Dans ce cas, il se fait une décomposition totale du premier composé, & une nouvelle combinaison du principe restant avec le principe survenant. Cela arrive lorsque le principe survenant n'a que très peu ou même point d'affinité avec un des principes du composé, & qu'il en a avec l'autre une beaucoup supérieure à celle qu'ont ensemble les deux premiers principes. (62–63) [85]

Macquer posits that qualitative differences can be understood as the macroscopic or visible manifestations of the varying intensities of affinity that different principles have for each other. This intensity cannot be measured directly, but is only assumed or postulated, in order for Macquer to be able to continue to explain the behavior of increasingly complex systems. By the time he reaches complexes acting on complexes, Macquer's description is totally dependent on the theory; the principles that are separating and recomposing are never seen in their isolated states. Their existences—and especially their identities—are only deductions from the theory of affinity:

> Les affinités de quatre principes formant deux nouveaux composés, pourront, par un échange mutuel, occasionner deux décompositions, deux combinaisons nouvelles. Cela arrive toutes les fois que *la somme des affinités, que chacun des principes des deux composés a avec les principes de l'autre, surpasse celle des affinités qu'ont entre eux les principes qui forment les deux premiers composés.* Cette sorte d'affinité où il se fait un double échange de principes, peut se nommer *Affinité double.* (63; my emphasis) [86]

It is clear that Macquer's concept of chemical combination is that of scalar compositions of discrete heterogeneous principles. He logically ascends the ladder of complexity from mechanical combinations of bodies of the same substances, which dissolve into each other and in which the original bodies are no longer distinguishable, to chemical combinations of two and more unlike principles which, even when in compounds, retain a certain recognizable qualitative character. It is at this point that the progression becomes problematic. Macquer has proceeded logically in his description of the many possible effects of affinity that lead to the "petites loix" which are nothing more than the effects of a single property common to all substances. But each logical advance in the arithmetic progression is accompanied by increasing dependence on analogy with the behavior of affinity in the less complex level preceding it, and a decreasing dependence on directly observable experiment. By the time he reaches the double affinities, Macquer is in the realm of pure speculation; even though his theory may be essential to the production of *Bleu de Prusse* or *Sel Neutre Arsénical* (the only two cross-references in the article), his perception of the events involved is entirely conditioned beforehand by what his theory has analogically led him to expect. This theory has several possible consequences, which Macquer states as follows:

> La dernière remarque qu'on peut faire sur l'affinité simple de composition, fournit une loi fondamentale très générale, & d'un très grand usage, pour reconnoître, *même sans décomposition,* les principes dont les corps sont composés. Voici cette remarque: *c'est que tous les corps composés ont des propriétés qui participent de celles des principes dont ils sont composés.* Ainsi, par exemple, l'union de deux principes, dont l'un est fixe & l'autre volatil, forme un composé qui a un degré de fixité ou de volatilité, moyen entre celles de ses principes.
> Il en est de même de toutes les autres propriétés, telle que la pesanteur, l'opacité, la transparence, la ductilité, la dureté, la fluidité, &c., & même des

affinités; en sorte *qu'en supposant qu'on connoisse parfaitement les propriétés des principes d'un composé, on pourra, en examinant les propriétés de ce composé, reconnoître quels sont ses principes quand même l'analyse en seroit impossible.* (61; my emphasis) [87]

Here we have Macquer's justification for his statement that "ce grand effet ... est si général qu'il peut être regardé lui-même comme cause de toutes les combinaisons, & *servir à en rendre raison*" (57; my emphasis) [88]. But it is now easy to recognize the assumptions that make this statement possible.

Chemical principles are not elements in a modern sense, defined by the internal structure of their constituent particles, but substances which support *an observable identifying property or quality.* The presence of a particular principle in a compound is recognizable by the presence of its characteristics in that compound, and the intensity of these qualities is an indication of the quantity of the principle present.

The possibility of adding the principles' qualities to each other to read a compound is directly analogous (although not reducible) to the concept of scalar combinations that makes the theory of affinity acceptable in logical terms. The principles in a heterogeneous compound maintain their integrity in the various compositions and decompositions that their affinities produce, and this integrity is *read* by the experimenter through his observation of the characteristic properties of each principle in the compound. But this integrity is perceivable only if affinity operates as postulated, and the abstraction from the data to produce the theory of affinity is possible only if it is postulated that principles keep their characteristics intact in composition. Neither the definition of *affinity* nor the definition of *principle* can exist outside the context of the other; they are mutually defining terms.

Behind these two definitions, supporting them but nonetheless relying on them, is an implicit definition of chemical analysis. As discussed earlier, Macquer's definition of *analysis* is reducible to the standard eighteenth-century concept of analysis as the organized decomposition of an object into its constituent parts and the description of the links between them. But that definition was always derived using a static visual field as the example of an object to be analyzed. The object of chemical analysis is not as easily characterizable. Even if one takes as object a single compound, a simple visual description of its most striking characteristics and the relationships between these characteristics does not constitute a chemical analysis. A chemical analysis attempts to separate out and recognize the different substances that make up the compound and to describe the relationships between them. At best, this information should be acquired materially through physical and not visual decomposition. But often, as in the case of the double affinities, the compound can be decomposed only in the presence of another compound, but at the same moment a recomposition with part of the second compound is effected. The researcher has to visualize the intervening states indirectly.

However, in the article "affinity," this problem is resolved. If a principle is a *carrier of a quality,* and if the presence of that observable quality in a compound indicates the presence of its carrier principle, then the possibility for directly observable analysis is reinstituted. But this is possible only through the grid of the affinity theory that makes this definition of a principle logical. And conversely, it is only through analogy with the general logical structure of philosophical analysis that it is possible for Macquer, when building up the definition of the combinations and permutations of affinities, to deduce the existence of the distinct chemical principles. Chemical principles are merely the mentally accomplished materializations of observed (or observable) qualities.

Just where the intersection of the theories of chemical and philosophical analysis lies is quite clear, and so are the implications of this intersection: "En supposant qu'on connoisse parfaitement les propriétés des principes d'un composé on pourra, en examinant les propriétés de ce composé, reconnoître quels sont ses principes, quand même l'analyse [matérielle] en seroit impossible" (61) [89]. The philosophical or logical analysis has priority over the material analysis of the laboratory; the goal of the chemist is to be able to *name* the constituent parts and their relationships rather than to be able to physically separate them. The privilege accorded to the process of reading compounds to perform their analysis provides one more insight into Macquer's fascination with the dictionary format. The complementary synthesis is performed by the chemist, in his armchair, as he reads the dictionary. The mental equivalent of the physical force of affinity is the establishing of the "cross-references" that combine term to term to form the philosopher's systems.

But the weak point of the analytic system is also signalled by Macquer, for it is almost impossible ever to perform the analyses definitively. "En supposant qu'on connoisse *parfaitement* les propriétés des principes...." It is not for nothing that the theory of mutual attractions is called "affinité." This word is at the center of the long alchemical tradition,[4] in which the relationships of all objects (including the names of the things) to each other were determined according to a complex of different relationships of similarity, each one serving as the epistemological basis and signature of another. At the heart of these poetic similitudes is the relationship of affinity, a sort of hidden metaphysical attraction of certain objects for each other, which can be perceived only in the context of, or in juxtaposition

4. See on this topic Owen Hannaway's *The Chemist and the Word* (Baltimore: Johns Hopkins University Press, 1975), which elaborates upon Foucault's definition of the Renaissance *épistémè* in "La Prose du monde," chapter 2 of *Les Mots et les choses.*

with, the other similitudes.[5] Affinity for the post-alchemical eighteenth-century chemists also reveals hidden similarities between distinct substances and the diversity which covers the similarities binding all things together. It ties together *principle* and *analysis.*

Analysis, principle, and affinity work only as a complex, each term defining and justifying, or serving as the reference for, the others in order to map out the boundaries of a conceptual field called chemistry. From this perspective, it becomes clear why Macquer attributes such overwhelming importance to the "Tables of Affinity" of Geoffroy, incomplete as they are. They constitute, for him, the first attempt to sketch out a theory of chemistry in which the formal structure of the presentation coincides with the methodological and material structures in which analysis, affinity, and principle work in harmony to demonstrate each other. "Mais personne, que je sache, n'avoit eu, avant feu *M. Geoffroy* le Médecin, l'idée de présenter dans un tableau très précis & très court, les effets des principales combinaisons & décompositions qui sont et seront toujours le fond & la base de toute la Chymie" (65) [90].

The fault and the strength of Geoffroy's tables, interestingly enough, lie in precisely the same qualities: "La table de *M. Geoffroy* avoit deux défauts, l'un d'être incomplette, & l'autre qui prouve que l'auteur étoit un homme de génie, de présenter quelques propositions qui ne sont point entièrement justes à cause de leur trop grande généralité" (65) [91]. These two flaws are actually due to a quirk in the concept of the scientific table. Geoffroy generalized the system of affinity to produce the structure of the scientific table. Theory or system seems to become fact. The theory of analysis that the general idea of a table depends on is present here only as the structure of his specific tables and is not explicitly explained. The incompleteness of Geoffroy's tables, the blank spaces, therefore, are less a flaw of the theory than an indication to later researchers as to where work remains to be done; the "too great generality" is not an immediate litmus test for a reprehensible act of theorization, but simply an indication that Geoffroy was a "man of genius." But according to Macquer's description of the modern chemist in the preface to the *Dictionnaire de chymie,* "genius" is a characteristic of the person who is able to perceive all of the facts at once and to link them together into a coherent "philosophy"—to analyze them. It is clearly a theory of chemistry that Geoffroy is encoding into the tables, according to Macquer's previous definitions.

But Macquer persists in calling the tables of affinity *a fact.* What he seemed at first to have defined as a fact was a simple and directly observable

---

5. The illusory nature of the crucial term *affinity* is most poignantly signalled by Bachelard in a discussion of Berthollet: "L'affinité serait radicalement indéfinie. C'est vraiment un désir." *Le Pluralisme cohérent de la chimie moderne* (Paris: Vrin, 1973), 52.

physical attribute that led to a single perception and hence to a single image in the mind of the philosopher. This single physical quality was equivalent to the single term that named it. No judgment was involved in this process; judgment enters only on the level of the links made between facts in the constitution of a system. The equivalence between single fact and word, a result of the analogous parts they play in systems of analysis (what Dagognet calls the "parallélisme physico-grammatical,"[6] which is the same parallel upon which the structure of the *Dictionnaire* is based) actually helps to hide the logical inconsistency embedded in the article "affinité." In steadfastly calling affinity a fact, Macquer is not merely attributing to it the simple conceptual status of a perception. Unwilling to admit that affinity is a product of analogical reasoning, and hence is artificial rather than natural, he has created a new type of fact: it is the *link between perceptions* (of which affinity is but one example) that is defined as being as true as the simple data from which it is derived.

Bachelard will say (talking about the alchemists), "Une science qui accepte les images est, plus que toute autre, victime des métaphores" [92].[7] In the case of Macquer, the image is not a simple metaphor, but, more subtly, the structure of the analytical system, repeated on every level. The language of philosophy that Macquer wanted to order according to a carefully maintained distinction between what is true and what is the result of artificial judgment, between what comes from the world and what comes from the mind, would have allowed him to move on the several levels of analysis at once (the physical, the linguistic, and the philosophical), or to move from one level of analysis to another, while remaining securely inside the same language. Language was always to be privileged over all of the other types of analysis, because Macquer shared the definition of language as the paradigm of all types of analysis. The *Dictionnaire* was the tangible presence of the being of language, waiting to be organized into an infinite number of equally valid "sentences," or systems, or compounds. As such, as the formal transcending of the linear argument of the treatise, the dictionary format was the final alignment of the rhetorical presentation with the physical, grammatical, and logical procedures. In this way, the language of science *was* the language of philosophy; language about the world was language working on itself.

It is therefore ironic that, in the article "affinité," the final focusing of all of the various structures of analysis to coincide with each other immediately brings into view the flaw that had previously been disregarded: at the initial point the posited relationship word-perception-object is equivocal. In order for all the structures of· analysis to be homologous, the

6. Dagognet, *Tableaux et langages de la chimie,* 27.
7. Bachelard, *La Formation de l'esprit scientifique,* 38.

perception must drop out to make the relationship a one-to-one identity: the word is effectively transparent to the thing. However, the perception is only a partial knowledge of the thing perceived; no number of perceptions can ever totalize the essence of an object perceived. Although Condillac acknowledges this, Macquer proceeds as though the act of naming—of constituting a fact, as he would have it—creates objective knowledge. But this objectivity is purely illusory, for "une connoissance immédiate est, dans son principe même, subjective" [93].[8] The nature of this subjectivity is obvious in the demonstration, in the article "affinité," that even the most immediate perception is made by analogy with previous perceptions; one never sees through innocent eyes. From the very first, Macquer's description of affinity clearly is dependent on unfounded analogies; all perception is already judgment.

There are two conclusions that can be drawn from this point. First, if all perception is already judgment, then the experiential basis of scientific research is highly mediated by the intellectual past of each researcher.[9] There is no simple qualitative difference between philosophical and scientific reasoning. No process of reasoning can escape from subjectivity. But to operate in the material world, the scientist needs a dependable point of contact with it; he needs at least the working assumption of verifiable objective knowledge. Macquer's philosophical position is ultimately untenable, as the practitioners of the chemical arts had to have some way of distinguishing between pragmatic and philosophical or literary operations in language.

This dilemma leads to the second conclusion: it is possible to draw a distinction between philosophical and scientific truths. Philosophical truth or judgment is involved in abstract, all-encompassing categorization which returns to talk about the operations of its own language. Scientific truth is of a more pragmatic order; it serves the needs of the researcher in a more complicated way. It is therefore doubly ironic that Macquer quite pragmatically demonstrates the logic of *the scientific hypothesis* on the microcosmic level of the article "affinité" and at the same time attempts to deny the necessary implications of this logic on the macrocosmic level of the *Dictionnaire*.

To be able to carry out work in a science rather than just theorize about ideal procedures, one must, as Macquer demonstrates in the article "affinité," be willing to disregard the differences of kind that Macquer himself postulates between the term that stands in for the fact/principle (as singular, "objective," or immediate reality) and the system or theory (as complex,

8. Ibid., 211.

9. Ludwik Fleck, *The Genesis and Development of a Scientific Fact* (Chicago: University of Chicago Press, 1979), 133.

"subjective," or derived reality). To deal with a system as a term, as he does using the noun "affinity," is to confer on a theoretical system a coefficient of truth denied to it under normal circumstances. It is precisely in his description of the mechanism of analytic naming that the significant change of procedure takes place.

Macquer does not want to adopt either extreme position—that system can be true or that all perception is already judgment. There must be objective knowledge that is primary to an artificial system. If there is no objective knowledge, the words cannot stand in for the things, and hence they cannot be manipulated as though they were the objects themselves. On the other hand, if there is no longer a distinction between theory and fact, then there can be only one true theory. The multiplicity of systems made possible by the dictionary format is at best a collection of just so many pretty stories that contradict the one true theory, but at worst, they are impossible. The *Dictionnaire de chymie,* in either case, cannot be used as a philosophical laboratory.

Macquer avoids, in the short run, this contradiction between the project of the dictionary and the pragmatic demands of his research. Instead of abandoning the idea of the scientific fact, he redefines it in practice to cover several of what, in his earlier work, he would have called artificial systems. By combining several discrete facts, he arrives at, not a theory, but simply a complex fact, at something which is both complex and derived, but which is not recognized by the reader as having been reached either through judgmental or combinatorial processes. He then gives a simple name to this complex fact, a name like *affinity.* By this process of renaming, the "glue" that holds the individual facts together, which is actually the process of systematization, becomes invisible. Instead of being seen as complex and *derived,* such constructions are now recognized only as complex. Hence for Macquer, Geoffroy's "Tables of Affinity" are not homologous to, nor a simplified version of, the dictionary. They are of a different order: they are fact and not theory. In this way, greater and greater complexes of scientific "truth" can be generated; Macquer proceeds in the application of his theory without having constantly to justify and qualify his reasoning.

Macquer has barely missed the way out of his dilemma. He does not recognize the possibility of working provisionally *as though* system or theory were true; that is, instead of working with a scientific hypothesis, he defines his system as a complex of truths. Rather than abandon the distinction between term and system, he simply *redefines* it in such a way that what was before only system can now be seen as fact.[10] He does not

10. Dagognet signals a similar and crucial event in the later history of chemistry in his discussion of the periodic table of the elements: "On ne peut ni l'affadir ni l'écarter: il ne faut que le regarder, apprendre à le lire, ou à le déchiffrer. *Table de la loi,* ou plutôt *Loi*

see that term and system imply each other, that the extremes of subjectivity and objectivity have a dialectical relationship in the formulation of a hypothesis and lead neither to one extreme nor to the other, but to the constitution of *scientific judgment.*

The real problem for Macquer lies with the inevitable implications that such a change in the procedures of naming holds for projects like his dictionary. The structure of these "complex facts," after all, implies a reasoning process that is not subject to challenge on its own ground; although the complex fact is complex and derived, it is perceived as true. More precisely, the links connecting the separate constituent facts are no longer seen at all. The treatise as persuasive argument or its spatial correlate, the table (whose persuasion is even more effectively masked or made to seem natural by the self-effacing tabular structure), has thus been reinstated into the body of the *Dictionnaire.*

If the process begun in the article "affinity" is allowed to continue unchecked, then all of the articles (facts or terms) could potentially crystallize into a rigid but coherent system of complex fact that gives itself for true. There would no longer be any room for the free play of the reader's imagination, for a multiplicity of readings of the data. The *Dictionnaire* would, in effect, become inoperative; it would be reduced from a combinatorial space to a very complex table.

But by using the specious distinction between complex fact and theory, Macquer hopes to maintain the illusion that he has not abandoned the theory of language that he must support for the *Dictionnaire* to be a valid project. It was to be hoped that the reader would not notice that he could no longer construct just any system. Invisible limits are instantly imposed on his imagination *not* by the exactitude with which principles are first observed and then encoded as object terms in the dictionary, but by the chemical theory imposed by the use of theory terms like *affinity.* These theory terms have the enormous advantage of providing a definition of both the objects and the limits of chemistry as a field. They therefore provide criteria for the selection of the subjects of the articles and place corresponding limits on the size of the dictionary.

However, the ruse is only too obvious and, in fact, made more apparent by every attempt to mask it. If Macquer refuses to give up his project, then he also must dispense with selection criteria. Hence there is no way to avoid the need for a second, enlarged edition to include more of the potentially chemical subjects. Neither, however, is there any way to check

---

devenue Table ... Il n'est pas un seul laboratoire où le Tableau périodique ne soit accroché au mur ... A l'heure où certains ne jurent que d'une science relative (et par conséquent fugitive), il est salutaire de relever cette fixité: une pure théorie s'est en quelque sorte fichée dans l'histoire et celle-ci s'enroule autour d'elle sans pouvoir l'arracher." *Tableaux,* 99 [94].

the number of subjects or to judge when a subject has been sufficiently explained; there is no way to judge when the definition of the term slips into the development of a system.

Although Macquer tries to "name away" his problem in the article "affinité," it is clear that what he has pointed out is the impossibility of maintaining the fiction of the unproblematic parallel systems that he calls philosophy. Early on, the superimposition of the various analytic structures that are embodied in the *Dictionnaire,* language about the world (science), and language about language (literature and philosophy) could happily coexist (and even, in the Renaissance *épistémè,* have any distinctions between them be meaningless). But Macquer pushes the implications of analysis to the limit; suddenly the language of philosophy splits into all of its constituents, and the fiction of the totalizing language of philosophical analysis is shattered. A choice must be made; one can no longer be a philosopher—that is, one can no longer be at the same time a scientist and an author. One must either utter scientific truths or philosophical opinions, and the systems can no longer be equated.

Macquer tries not to make this choice. In order to avoid it, he resorts to a devious maneuver.

The article "affinité" is eighteen pages long. The section I have just discussed, in which the tables of Geoffroy are explained, comprises the first ten pages. The last eight pages (almost half of the article) have nothing to do with affinity at all. They are a recapitulation of the distinctions between the alchemists who believed that their analogies were true and the modern chemist who knows that his systems are not true, but who sees them as useful—to create products to facilitate further research.

In the "Préface de l'Auteur," the distinction alchemist/chemist was carefully worked out through a rhetorical structure in which the existence of enlightened modern chemists was derived neither from factual historical descriptions nor, more importantly, from any explanation of a theory of chemistry that would define it as a coherent field of study. The chemists were defined purely as the locus of a series of epithets opposed, point by point, to the irrational qualities of the alchemists whose thinking patterns Macquer found both unethical (antisocial) and analogical to the point of incomprehensibility. The lack of a definition of chemistry in the preface parallels the reluctance to adopt a theory of chemistry in the body of the *Dictionnaire.*

Interestingly enough, it is precisely at the point in the article "affinité" at which Macquer's discussion obviously transforms itself into scientific theorizing that Macquer breaks off and turns to a restatement and reelaboration of the preface. He presents the objections of another chemist (*feu* M. Baron): "[Il dit que] le système des affinités est une belle chimère plus propre à amuser nos Chymistes scholastiques, qu'à avancer cette science;

[il les appelle] nos raisonneurs, nos faiseurs de tables, &c." (67) [95]. Macquer immediately counters with:

> Je remarquerai seulement ici, puisque l'occasion s'en présente, que les affinités plus ou moins grandes des différentes substances qui agissent les unes sur les autres, sont des choses de fait & d'expérience auxquelles on ne peut pas donner le nom de système, parce qu'en Physique ce nom ne peut s'appliquer qu'à des raisonnemens & à des conjectures & point du tout à des faits. D'ailleurs, quels peuvent être les chymistes que l'Auteur a voulu désigner par l'épithète méprisante de Scholastiques? (67) [96]

Notice here the use of another purely rhetorical move: Macquer frames the most unfounded of all of the conclusions in the article with the condescending "je remarquerai seulement ici … que" and "d'ailleurs." He at once avoids having to confront or explain the implications of the sudden collapse of theory onto fact by implying that what he states so baldly needs no explanation, and then he changes the subject quickly to discuss a minor point of the accusation. The unwary reader will think that, because the next seven pages are spent refuting the charge of "scholasticism," Macquer has refuted the charge that Geoffroy's tables are a theory, whereas the arguments are not substantively related. He also describes the chemists of whom he does approve in the same series of laudatory adjectives—"les plus illustres & les plus estimables que nous ayons eus jusqu'à présent en Physique & en Chymie" (67) [97]—that he had relied on so heavily in the preface.

Finally, Macquer instructs the reader, as final proof, to reread the preface. It is here that we understand one part of the great importance of the preface for the body of the *Dictionnaire*. It does not serve simply as an entertaining or elegant introduction to an otherwise stuffy or obscure subject but, on the contrary, as a rhetorical mechanism through which Macquer can always manipulate the reader into believing that he is holding to the rules he has established at the precise moment when he *must* let them go to function as a chemist at all. The preface is a kind of cul-de-sac into which Macquer sends the reader, knowing that the only way out is back into the body of the *Dictionnaire*.

Now, as we saw, the preface itself is very carefully constructed rhetorically, precisely so that it will mask the willed nonexistence of a theoretical foundation for chemistry. The social/moral and philosophical/analytical arguments are played against each other in such a way that the reader never perceives the lack of either a logical or formal connection between the two. They are linked only through the rhetorical emplotment, which convinces the reader through polemic when the logic is faulty. Out of the preface, the reader has generated a chemistry of whose presence he is aware only as a locus of the figurative language. He is not aware that behind the figures, there is nothing *figured:* the language does not point to anything. Chemistry has neither a positive philosophical, historical, nor scientific existence; it is cleverly derived from the reader's assumption that it must be there if the language can figure it.

The rhetorically entwined social and philosophical discourses of the preface are woven very carefully into the structures supporting the body of the *Dictionnaire*. But again, though they are linked to each other, they do not support each other substantively. Instead of serving as logical demonstrations, the cross-references are a maneuver to avoid facing the real issue—namely, that philosophical truth has no meaning in terms of such systems. Macquer's rhetorical detours mask the insufficiency of each train of thought, whether chemical, historical, social, or "scientific." When one system fails, he falls back on another; he escapes his predicament instead of solving it. And although each system is given as depending on the procedure of analysis, as being a positive manifestation of the generalized system of representation, Macquer has been forced, in order to support the specious logic behind the project of the *Dictionnaire,* to make the language structure of analysis only one discourse among several systems. It still supports and justifies them, but now only insofar as they in turn can support or justify it through the same rhetorical mechanism of weaving back and forth.

What Macquer has attempted to provide is, in effect, a series of different but related perspectives from which to look at and discuss chemistry. He has not even given a substantive description of the object of his science, for in order for his project in the *Dictionnaire* to be maintained, for each reader to be able to constitute his own object, this object must remain undefined. Macquer has therefore privileged the reader's liberty over the coherence of the science, a move very much of a piece with the idea of the philosopher as good citizen, as he who does not impose his will on others. He has attempted to incorporate certain attitudes into each perspective on chemistry in order to moderate the reader's imagination without dispensing with it altogether. This is one reason why the image of the "bon citoyen" who lives by the golden mean recurs constantly, although it is not substantively related to the object of chemistry.

For Macquer, the opposition alchemist/good citizen is one based on degree rather than on kind, one of moderation rather than self-indulgence. Unfortunately, what is actually at stake in the project of the *Dictionnaire* is not how much the reader can manipulate the language of chemistry but whether he should control it at all. In the slippage point of the article "affinité," during the one moment in which Macquer claims that the system of affinities is not an artificial system but is scientific truth, he reverses the dominance of the practitioner over his language utterances. The working definition of scientific truth is in this instance a function or an operator rather than a value judgment on experimental data. When, in order to advance to more complex work, the researcher accepts to privilege a prior scientific statement and rejects the possibility of continuing to rethink its givens, then he has defined it as scientifically true. The fact that it remains nonetheless a product of language, a judgment or systematization, becomes irrelevant or, in the case of Macquer's discussion of Geoffroy's "Tables of Affinity," invisible. Although the actual functioning of the language may not have changed, the relationship of the practitioner to his language has. The language of literature is subjective and the author its master, whereas the language of science is objective, and the scientist accepts being mastered by his language. But if science is a language that rules its practitioners, the *Dictionnaire de chymie* is not a scientific tool. The kind of freedom for innovation that the *Dictionnaire* embodies is precisely the kind of freedom that scientific language denies.

Instead of making the jump to the language of science, Macquer has chosen to rely on rhetorical structures to create the illusion of a "belle science" that, however, cannot exist according to the rules he has established. Macquer has made a choice; he will not become a scientist. He will, after having most ably played out the implications of his theories of language, after having so clearly demonstrated the inadequacies inherent in his own highly ordered example of the classical *épistémè's* theories of order, refuse to accept the obvious conclusions, and he will therefore remain an Enlightenment author. When the logic of order fails him, he turns to rhetorical and polemical figures of language to try to patch together the pieces of a project that is falling apart, but the definitions then become the dissertations that he was trying to avoid all along. The simple relationship between a word and its definition breaks down inevitably, and every attempt to recreate the illusion of order creates only more disorder. It makes the information harder to locate and harder to understand. Ironically, every reference to the alchemists, whose abuse was to weave worlds of thought unconnected to the physical world, instead of restoring Macquer to the role of the philosopher, only points up that much more clearly his dependence on figures of language at the expense of "objective" proofs, and marks ever more clearly the choice he has made between the language of science and the language of literature.

PART II

THE LANGUAGES
OF THE LABORATORY

CHAPTER 5

Lavoisier's Critique
of Philosophical Chemistry

THE TERMS *ANALYSIS* AND *AFFINITY* PROVIDE, FOR MACQUER, MORE than a workable theory of chemical combinations. Relationships between these two concepts form the philosophical groundwork out of which both a picture of the chemical world and a corresponding delimitation of the goal of chemical research are generated. Both are dependent on their isomorphism with the analytical theory of naming, the system of representation, that is embodied in the format of the *Dictionnaire de chymie*. The theory of affinity, as Macquer has outlined it, serves not only as a collection of answers to chemical questions, but also as a philosophical method. It prescribes patterns of reasoning that determine how the chemist can conceive of and, even more importantly, read the data of his laboratory experiments. *Analysis* tells one to take apart, to decompose a compound into its constituent principles; *affinity* provides the interpretation system that shows how to read where one principle begins and where another leaves off. Together they enable the chemist to attribute a substantive existence and then a name to a selected set of qualities. As we saw, one of the assumptions that was necessary for Macquer's representational system to work hand-in-hand with his concept of chemical procedure—for the *parallélisme physico-grammatical* to be dominant—was the double nature of the concept of affinity. Affinity is not only the name for a force that draws substances together; elective affinity is also the function through which repeatable sets of visible qualities or properties separate each other out of compounds. The integral nature of a principle is thus read through a series of decompositions and recompositions determined by the "laws of affinity," and it therefore becomes *intelligible*. Affinity ties together both experimental procedures and the reading of them. It is the operator through which the linguistic and chemical philosophies close on each other; the

73

chemist is working at the same time in the realm of names and the realm of things.

The affinity theory provided the philosophical framework for the phlogiston theory of the seventeenth and eighteenth centuries, as it was precisely this working assumption of intelligible decompositions and recompositions, of readable compounds, that made the existence of phlogiston logically tenable. According to this theory, fire, as a chemical substance, cannot exist in isolation. It exists only in the combined state, in a compound with other chemical principles; and in this state it is called phlogiston.

Macquer was a confirmed phlogistonist, a disciple of Stahl, and in this, as in many other things, he represented the general view of chemistry of his time.[1] His description of this theory picks up terms which are by now familiar:

> Je n'ai pu appercevoir d'autre différence entre l'ancienne idée du feu combiné dans les corps, et [le phlogistique] de Stahl, si ce n'est celle qui se trouve nécessairement, entre une assertion en l'air, absolument gratuite et dénuée de toute espèce de preuve, et une théorie solidement fondée sur un des plus grands et des plus beaux ensemble de faits positifs qu'on pût réunir pour lui servir de base. Il est bien aisé, sans doute, d'avancer d'une manière vague, que le feu est un des principes des corps, comme les anciens Philosophes l'ont dit, bien longtems avant qu'on eût la moindre idée de Physique. Mais le prouver, c'est autre chose; il falloit pour cela qu'il parût un homme de génie, un aussi grand Chymiste que Stahl, qui pût en considérer toutes les preuves d'un coup d'oeil général dans le détail immense des faits chymiques connus jusqu'alors, augmenter le nombre de ces preuves par une grande quantité de ses propres expériences, et mettre enfin le comble à la démonstration, par la découverte à jamais mémorable de la production artificielle du soufre ... Je ne connois point, je l'avoue, d'autre Chymie que celle-là. (*Dict.,* 2:352–53, s.v. "gas nitreux") [98]

For Macquer, Stahl's phlogiston theory, albeit in much-revised form, is the closest thing to a general theory of chemistry that he can imagine.[2] It is not surprising to find that this theory fits the requirements for a science— philosophical, logical, and experimental—described in the *Dictionnaire*

1. For discussions of the phlogiston theory from both historical and philosophical viewpoints, see, among many works on the subject: J. B. Conant, *The Overthrow of the Phlogiston Theory* (Cambridge: Harvard University Press, 1950); A. R. Hall, *The Scientific Revolution, 1500–1800* (Boston: Beacon, 1954), 305–40; H. R. Leicester, *The Historical Background of Chemistry* (New York: Dover, 1936), 119–49; Hélène Metzger, *Newton, Stahl, Boerhaave* (Paris: Blanchard, 1930) and *Les Doctrines chimiques en France* (Paris: Presses universitaires de France, 1923); and J. R. Partington and Douglas McKie, "Historical Studies on the Phlogiston Theory, IV: Last Phases of the Theory," *Annals of Science* 4 (1939): 113–49.

2. It is this theory that is indirectly presented by the series of cross-referenced articles (the major ones being "affinité," "analyse," "causticité," "gas inflammable," "feu," "gas déphlogistiqué," "gas nitreux," and "phlogistique").

de chymie. Most important is the fact that the logical development of Macquer's description of phlogiston, or of the series of experiments through which Stahl "discovered" phlogiston, follows the process of reading qualitative analyses institutionalized in the affinity/analysis/principle matrix of chemical methodology:

> Stahl a démontré de plus, que ce principe igné, semblable en cela aux autres principes des corps composés, peut passer, et passe en effet d'une combinaison dans une autre, sans devenir libre, sans reparoître dans son état de feu actif ... et c'est en suivant, pour ainsi dire, ainsi pas à pas le feu combiné dans les différens mixtes, que ce Chymiste est parvenu à faire connoître de la manière la plus satisfaisante, les grands effets que produit cet élément lorsqu'il est lié avec différentes espèces de substances. (*Dict.,* 2:354) [99]

The concept of a readable chemical analysis, in which a substance or principle is defined in terms of qualities that persist throughout a series of affinity-ruled decompositions and recompositions, is the only rigorously logical context in which the property of inflammability can be followed from compound to compound, be stubbornly unisolable, and yet still be granted a chemically distinct identity. It becomes not a quality that these substances have in common, but an actual substance with which they are all compounded: the principle (element, in our terms) of inflammability, *phlogiston.*

It was the phlogiston theory that Antoine-Laurent Lavoisier overturned on the eve of the French Revolution, thus guaranteeing himself immortality as the father of modern chemistry. But the phlogiston theory is only the most visible aspect of the Enlightenment epistemological construct that could be read through the field of chemistry but which was by no means limited to the kind of questions today regarded as specific to the chemical domain. In taking on the phlogiston theory, Lavoisier was putting into question much more than simply the existence of the matter of combined fire.

His "new science," as he called it in a letter of February 2, 1790, to Benjamin Franklin,[3] can be discussed initially in terms of three distinct but tightly related reformations in chemistry: his own theory of heat and causticity (the oxygen-caloric theory of combustion), his insistence on highly refined quantitative experimental methods, and his creation of a new chemical nomenclature to house his new science of chemistry. It has been pointed out time and again that Lavoisier's combustion theory, which posits caloric as the fluid of heat and oxygen as the cause of acidity, is wrong and did not fit much of the experimental data available to him.[4] It

3. Quoted in Guerlac, *Antoine-Laurent Lavoisier,* 112.
4. Cf. for example Berthelot, *La Révolution chimique: Lavoisier,* 139–40. See also Dagognet, *Tableaux,* 59.

has also been pointed out that his quantitative results are not as exact as had once been believed, and that many of his experimental procedures not only give equivocal, but sometimes out-and-out incorrect data.[5] The nomenclature which is ascribed to him is to a great extent the work of a group of chemists of which he was a member, but the project was begun by another of the group, Guyton de Morveau, and the initial process of refining the terminology of chemistry and especially of making it into an analytical tool was begun by Geoffroy and eventually Macquer.

> Si donc Lavoisier—on peut nous l'accorder—n'a pas conçu ce projet d'un langage chimique articulé et systématique, il ne faut pas lui attribuer davantage l'idée qui le sous-tend: la conception scalaire des substances. Macquer, en effet, l'avait développée avant lui et aussi nettement ... La seule différence entre Macquer et Lavoisier—encore doit-elle être affaiblie—vient de ce que le premier tient pour fondements "le feu, l'air, l'eau et la terre," que le second cherche à les dissocier. [100][6]

So what is it that explains Lavoisier's importance? To see where Lavoisier himself situates the reform he is attempting, it is useful to examine the position paper that he wrote in 1783 and presented to the Academy of Sciences, the "Réflexions sur le phlogistique"[7] This paper is to a great extent an attack on Macquer's presentation of the phlogiston theory as it appears in the first and especially in the second edition of the *Dictionnaire de chymie*. Macquer's discussion in the second edition, especially in the articles "phlogistique" and "gas nitreux," is a complicated reformulation of the phlogiston theory in response to the papers on the reduction of nitric oxide in the presence of water and mercury that Lavoisier had presented as the set pieces in his theory of combustion in 1773 and in the *Opuscules physiques et chimiques* of 1774. Lavoisier answers Macquer that, as he had shown in his earlier work,

> Si tout s'explique en chimie d'une manière satisfaisante sans le secours du phlogistique, il est par cela seul infiniment probable que ce principe n'existe pas; que c'est un être hypothétique, une supposition gratuite; et, en effet, il est dans les principes d'une bonne logique de ne point multiplier les êtres sans nécessité. Peut-être aurais-je pu m'en tenir à ces preuves négatives, et me contenter d'avoir prouvé qu'on rend mieux compte des phénomènes sans phlogistique qu'avec le phlogistique; mais il est temps que je m'explique d'une manière plus précise et plus formelle sur une opinion que je regarde comme une erreur funeste à la chimie, et qui me paraît en avoir

5. Guerlac, *Lavoisier—The Crucial Year,* xvi-xvii.
6. François Dagognet, "Sur Lavoisier," *Cahiers pour l'analyse* no. 9 (1968): 183.
7. "Réflexions sur le phlogistique, pour servir de suite à la théorie de la combustion et de la calcination, publiée en 1777," *Mémoires de l'Académie des sciences,* 1783, 505ff, in *Oeuvres de Lavoisier* (Paris: Imprimerie Impériale, 1862), 2:623-55. Hereafter cited as "Réflexions."

retardé considérablement les progrès par la mauvaise manière de philosopher qu'elle y a introduite. ("Réflexions," 623–24) [101]

What is under challenge in this paper, Lavoisier explains, is not the body
of experiments and their isolated interpretations, but the particular method
of reasoning, the "mauvaise manière de philosopher," that makes the
theory possible: the analysis/affinity/principle complex that is derived from
the logical concept of *philosopher* in Enlightenment France. Lavoisier is,
therefore, challenging not only the content of this chemical theory, but
the much broader epistemological basis for it as well.

The "Réflexions sur le phlogistique" uses several arguments at once:
the technical, the theoretical/logical, and the rhetorical. It is necessary to
discuss the technical aspects of the experiments Lavoisier relies on only
in passing; their interest in the "Reflections" lies primarily in their providing the subject matter for a "philosophical" debate between the philosophical chemists and Lavoisier. Lavoisier redescribes in the following
terms the artificial production of sulfur that Macquer felt was the experimental basis of Stahl's "discovery" (actually his hypostatization) of the
existence of phlogiston (cf. *Dict.*, 2:354, s.v. "gas nitreux," quoted above):

> La seconde découverte, c'est que la propriété de brûler, d'être inflammable,
> peut se transmettre d'un corps à un autre: si l'on mèle, par exemple, du
> charbon, qui est combustible, avec de l'acide vitriolique qui ne l'est pas,
> l'acide vitriolique se convertit en soufre; il acquiert la propriété de brûler,
> tandis que le charbon la perd. Il en est de même des substances métalliques:
> elles perdent par la calcination leur qualité combustible; mais, si on les met
> en contact avec du charbon, et, en général, avec des corps qui aient la
> propriété de brûler, elles se revivifient, c'est-à-dire qu'elles reprennent, aux
> dépens de ces substances, la propriété d'être combustibles. *Stahl a conclu
> de ces faits* que le phlogistique, le principe inflammable, pouvoit passer d'un
> corps dans un autre, et qu'il obéissait à de certaines lois, auxquelles on a
> donné depuis le nom *d'affinité*. ("Réflexions," 625; my emphasis) [102]

Lavoisier, even more explicitly than Macquer, makes the point that the
affinity theory and the postulation of the existence of phlogiston are part
of the same general physicochemical theory, or more precisely, are part
of the same natural philosophy. He also accepts Macquer's reading that
the property of inflammability is transmitted from one substance to another.
He shies away, however, from ascribing the status of physical element to
this quality and tells us only that "Stahl [l'a] conclu de ces faits" using the
theory of affinity.[8] Lavoisier rejects Stahl's or Macquer's conclusions, although
he has used basically the same language to describe it. Why?

8. A provisional remark: Lavoisier's uneasy relationship to the theory of affinity, which
has been noted by most of his commentators with some uncertainty as to its cause, is not
dealt with directly in the "Réflexions sur le phlogistique," and hence I will put off my
discussion of it until I deal with his cryptic note in the *Traité élémentaire de chimie.*

It is interesting and instructive to note first of all *how* he rejects Macquer's reading.[9] He begins with a plea to the reader, which serves two functions: "Je prie mes lecteurs, en commençant ce mémoire, de se dépouiller, autant qu'il sera possible, de tout préjugé; de ne voir dans les faits que ce qu'ils présentent, d'en bannir tout ce que le raisonnement y a supposé, et d'oublier, pour un moment, s'il est possible, qu'une théorie a existé" (624) [103]. Here Lavoisier, echoing Macquer's general procedures, clearly makes the distinction between the data, the experimental facts, and the *raisonnement,* the theory, that encloses them. He implies that the facts (and the mysterious "ce qu'ils présentent") can actually be dealt with as if Stahl had never existed, as if the theory of Stahl were merely a widespread prejudice of fairly recent origin. Lavoisier is not only asking the reader to be impartial, a standard rhetorical request; the terms in which he requests this impartiality already incorporate the reason for the denunciation of Stahl that will be used to structure his argument: "d'en bannir tout ce que le *raisonnement* y a supposé."

After requesting the reader to forget that Stahl ever existed, Lavoisier proceeds, for fifteen pages, to discuss in detail the *doctrine* of Stahl, the *theory* of Stahl, the *disciples* of Stahl. He specifically goes on to discuss the phlogiston theory in "la manière dont M. Macquer a présenté la doctrine de Stahl dans son Dictionnaire de chimie" (624) [104]. He describes it, as we have suggested, primarily through a critique of the reasoning process:

> A l'époque où Stahl a écrit, les principaux phénomènes de la combustion étaient encore ignorés. Il n'a connu de cette opération que ce qui frappe les sens, le dégagement de la chaleur et de la lumière … Rien n'était plus naturel, en effet, que de dire que les corps combustibles s'enflamment parce qu'ils contiennent un principe inflammable; mais on doit à Stahl deux découvertes importantes, indépendantes de tout système, de tout hypothèse, qui seront des vérités éternelles: premièrement, c'est que les métaux sont des corps combustibles, [deuxièmement,] que la calcination est une véritable combustion, et qu'elle en présente tous les phénomènes. Ce fait constant, que Stahl parait avoir reconnu le premier, et qui est aujourd'hui généralement avoué de tout le monde, le mettait dans la nécessité d'admettre un principe inflammable dans les métaux. (624–25) [105]

On the one hand, Lavoisier points out that Stahl was the first to *recognize* that metals oxidize. On the other hand, Stahl had mistakenly allowed his senses to persuade him that behind the visible phenomena he could deduce the existence of a carrier substance for the property of inflammability. This deduction is given by Lavoisier as the only logical interpre-

---

9. For Lavoisier's discussion of the experimental data, see his article on *gas nitreux,* "Mémoire sur l'existence de l'air dans l'acide nitreux, et sur les moyens de décomposer et de recomposer cet acide," printed at the end of the *Recueil de mémoires et d'observations sur la formation et sur la fabrication du salpêtre* (Paris: Lacombe, 1776).

tation that Stahl had available to marshal the experimental data into his theory of phlogiston. However, Lavoisier has here already rephrased Stahl's interpretation in the language of his own theory. The fact is that Stahl had recognized two different phenomena; he made readings on two different levels. It is helpful to depart here from Lavoisier's misleading narrative to emphasize that Stahl had already performed two interpretations. First, he had generalized from the data the interpretation that metals burn. Only secondly had he generalized the phenomena of burning from this first interpretation and from the experiments on carbon and sulfur in order to interpret them on a more abstract level, in order to arrive at the logical existence of a principle of flammability always *combined* with the burning substances. Lavoisier masks one of these two interpretations, the one he wishes to use himself, under the guise of fact, of a *vérité éternelle* that Stahl has not reached using interpretation (i.e. it does not come from theory), but which he has recognized. And there is, in effect, an important difference between these two kinds of interpretation, one that will enable Lavoisier to avoid the pitfalls of chemical analysis as Macquer had set it up. A generalization is an operation of the mind on the stimuli received from the external world. In the first interpretation, Stahl is remarking only on similarities between repeatable and observable phenomena. But the second interpretation which, interestingly enough, Lavoisier qualifies as natural or unavoidable even though incorrect—is an operation of the mind on ideas that it itself has formulated and that do not come directly from exterior sensations. Furthermore, this operation is questionable in its very "naturalness": it seems that Stahl has attributed to a property the status of a substance in the physical world. This attribution is both protected from experimental challenge and designated as a logical derivation by the explicit qualification of phlogiston as the principle of *combined* fire. The fact that phlogiston can exist only in a combined state should have been the clearest suggestion that what was present was not a material substance. Phlogiston is, on the contrary, a logical entity. The concept of *principle* that belongs to the analysis/affinity/principle epistemology operates in eighteenth-century chemistry in this way to endow a wide range of properties with the status of "substance." In the decompositions and recompositions of compounds governed by the rules of affinity, the identity of a substance is deduced by following the transmission of the quality that serves as its sign from one compound to the next and the next, whatever that quality may have been. A material substance was posited to account for the enduring visibility of the quality. Phlogiston's existence was of course deduced in exactly this way by Stahl, according to Macquer. Phlogiston is a category that can exist by itself as a substance, but only if substance indicates an operation of ordering qualities performed in the mind rather than an assertion about the nature of the material world.

Lavoisier points out that the mistake of Stahl and the later phlogistonists was to have let a logic of deduction carry them away: they moved from the assertion of the existence of a simple *category* of inflammability and its metaphorical analogues to the assertion of the existence of a material substratum for this one property.

Lavoisier's emphasis on this "carelessness" serves two functions. Lavoisier has pointed out the equivocal nature of the word *principle,* which is defined both from a material point of view and from a logical standpoint (it is a carrier of a property or quality, not only a simple substance or the end point of a decomposition). A principle embodies a category. Principles thus lead a precarious existence in a no-man's-land between the realm of words and the realm of things. For the phlogistonists, they provide the necessary bridge between philosophical and material analyses of compounds; for Lavoisier they are suspect entities, leaning towards the realm of logic when chemical analysis falters, and towards the material when the logical deduction is weak.

The greatest abuse, of course, is the one perpetrated quite literally in the name of phlogiston. The physical procedures are so inconsistent that the principle is in practice replaced by the word *phlogiston* itself. Its entire sphere of operations is limited to that of the imagination. Lavoisier had said that not only is there no demonstrable proof of the physical existence of phlogiston, but that even its status as a useful hypothetical body had been outlived. "Mais si tout s'explique en chimie d'une manière satisfaisante sans le secours du phlogistique, il est par cela seul infiniment probable que ce principe n'existe pas; que c'est un être hypothétique ... je regarde [le phlogistique] comme une erreur funeste à la chimie, et [il] me parait en avoir retardé considérablement les progrès par la mauvaise manière de philosopher qu'elle y a introduite" ("Réflexions," 623–24) [106]. This "defective manner of philosophizing" lies precisely in the fact that the word *phlogiston* is no longer rigorously defined by any particular set of qualities; on the contrary, even the most contradictory of qualities will be ascribed to it, depending upon the logical exigencies of the chemical arguments of Stahl's followers. In describing two contemporary experiments performed by phlogistonists and interpreted according to the phlogistonic doctrine, Lavoisier says: "Voilà donc deux substances bien distinctes que confondent les disciples de Stahl; un phlogistique non pesant et un phlogistique pesant; l'un qui est la matière de la chaleur, l'autre qui ne l'est pas; et c'est en empruntant les propriétés tantôt de l'une, tantôt de l'autre de ces substances, qu'ils parviennent à tout expliquer" (635) [107]. Lavoisier insists on the contradictory nature of the concept in many other places, and with even less restraint (see esp. 637 and 639). He also brings in the fact that Macquer had made a last-ditch effort to save Stahl's theory by relying precisely on the *undefined* nature of phlogiston.

Ces nouveaux faits déconcertaient et le système de Stahl et celui de M. Baumé. M. Macquer le sentit; mais il crut en même temps qu'il n'était pas impossible de concilier les expériences modernes avec la doctrine du phlogistique. La théorie nouvelle qu'il imagina pour remplir cet objet se trouve savamment exposé dans la seconde édition de son Dictionnaire de chimie ... On est étonné d'y voir M. Macquer, tout en paraissant défendre la doctrine de Stahl, en conservant la dénomination de phlogistique, présenter une théorie toute nouvelle, et qui n'est point celle de Stahl; au phlogistique, au principe inflammable, à ce principe pesant, composé de l'élément du feu et de l'élément terreux, il substitue la pure matière de la lumière; en sorte que M. Macquer a conservé le mot sans conserver la chose, et qu'en paraissant défendre la doctrine de Stahl, il y a porté une véritable atteinte. (629–30) [108]

But Lavoisier points out that Macquer's efforts, while almost creating a coherent theory for phlogiston, had had to go so far afield that they only served to demonstrate more fully the real problem with the theory of phlogiston: that it is not actually a chemical theory. It is, according to Lavoisier, a logical perversion in the deductive processes of the natural philosophers; it is a strategem to appear to explain something without ever talking about chemical phenomena at all, it is a defective manner of philosophizing. "Toutes ces réflexions confirment ce que j'ai avancé, ce que j'avais pour objet de prouver, ce que je vais répéter encore, que les chimistes ont fait du phlogistique un principe vague qui n'est point rigoureusement défini, et qui, par conséquent, s'adapte à toutes les explications dans lesquelles on veut le faire entrer ... C'est un véritable Protée qui change de forme à chaque instant" (640) [109].

Lavoisier argues that Stahl and his successors like Macquer are basically proponents of a faulty system that has very little to do with chemistry as he wishes to understand it. The epistemological groundwork that enables Macquer to justify the existence of Stahl's phlogiston is the same that enabled him to combine the structures of affinity and analysis and bridge them with the notion of chemical principle. In discarding phlogiston, Lavoisier is undermining not an isolated chemical concept, but an entire series of related epistemological stances: those that make up the "liberal" natural philosopher's approach to his experiments, his writings, and his definition of the chemical art as a field of study and practice.

That Lavoisier recognized very well the implications of this attack is indicated by the polemical rhetoric that supports his condemnation of the illogical status of the concept of phlogiston. From the very beginning of the "Reflections," he makes a distinction between the interpretations given by the proponents of phlogiston and those of the anonymous practitioners of chemistry, whose conclusions are qualified as "natural" or "inescapable" recognitions of "facts."

In summary: from the beginning of the article, Lavoisier has attacked the followers of Stahl on two grounds. First, their concept of phlogiston is an empty one, and second, they are partisans of a school, defenders of a theory, rather than objective researchers concerned with the collection of empirical data. These two charges are substantively related; the real problem with the phlogistonists lies in their background, in a quality that makes both of these charges possible: the disciples of Stahl work primarily in the realm of logic and language. They are not good savants, but bad philosophes. As with Macquer, their logical analysis may sometimes take priority over the experimental evidence that threatens its foundations; it almost seems to preserve itself in the face of hostile experimental data. It is in this sense that Lavoisier's statement concerning Macquer takes on its full import: "Il a conservé *le mot* sans conserver *la chose"* [110] (which is, in effect, not only phlogiston, but even Stahl's theory).

Lavoisier challenges the theory of phlogiston by rereading experimental data to propose two simultaneous changes in the discipline. One is to deny the existence of phlogiston itself; the other—the more radical and more important one—is to challenge, through the exposure of phlogiston as a rhetorical strategy rather than a material substance, the theories of knowledge that delimit the field of chemistry. That this is the level on which Lavoisier expends his efforts is brought out explicitly at the end of his discussion of Stahl and Macquer. It is a call to arms on methodological rather than on philosophical grounds.

> Il est temps de ramener la chimie à une manière de raisonner plus rigou-
> reuse, de dépouiller les faits dont cette science s'enrichit tous les jours de ce
> que le raisonnement et les préjugés y ajoutent; de distinguer ce qui est de
> fait et d'observation d'avec ce qui est systématique et hypothétique; enfin, de
> faire en sorte de marquer le terme auquel les connaissances chimiques sont
> parvenues, afin que ceux qui nous suivront puissent partir de ce point et
> procéder avec sureté à l'avancement de la science. (640) [111]

Lavoisier's statement must be compared with the following passages from the article "gas nitreux" in Macquer's *Dictionnaire.*

> Quoique M. *Lavoisier* semble porté à croire que son expérience tend à
> renverser entièrement cette théorie, il est cependant trop éclairé, pour l'as-
> surer positivement et d'une manière tranchante; ... je n'ai pu appercevoir
> d'autre différence entre l'ancienne idée du feu combiné dans les corps, et
> celles de Stahl, si ce n'est celle qui se trouve nécesssairement, entre une
> assertion en l'air, absolument gratuite et dénuée de toute espèce de preuve,
> et une théorie solidement fondée sur un des plus grands et des plus beaux
> *ensemble* de faits positifs qu'on pût réunir pour lui servir de base ... Ce
> qu'il y a dans les travaux de *Stahl* sur le phlogistique, de plus satisfaisant
> pour les Chymistes qui ont vraiment l'esprit de leur science, c'est cette

abondance de preuve qu'il a su réunir, et dont l'ensemble porte la lumière avec la conviction. (2:352–53) [112]

Both Macquer and Lavoisier attribute to their own side of the argument the positive qualities of experimental proofs, *sang-froid,* and so on. To the other side belongs the stigma of haste, imagination, poor logic, and a cavalier attitude towards empirical data. So what is the real difference between the two? What determines the weight of necessity? Where does Lavoisier get the justification for his claim that his readings are natural, inescapable facts, not to be doubted, rather than hypothetical judgments like those of the phlogistonists ("Réflexions," 628, 634, 637, 639, 641)? Lavoisier's condemnation of the phlogiston theory begins in an equivocal passage. He wants his readers to maintain a distinction between the "fait constant, que Stahl paraît avoir reconnu le premier et qui est aujourd'hui avoué de tout le monde" (that metals are combustible), and what "Stahl a conclu de ces faits: que le phlogistique, le principe inflammable, pouvait passer d'un corps dans un autre, et qu'il obéissait à de certaines lois, auxquelles on a donné depuis le nom d'affinité" (624) [113].

Lavoisier disguises the first interpretation by calling it a natural *fact* and by defining Stahl's act as one of recognition rather than one of judgment. He wishes to retain some of Stahl's conclusions while discarding those that imply accepting the phlogiston theory and its epistemological support, the affinity theory. While the second interpretation, an abstraction, is proclaimed by Lavoisier to be a dangerous abuse of chemistry by logic, the first interpretation, only a generalization, is to be admitted into the corpus of acceptable "scientific" thought.

For Macquer, there is no easy distinction to be made between generalization and abstraction, given the pyramidal structure of knowledge in an ideal analytic system. Either an utterance represents one of the simple empirical "connoissances," or it represents the links that can be imagined or logically deduced between them. These two categories must be maintained utterly separate, facts belonging to the real world (or to the world of experience) and judgments (both generalizations and abstractions) belonging only to the world of the mind (the world of artificial constructs, always subject to challenge.) If within this framework one tried to introduce complex facts in which the relationships between facts were true in the same way as the discrete facts they linked together, then there would be no way to distinguish between complex fact and judgment. The epistemological stance of the scientist would then become nonsensical, as Macquer himself mournfully demonstrates.

Lavoisier discards the pyramidal image of knowledge by accepting generalizations as true. In the passage cited above, he marks the divergence of the two forms of judgment, incorporating the complex or aggregate fact (generalization) into the realm of the natural fact and defining the abstraction as theory. Abstraction becomes an invalid scientific procedure on the grounds that the links that go into making an abstraction coherent are willed (i.e., "prétendus") by the philosopher rather than passively received (i.e., "reconnus").

How, then, does Lavoisier go about explaining his theory of caloric, and just what is the value of such a theory for the science of chemistry that Lavoisier is reformulating? Significantly enough, Lavoisier ends his discussion of the phlogiston theory with a plea for a return to a kind of empiricism and a rejection of theorizing. Reason and theory, he tells us, tend to lead themselves along according to their own internal rules of logic and coherence. They make a good story but do not necessarily say anything about the real world. One must always be led by the data and not by the rules of logic or reason. He then gives us some "considerations on the nature of heat and its effects":

> Lorsqu'on échauffe un corps quelconque, solide ou fluide, ce corps
> augmente de dimension dans tous les sens ... On ne peut guère concevoir
> ces phénomènes qu'en admettant l'existence d'un fluide particulier, dont
> l'accumulation est la cause de la chaleur et dont l'absence est la cause du
> froid; c'est sans doute ce fluide qui se loge entre les particules des corps,
> qui les écarte et qui occupe la place qu'elles laissent entre elles. Je nomme,
> avec le plus grand nombre des physiciens, ce fluide, quel qu'il soit, *fluide
> igné, matière de la chaleur et du feu.* ("Réflexions," 640–41) [114]

Clearly, we are dealing not simply with a theory but with a highly abstract one at that. After a paragraph full of conditionals in which Lavoisier postulates three forces (heat, attraction, and atmospheric pressure) that operate in balance to produce the closed physical system of the earth, we are given the most telling indication of the genre of this example. "Pour nous former des idées nettes sur une matière aussi abstraite, empruntons une comparaison des objets qui nous sont les plus familiers: supposons pour un moment un espace, une caisse si l'on veut, dont ..." (642) [115]. From here on, the reasoning is purely by analogy. Lavoisier does not ask his reader to consider empirical data; he is working with an imaginary closed system whose behavior can be modified and on which he performs experiments purely in the realm of the imagination. This imaginary experimentation makes possible the postulation of certain abstract physical categories— such as heat capacity—solely on the basis of an analogy between material bodies (full of Cartesian "pores") and a familiar object. He has produced the metaphor of the sponge.

> La mesure de cette quantité de matière de la chaleur ... a été nommée
> *capacité* pour contenir la matière de la chaleur; un moment de réflexion sur
> ce qui se passe dans l'eau rendra tout ceci beaucoup plus sensible.

> Si on plonge dans ce fluide des morceaux de différents bois égaux entre
> eux, par exemple, d'un pied cube, l'eau s'introduira peu à peu dans leurs
> pores, ils se gonfleront et augmenteront de poids; mais chaque espèce de
> bois admettra une quantité d'eau différente ... On pourra donc dire que
> chaque espèce de bois a une capacité différente pour recevoir de l'eau.
> Toutes les mêmes circonstances se retrouvent dans les corps qui sont
> plongés dans le fluide igné, dans le fluide de la chaleur. (642–43) [116]

Always using this image to first propose the concepts, Lavoisier proceeds
to speak of the quantity of heat and of the specific heat of a body. Only
after giving a metaphorical explanation of the concept he wishes to introduce does he fill the paragraphs with quantitative experimental findings.
It is clear from his descriptions that the ice calorimeter that he designed
with Laplace is conceivable only if the image of heat as a flowing liquid
already exists.

> Il est clair, *a priori,* indépendamment de toute hypothèse, que plus les molé-
> cules des corps sont écartées les unes des autres, plus elles doivent laisser
> entre elles de capacité pour recevoir de la matière de la chaleur, et plus par
> conséquent leur chaleur spécifique sera grande; ainsi la chaleur spécifique
> d'un corps liquide doit être moindre que celle du même corps dans l'état
> solide, et c'est en effet le résultat constant des expériences qui ont été faites
> jusqu'à présent sur ce sujet. (644–45) [117]

The hypothesis, of course, resides in the postulation of the analogy
between matter and sponge; what is "clear, *a priori,*" is not *a priori* at all,
but is deducible from the given metaphorical system. What is being proven
is that by the choice of the initial analogy, Lavoisier has already predetermined in great detail what interpretations are possible of the empirical
data—a flagrant case of the reasoning leading the data.

From the initial definition of heat[10] Lavoisier derives the pattern for his
explanation of causticity and combustibility. It is therefore at this point
that he introduces his theory of oxygen. Basically, he splits phlogiston
between, at this point, two entities (later, as we shall see, he divides it up
into caloric, hydrogen, and oxygen). He sorts out the matter of heat (which
contains the properties of heat and fire) from vital air or oxygen (containing
the properties of fire and causticity). "J'ai déduit toutes les explications
d'un principe simple, c'est que l'air pur, l'air vital, est composé d'un
principe particulier qui lui est propre, qui en forme la base, et que j'ai
nommé *principe oxygine,* combiné avec la matière du feu et de la chaleur"
(623) [118]. Any time there is a problem that Lavoisier cannot explain in

10. Contrast his matter of heat with Macquer's equally imaginative—and equally logical
and coherent—description of heat as a form of motion between particles in the article "feu"
in the second edition of the *Dictionnaire.*

chemical terms, he again refers to the image of the sponge:

> Si donc l'air vital ne laisse échapper la matière du feu qui lui était unie
> qu'autant qu'il perd l'état aériforme, il ne devrait pas y avoir de dégagement
> de chaleur dans la combustion du charbon; cette circonstance, qui semble
> contrarier les idées générales que j'ai cherché à donner de la combustion,
> exige quelques détails particuliers.
>
> J'observai d'abord que, dans la formation de l'air fixe, ... le charbon
> disparait en entier, et que la quantité de cette substance qui se trouve
> dissoute ainsi dans l'air vital est de plus du tiers de son poids; mais, loin que
> l'air qui a reçu une aussi grande quantité de matière et qui l'a logée entre
> ses molécules constituantes ait augmenté de volume, il se trouve au
> contraire diminué d'un dix-neuvième; il est donc évident que les particules
> de l'air vital se sont rapprochées, que les intervalles qu'elles laissent entre
> elles ont été diminués. (647–48) [119]

A few pages later, however, Lavoisier tells us: "Mais ... l'expérience et
l'analogie prouvent *également* que la chaleur spécifique de l'air, et celle
qui lui est combinée, est infiniment plus abondante que celle de quelque
corps combustible que ce soit" (652) [120]. In this argument, the experiment and the analogy are, for the first time, on an equal footing. Then
Lavoisier finally does reverse the process, moving from analogical explanations of experimental data to experiment used to support the analogical
model. "N'est-ce pas une nouvelle preuve que le fluide de la chaleur
occupe les interstices des corps; que, toutes les fois que les interstices
diminuent, il y a de la chaleur qui en est chassée et qui devient libre?"
(653) [121]. The experiments and their interpretations, both of which were
dependent for their initial exposition on the image of the sponge, are now
themselves used to justify the analogy that made them possible. That analogy is presented again in conclusion as though it had only just been derived
from the empirical data, rather than having been used to structure the
argument from the beginning. *"Je dirai presque que tous les corps de la
nature sont pour la matière de la chaleur, ce qu'une éponge est pour
l'eau:* pressez l'éponge, vous diminuez les petites cellules qui retiennent
l'eau; faites en sorte de la dilater, aussitôt les cellules augmentées se
trouvent en état de loger une plus grande quantité d'eau" (653; my emphasis) [122]. But Lavoisier ends on another note entirely, one that can only
be read ironically, given the procedures by which he has just "proven"
his theory of the fluid or principle of heat, to which he will later give the
name of caloric:

> Je n'ai eu pour objet dans ce mémoire ... que de faire voir que le phlogis-
> tique de Stahl est un être imaginaire dont il a supposé gratuitement l'exist-
> ence ... que tous les phénomènes de la combustion et de la calcination
> s'expliquent d'une manière beaucoup plus simple et beaucoup plus facile
> sans phlogistique qu'avec le phlogistique. Je ne m'attends pas que mes idées

soient adoptées tout d'un coup; l'esprit humain se plie à une manière de
voir, et ceux qui ont envisagé la nature sous un certain point de vue,
pendant une partie de leur carrière, ne reviennent qu'avec peine à des idées
nouvelles; c'est donc au temps de confirmer ou de détruire les opinions que
j'ai présentées. En attendant, je vois avec une grande satisfaction que les
jeunes gens qui commencent à étudier la science sans préjugé, que les
géomètres et les physiciens qui ont la tête neuve sur les vérités chimiques,
ne croient plus au phlogistique dans le sens que Stahl l'a présenté, et regar-
dent toute cette doctrine comme un échafaudage plus embarrassant qu'utile
pour continuer l'édifice de la science chimique. (654–55) [123]

Much of what Lavoisier says in condemnation of Stahl's theory applies
to his own theory of combustion. Where he sees his opponents as "ceux
qui ont envisagé la nature sous un certain point de vue," he sees those
who adopt his own thoroughly imaginary model as "sans préjugé." Yet it
is clear that the caloric theory being expounded here shares the same two
major faults that Lavoisier ascribes to the phlogiston theory. It is certainly
hypothetical in both of the senses that he points out. It gratuitously supposes
the existence of a heat substance (here the *fluide igné,* elsewhere *calorique)* which quite simply borrows the properties of phlogiston that derive
from fire, including its equivocal imponderability (see 643), and ascribes
phlogiston's caustic qualities to another body, oxygen. He speaks in terms
that echo the nondistinction between principle as category and principle
as material substance decried in the case of phlogiston (623). Secondly,
his reasoning does not rely on empirical data, but on abstract, even metaphoric logic ("raisonnement"). His argument may be logically less self-
contradictory and more coherent than Stahl's, but that does not make it a
different *kind* of argument. He is still working within the realm of analytic
logic and analogy. On both the level of the word itself and its complementary methodology, we can paraphrase Lavoisier's condemnation of
Macquer and turn it back on Lavoisier. Whereas he claims that Macquer
"a conservé le mot sans conserver la chose," we must conclude that Lavoisier "a conservé la chose sans conserver le mot" [124].

Let us, therefore, return to the distinction raised before between levels
of theory or levels of fact to see if they can explain the peculiar statements
with which Lavoisier both begins and ends his exposition of this theory
of combustion. He begins his own process of reasoning-by-metaphor with
the following equivocation: "Je ne nie pas que l'existence de ce fluide ne
soit, jusqu'à un certain point, hypothétique; mais, en supposant que ce
soit une hypothèse, qu'elle ne soit pas rigoureusement prouvée, c'est la
seule que je sois obligé de former. Les partisans de la doctrine du phlogistique ne sont pas plus avancés que moi sur cet article, et, si l'existence
du fluide igné est une hypothèse, elle est commune à leur système et au
mien" ("Réflexions," 641) [125]. Contrast this statement with one of his

final comments on his own *systematic* reading: "Il est aisé de voir que cette doctrine est diamétralement opposée à celle de Stahl et de ses disciples" (652) [126].

In what way is Lavoisier's doctrine diametrically opposed to that of the phlogistonists? After all, his theory is equally as doctrinaire as Stahl's, and perhaps even more so, to judge by the polemic with which he always accompanies his work. It is difficult not to recall ironically the break with all past chemical philosophies with which he seemed to begin his article: "Je prie mes lecteurs, en commençant ce mémoire, de se dépouiller, autant qu'il sera possible, de tout préjugé; de ne voir dans les faits que ce qu'ils présentent, d'en bannir tout ce que le raisonnement y a supposé, de se transporter aux temps antérieurs à Stahl, et d'oublier pour un moment, s'il est possible, que sa théorie a existé" (624) [127]. If there is one thing that Lavoisier's reader is never allowed to do, it is to banish the operation of deductive reasoning or to forget for even one moment that Stahl's theory ever existed. On the contrary, Lavoisier's igneous fluid is just as hypothetical as, his theory perhaps even more imaginative and deductive than, phlogiston and its theory were for Stahl and Macquer. If Lavoisier's doctrine is diametrically opposed to Stahl's, it is not in terms of its theoretical content or its reasoning processes. It is constantly opposed via a *rhetorical strategy* to Stahl's theory throughout the "Reflections on Phlogiston." The opposition is that of counterpoint, of dialogue; in fact, the article is a dialogue between twins, and Lavoisier never allows the dialogue to become a monologue or a simple exposition. One theory is bad; the other, although sharing the same faulty qualities, is, through rhetorical opposition, affirmed to be good.

If the entire second half of the "Reflections" is devoted to a disguised if more rigorous restatement of a theory of phlogiston, then what has Lavoisier changed? Evidently, it is not only at the specific content of his theory that one must look to find the differences. Even more evidently, Lavoisier has not reversed Macquer's priority of logical over material analysis, of the systematic over the empirical, as his emphasis on quantitative studies is sometimes assumed to show. Yet it is clear from the description of the "good" theory that Lavoisier feels that there is a significant difference.

We have seen Lavoisier's insistence that the judgments made by the new chemists are "natural." The word that, interestingly enough, Lavoisier always uses to describe his observation of these natural facts is *hypothesis,* and this conjunction of previously unrelatable terms is the most persistent indication that the definition of hypothesis is itself undergoing a change for Lavoisier and for the practitioners of his chemical methods. There is a systematic insistence, in Lavoisier's judgment of himself and of his opponents, on determining the chemist who first *recognized* a particular cause for a chemical phenomenon rather than the one who first created a workable but artificial system to describe it. This point of view gives a serious meaning to a passage which might otherwise appear to be petty bickering on Lavoisier's part:

> Quelque démonstratives que fussent les expériences sur lesquelles je m'étais appuyé, on a commencé, suivant l'usage, par révoquer les faits en doute; ensuite, ceux qui cherchent à persuader un public que tout ce qui est nouveau n'est pas vrai, ou que tout ce qui est vrai n'est pas neuf, sont parvenus à trouver, dans un auteur très ancien, le premier germe de cette découverte. Sans examiner ici l'authenticité de l'ouvrage dont on s'est empressé de donner, à cette époque, une nouvelle édition, j'ai vu avec quelque plaisir que le public impartial avait jugé qu'une assertion vague et jetée au hasard, qui n'était appuyée d'aucune expérience, qui était ignorée de tous les savants, n'empêchait pas que je pusse être regardé comme *l'auteur de la découverte* de la cause de l'augmentation de poids des chaux métalliques. (629; my emphasis) [128]

Lavoisier implies that it is neither the brute production of the phenomenon in the laboratory nor its inclusion into an artificial even if coherent philosophy that is important. His scientist no longer chooses between the roles of inventor versus classical author as Diderot would have it. Nor is he faced with Macquer's opposition of the artisan to the philosopher; he is working neither in the realm of the simply empirical data nor in that of the idealistically systematic theory. He is working with a new category—the *natural*—in a strategically new field, one that displaces the relationships between the practitioner, his language, and his object of study. This new configuration defines the outlines of a transformed chemical discipline. The natural reading replaces artificial systematization, and hypotheses change status from being useful yet artificial systems to being dynamic strategies, rigorously distinguished from the natural readings. They will be positions adopted in order to force Nature to give up its secrets.

This new configuration, however, results in scientific writing that at first is almost indistinguishable from the writings of previous Enlightenment chemists such as Macquer. The emphasis on nomenclature is paramount in both cases, and in fact the reform of the chemical nomenclature was one of Lavoisier's most celebrated projects. To demonstrate the changes in chemical methodology suggested by the polemical article "Réflexions sur le phlogistique," we must turn to two other bodies of writings. The first group explores the problems of scientific interpretation as the recognition of the natural: Lavoisier's experiments on the decomposition and synthesis of water were the subject of a heated debate over his right, as opposed to Priestley's, to claim authorship for the discovery that water is not an element. The second group, which includes the *Traité élémentaire de chimie* along with the *Méthode de nomenclature chimique,* provides the context for a final discussion of chemical nomenclatures, in which the epistemological differences between Lavoisier's and Macquer's two scalar nomenclatures can finally be brought to light.

CHAPTER 6

"Water, Water Everywhere": The Shaping of the Concept of Scientific Experimentation

IN THE "RÉFLEXIONS SUR LE PHLOGISTIQUE," LAVOISIER HAD DEMON-strated that phlogiston was an empty concept. But Berthelot asserts that the stampede of respectable chemists to what Lavoisier calls "his side" was not provoked by such arguments; it was brought about, instead, by the presentation to the Academy of Sciences of the experiments on the decomposition and recomposition of water.[1] Lavoisier, of course, was not the only one to have concerned himself with investigating its elemental status. Joseph Priestley and Henry Cavendish were both involved more or less simultaneously with identical problems, and it has been convincingly argued that Priestley, and not Lavoisier, was the first to have systematically synthesized and analyzed water.[2] However, one can approach this unre-solved dispute from another perspective by changing the meaning of the basic assumptions used to define the problem. We know that Cavendish refused to admit that the decomposition of water proved that it is not an element; but it has been remarked at great length that Priestley did recog-nize, *although in phlogistic terminology,* that water was a chemical compound of hydrogen and oxygen.[3] I contend that this statement cannot be made

---

1. Berthelot, *La Révolution chimique: Lavoisier,* 134–44ff.

2. Daumas, in his *Lavoisier: Théoricien et expérimentateur.*

3. Berthelot, in *La Révolution chimique:* "Jusque là il semble que nous n'avons guère affaire qu'aux expériences de Priestley. Mais la différence réside dans l'interprétation et elle est capitale. Priestley, je le répète, regardait les deux nouveaux gaz comme résultant, l'un de l'union de l'air ordinaire avec le phlogistique, l'autre comme étant ce même air privé au contraire d'une partie de son phlogistique: opinion qui maintenait l'unité matérielle de l'air, sans conclure à sa nature composée" (64) [129]. Daumas points out the basic problem in

simply, because none of the essential terms—"chemical compound," "hydrogen," or "oxygen"—are used by Priestley. Rather, they belong to the antiphlogistic epistemological field being developed by Lavoisier.

To show how crucial this distinction is, to show, in fact, that the impact of the experiments on the decomposition of water was dependent precisely on the language in which they were described, I will refer to two basic texts by Lavoisier: the memoir "Sur la nature de l'eau et sur les expériences par lesquelles on a prétendu prouver la possibilité de son changement en terre,"[4] and the memoir "Dans lequel on a pour objet de prouver que l'eau n'est point une substance simple, un élément proprement dit, mais qu'elle est susceptible de décomposition et de recomposition" [131].[5]

In dealing with Lavoisier's work on water, it is necessary to keep in mind the centrality of water in the chemistry of the eighteenth century.[6] This is especially true for Lavoisier, who expressed early in his career his predilection for experiments performed "in the wet way".[7] In that sense, water was for him not merely one substance among many; it was a principle, or as he would later call it, an element, defined in a way similar to that found in Macquer's work:

> Les Chymistes considèrent le feu, ainsi que les autres élémens, sous deux aspects fort différens: savoir, comme entrant réellement, en qualité de principe ou de partie constituante, dans la composition d'une infinité de corps; et comme étant libre, pur, ne faisant partie d'aucun composé, mais ayant une action très marquée, et très forte sur tous les corps de la nature, et singulièrement comme un agent très puissant dans toutes les opérations de la Chymie. (*Dict.*, 2:163) [132]

---

assigning authorship to such a discovery as the decomposition of water: "Il faut se rappeler que Lavoisier et Priestley travaillaient chacun dans un état d'esprit particulier. Selon que l'on considère la chronologie des faits matériels ou l'ordre de l'interprétation de ces faits, on aboutit à des conclusions complètement opposées. La sagesse aurait été de donner aux deux sortes de considérations la place qui leur revient" *(Lavoisier,* 75) [130].

4. *Mémoires de l'Académie des sciences,* 1770, 73ff, in *Oeuvres de Lavoisier,* 2: 1–28. Hereafter cited as "Nature de l'eau." J. B. Gough, "Lavoisier's Theory of the Gaseous State" (in *The Analytic Spirit,* ed. Harry Woolf [Ithaca: Cornell University Press, 1981], 37), documents that Lavoisier did not actually read the first, historical, part of this memoir at the public meeting of the Academy of Sciences at which he read the second part of this memoir. He simply turned it in to the perpetual secretary a little earlier in November 1770.

5. Read in 1783, but published in the *Mémoires de l'Académie des sciences* for the year 1781. In *Oeuvres,* 2: 334–59. Hereafter cited as "Décomposition."

6. See Jacques Roger, *Les Sciences de la vie dans la pensée française du XVIIIe siècle* (Paris: Colin, 1963), esp. pt. 3, chap. 4.

7. Henry Guerlac, *Lavoisier,* 58. Guerlac presents Lavoisier's early work on gypsum, in which this quote appears: " 'I have tried to copy nature,' Lavoisier wrote. 'Water, this almost universal solvent ... is the chief agent she employs; it is also the one I have adopted in my work.' " Translated from the *Oeuvres,* 3: 112.

It is not enough for a substance to be merely indecomposable in order for it to be designated as an element. According to Macquer, the four basic elements, and especially fire and water, have two mutually exclusive fields of action: the physical and the chemical.[8] Lavoisier recognized the mutually exclusive nature of the two different kinds of fire as the conceptual problem in the definition of phlogiston, and it was partly this recognition that motivated his statement in the "Réflexions sur le phlogistique" that "phlogiston" is a vague term which covers contradictory phenomena. But this criticism is neither fully demonstrated for the case of phlogiston, nor extended to a more profound critique of the epistemological basis of the concepts of the four complementary chemical principles, without Lavoisier's discussion of his experiments decomposing water.

Let us start with a discussion of some of the basic problems of definition that Lavoisier had to deal with during the approximately ten years covered by these two memoirs. For it is the definitions of several key chemical concepts that are implicitly at stake in the first memoir, and these problems become explicit and crucial ten years later in the second memoir.

In the first memoir, "Sur la nature de l'eau," Lavoisier has set himself two tasks, and accordingly he divides the memoir into two complementary essays. The first essay gives a brief commentary on the major experiments conducted during the preceding hundred years or so to try to resolve the question of whether or not water can be changed into earth. The second essay is a detailed report on Lavoisier's own experiments proving that water cannot be transformed into earth and that the earthy substance found in continuously distilled water is dissolved out of the glass of the flask holding the water.

It would seem as though the second essay should stand on its own without the historical support provided by the first essay. The second is, after all, a beautifully specific recounting of one of the highly quantitative and precise experiments for which Lavoisier was famous. One by one, he reduces the variables in the experiment to the bare minimum until the final simple experiment leaves the reader with no choice as to the conclusion to be drawn from the data. But the second essay is deceptively simple. It would perhaps be more precise to say that for a modern reader, the second essay follows our expectations of the proper emplotment of scientific experimentation to the letter, so much so that we do not perceive what must have been the inherent conceptual difficulties for a contemporary chemist. These difficulties are elegantly dispensed with in the first essay; the first essay is in fact the necessary rhetorical and philosophical

8. Perhaps this explains Lavoisier's particular interest in fire and water as not merely simple substances, but as principles, a distinction that will be crucial to the method of his *Traité élémentaire de chimie* in 1789.

counterpart to the second. In it, Lavoisier uses an historical overview as a pretext to refine his definitions of the elements to the simplicity necessary to make sense out of any experimental data.

He begins his discussion with the following statement, whose themes are by now familiar: "Je ne parlerai point de ce qu'ont écrit sur les éléments les philosophes des premiers siècles; l'exposé que je pourrais faire de leur opinion me jetterait dans des détails trop étendus, ils répandraient d'ailleurs peu de jour sur la question que j'ai à traiter: je passe à ce qui intéresse plus particulièrement les physiciens; je veux parler des faits" ("Nature de l'eau," 1) [133]. In speaking of the "facts" of the experimenters whose work he is reviewing, Lavoisier does not question the accuracy of the data, but rather, the concept underlying the presentation of the data. It is around this problem that the overview is carefully plotted out. Van Helmont, he tells us, grew a slip of a tree in a pot of earth that at the end of five years weighed only two ounces less, whereas the tree weighed 162 pounds. Van Helmont drew the conclusion that the water with which the tree had been watered had been the only possible source of weight gain and hence that water had been transformed into earth. The weight change of the tree is denoted by Van Helmont as an increase of earth. But there is a certain conceptual difficulty in defining a complicated and varied substance like "tree" as a simple substance like "earth," which Lavoisier suggests in the language with which he describes the experiment: "C'étaient donc 162 livres de bois, d'écorce, de racines, en un mot, de parties solides qui devaient, suivant lui, leur origine à l'eau" (2) [134]. In Boyle's experiments, which he then describes, the same type of reasoning has been allowed: the weight change of cucumbers and squash grown in pots is attributed to the water with which they are furnished, and hence water is thought to have been transformed into earth.

An even more peculiar type of proof is used in the next experiment described: rather than the size of the plant, the undiminished strength of the fragrance of mint grown in water is given as an indication that water is transformed into earth.[9] Lavoisier makes it clear that the success of the experiment depends on the reader's being able to assume that the presence of a *plant* is an indication of the presence of *earthiness* without a more specific definition of the properties of the element earth.

> L'eau se transforme véritablement en terre par l'opération de la végétation; c'est ce qui ne parait pas aussi bien prouvé, et ce qui répugne même à l'idée

---

9. For Macquer, following Stahl, scent was, like color, an indication of the presence of phlogiston, not of earth, for it activated the senses. The metaphor underlying phlogiston seems to have been derived from: fire understood as producing intense sensation and motion. Hence causticity, bright color, smell, movement, and even quick and penetrating thought result from phlogiston *(esprit ardent* was more than a metaphor for the phlogistonists).

qu'on a coutume de se former de l'eau, et, en général, de tous les éléments
... les plantes ne sont pas seulement composées d'eau et de terre, elles
contiennent encore des huiles, des résines, des parties salines et odorantes
de sucs acides et alcalins, etc. Lorsque l'on combine en effet de l'acide vitriolique concentré avec de l'huile de tartre, il en résulte une masse concrète de
tartre vitriolique, quoique les deux êtres qui sont entrés dans la combinaison
fussent fluides avant le mélange; mais qu'une masse d'eau puisse, sans addition, sans déperdition de sa substance, se changer en une masse de terre,
c'est ce qui répugne à toute idée reçue, et ce qu'il ne serait possible d'admettre qu'autant qu'on y serait forcé par des expériences très-démonstra-
tives. (4) [135]

Hence the first series of experiments proves something, but that conclusion
is not that water can be transformed into earth. The experiments were not
set up in such a way that this assertion could even be tested. In fact,
Lavoisier tells us, "si Boyle eût fait l'analyse de cet arbre, il aurait retiré
presque tout en flègme [liquid], et la quantité réelle de terre qu'il aurait
obtenue se serait sans doute trouvée réduite à une très-petite quantité"
(5) [136]. More importantly, sufficient controls were not applied to the
experiment; it would have been necessary to block off all air from the
leaves to prove that only water enters into the composition of plants. In
fact, air is probably the source of much of the plant matter, and he suggests
that plants can be reduced back to "water" and "air" with little "earth" left
at all.

But Lavoisier's discussion of this traditional series of experiments implicitly
raises another question. What is the relationship between the *three* so-
called elements that go into making up vegetable matter: water, earth, and
air? How does one define these elements in such a way that the particular
qualities of each can be sorted out from those of the others, and so that
some kind of consistently identifiable substance will be referred to when
one uses the name of the element? For this primary inability to recognize
the possible chemical rôle of air in the growth of plants is brought about
by an inadequate definition of what any of the elements are and, in fact,
what it means to talk about an element at all. Lavoisier's definition of air
is in itself very interesting and informative. It mirrors Macquer's definition
of an element by deliberately drawing the analogy between the logical
and the material domains and by not distinguishing between physical and
chemical phenomena:

L'air existe de deux façons dans la nature: tantôt il se présente sous la figure
d'un fluide très-rare, très-dilatable, très-élastique, tel est celui que nous respi-
rons; tantôt il se fixe dans les corps, il s'y combine intimement; il perd alors
toutes les propriétés qu'il avait auparavant; l'air dans cet état n'est plus un
fluide, *il fait l'office d'un solide,* et ce n'est que par la destruction même des

corps dans la composition desquels il entrait, qu'il revient à son premier état de fluidité. ("Nature de l'eau," 7) [137]

Air is that substance which, when in its free or physical state, unites the quality of being fluid with the quality of being compressible (the equivalent for phlogiston is the free-fire state). In its fixed or chemical state, Lavoisier has not yet specified any particular identifying qualities for air except that it seems to solidify. But has the air, in combining with other substances to form a solid, therefore been transformed into the element earth? Does one define "earth" simply as the presence in a substance of the quality of solidity, or must this "earthiness" be the dominant quality of a *simple* (i.e., uncomposed) substance which is then by definition the element "earth"? How can one be certain that the compressible fluid called "air," which can become solid, is an element according to Lavoisier's definition, if its identifying qualities change with the circumstances? What does it mean to say that water itself is an element? Precisely what does it mean to talk about the "transformation" of one element into another? Underlying all of these experiments is a fundamental nondistinction between the idealist concept of readable chemical identities and the materialist concept of a chemical entity that subsists but is *unreadable* through its observable qualities. Given the complexity of the experiments themselves and, much more importantly, the lack of any concept of chemical identity or purity, it is impossible for the plant experiments to test anything at all.

Lavoisier's conclusion is basically that the experiments do not prove, one way or another, anything about the transformation of water into earth; at the most, they suggest that, using physical or state definitions of the elements, the transformation is *not* possible, rather than that it is.

He then begins the description of a very different series of experiments in which the vague nature of the problem under investigation can be at least attenuated. The first step is to attempt to reduce the experiment to procedures which will involve only two of the elements and not three. The second is to attempt to define what it means to refer to *water* and *earth,* and the third is to define what one means by *transformation.* The order in which Lavoisier describes the second series of experiments is significant; each new experiment brings one more parameter of control to the ongoing experiment. Each new parameter of control helps to refine further the necessary concepts (of the elements' identities and of transformation), and this refinement brings about the focusing on another parameter of control that can slowly winnow out the variables unnecessarily embedded in the experiments. For this is, in reality, the reason for Lavoisier's historical introduction. He is not simply presenting an accumulated body of data from which his generalizations can be deduced. On the contrary, his history of this series of experiments creates a slowly developing awareness of just what the *question* is that is being asked. The "language" of questioning is continually refined until, as Condillac would say, the final form of the question indicates precisely what the answer must be:

> Il y a donc deux choses dans une question: l'énoncé des données, et le dégagement des inconnues.
> L'énoncé des données est proprement ce qu'on entend par l'état de la question, et le dégagement des inconnues est le raisonnement qui la résout.
> Lorsque je vous ai proposé de découvrir le nombre de jetons que j'avois dans chaque main, j'ai énoncé toutes les données dont vous aviez besoin; et il semble par conséquent que j'aie établi moi-même l'état de la question. Mais mon langage ne préparoit pas la solution du problème. C'est pourquoi, au lieu de vous en tenir à répéter mon énoncé mot pour mot, vous l'avez fait passer par différentes *traductions,* jusqu'à ce que vous soyez arrivé à l'expression la plus simple. Alors le raisonnement s'est fait en quelque sorte tout seul, parce que les inconnues se sont dégagées comme d'elles-mêmes. Etablir l'état de la question, c'est donc proprement traduire les données dans l'expression la plus simple, parce que c'est l'expression la plus simple qui facilite le raisonnement, en facilitant le dégagement des inconnues. *(Logique,* 273–74) [138]

Translation, the continual "restating" of the same with increasing precision, is not a metaphor for reasoning. It is the linguistic analogue of analysis and hence *is* reasoning.[10] The concept of "simple" that Condillac is using therefore derives from this definition of the process of analytical thinking. The reasoning person reduces his question not to the shortest but to the simplest—that is, *most fully analyzed*—translation of it. Each term must be "elemental": it must be fully defined so that it embodies only one unit of learning, and its relationship to the other terms should be very clear and explicitly designated by the grammatical structure of the statement. Only then can the unknowns be recognized. The real field of inquiry is thus not primarily the laboratory; much of the difficult work is performed first through this process of refining the language in which the question is asked. The laboratory work must be only the simplest inquiry, yielding only the simplest of answers, preferably of an "either/or" or "yes/no" type. Its inevitability and hence its impact are totally determined by the invisible mass of "philosophical" jockeying and winnowing away that has preceded it. The laboratory data is not empirical evidence out of which generalizations are made; on the contrary, the experiment, no matter how complicated it is to perform in practice, should be constructed so as to yield results all of one conceptual order. Only then can they indicate inescapably the answer to a prior and primary question properly phrased. What is, in

---

10. In the *Langue des calculs,* the definition of conceptual clarification as a process of translation is worked out in much greater detail, almost to the point of tautological absurdity. See chap. 2, 4–8, in *Oeuvres de Condillac,* vol. 23.

effect, being tested is precisely the "grammar" of this question. Lavoisier's discussion of the first series of experiments on plants grown in water can be characterized as a demonstration of the inadequacy of the way the question is being asked: can water in fact turn into earth?

Therefore, in the second series of experiments, Lavoisier reduces the number of elements to two and proceeds to the refining of his definitions of the elements. He eliminates at once the problem of the chemical interference of the air and the entirely inadequate definition of earth by eliminating the intermediary function played by the plants.

In the first experiment described, another well-known chemist, Borrichius, repeatedly distills water from supposedly pure sources, always obtaining a small quantity of powder; he interprets his results to mean that some water has turned itself into earth. Boyle performs his own distillations and evaporations two hundred times on the same water and he, also, obtains a considerable quantity of powder. But although the overall experiment has been greatly simplified with respect to the number of active components that are intentionally brought to it, it is still conceived of in fundamentally nonscientific terms. For it is not until this point that the idea of experimental closure is introduced. There is no concept of equivalent weight or of the conservation of matter, because there is no closed physical system operating here. Such an idea is not possible within the confines of this experiment, for the mere transformation of qualities is all that is being looked for. The proof of the transformation's having occurred is read in the production of a new substance which has none of water's identifying qualities but which does have properties recognizable as "earthy."

Without discussing the problem directly, Lavoisier makes it clear that the idea of complete scientific control is the next logical step in the refinement of the "question." It is not enough merely to eliminate sources of possible error in the experiment. One must be able to conceive of an experiment as a totally determined system in which every component has been recognized and taken into account by the experimenter. The main weight of theorizing and interpretation must be displaced to take place before the experiment is performed, not after.

Lavoisier therefore tells us that two of Macquer's favorite authorities, Beccher and Stahl, performed no experiments of their own to back up their published opinions on the subject, but that Boerhaave did, and the description we are given of the experiment is peculiar and significant:

> Il était réservé à M. Boerhaave d'apprécier toutes ces idées et de les réduire à leur juste valeur. On peut voir, à la fin de son Traité sur l'eau, les expériences qu'il a faites sur cet objet; il en résulte que l'eau ne change point de nature par la distillation, qu'elle ne devient ni acide, ni alcali, ni plus corrosive, ni plus pénétrante ... il rapporte qu'une once d'eau avait donné 6

dragmes de terre par deux cents distillations successives, sans se décider formellement sur cet objet. M. Boerhaave présume que la poussière qui flotte continuellement dans l'air a pu se mêler avec l'eau pendant la distillation, et former la petite quantité de terre qui y a été trouvé par les chimistes. ("Nature de l'eau," 9) [139]

The different types of possible error are posited in this text. The distillation vessels must have been open, as dust settling on the water is suggested by Boerhaave as a source for the very small amount of powder that is named as "earth." Moreover, Boerhaave recognizes the insufficiency of the experiment to give data from which conclusions can be drawn, and this insufficiency is couched in quantitative rather than qualitative terms. Not *enough* earth was produced for him to be able to say that it was from the distillation of the water that the earth resulted. The condition, which had been sufficient before, of merely observing the qualities of earthiness in any product, is no longer considered adequate to conclude that the water was its only possible source. The concept of an element as a physically definable identity that subsists from compound to compound has begun to displace the idea of the mere observability of one particular quality among the mix of other qualities, and to make the consideration of the closed, controlled system an active necessity.

To reduce the question still further, Lavoisier describes two final experiments. In the first, the distillation is performed in a closed vessel, which disproves the claim that the presence of the powder comes from dust; then the second "experiment"—which is actually only a second interpretation of the first one—claims that the earth could have been present in the water to begin with, so closely dissolved in the water that only a fraction sorts out with each progressive distillation. What Lavoisier then proposes to do first himself is to ascertain that his water sample is nothing *but* water.

To have been able to speak in such terms is to have already proposed a definition of a chemical element and its behavior in a chemical compound that would preclude the idea of transmutation. What Lavoisier has done is to progressively redefine *water* and *compound* (interestingly enough, he did not need to define *earth* so long as it is perceived as "not-water") until he has specified a new meaning for the term *chemical element*. This new meaning is no longer dependent on the definition of the specific qualities of the water itself; it is, on the contrary, the gradual clarification of precisely the term that Lavoisier uses in the title of his memoir, and which it is easy to overlook: *nature*. When one speaks about the *nature of water,* one is actually talking about a general concept of enduring identity, and hence of an element, whose test lies in the verification of its purity, its *sameness,* rather than merely in the recognition of *observable* qualities which may or may not derive from the same material source. The concept of nature is essentially unthinkable in tandem with the concept of transmutation. Transmutation means that the nature of something has been changed, but by definition, an enduring nature cannot change. Hence, the progressive refinement of terms, the progressive "translation" of the sentence, must move from "Can water be transmuted into earth?" into "Can any element be an element and still change its nature through chemical means?"[11]

What was at stake in the two series of experiments that Lavoisier has described was precisely this last question. The experimenters move progressively away from the experiment in an open system which is not a system at all. The experiment with the tree in the tub is an observation of Borrichius' that he calls an experiment because he interferes at one point to limit the quantity of earth to which the tree has access. But it is not sufficient, as Lavoisier slowly but convincingly demonstrates, to intervene actively in order to perform an experiment in the modern sense of the word. The active intervention must be generalized to a philosophical ideal: *every* condition of the experiment must be controlled *except* one, and that one must be the one that is being tested, that one being the *unknown* of which Condillac speaks. The crux of this problem, however, lies in the fact that in order to be able to recognize, to denote, and to control the conditions of the experiment, the conceptual apparatus must be able to furnish definitions of these separate components that are of the same order: they must be interlocking definitions grounded in a common logical matrix or conceptual field. Only when the language has been sufficiently retranslated so that Lavoisier's experimenters perceive what they are asking can an experiment to test the question generate "facts": *experimental closure is a function of the epistemological or conceptual closure.*

These facts, then, the facts on which Lavoisier calls so often as his final judges, reveal their own true nature. A fact is not a simple entity, a single isolated empirical (and even more certainly, *not* accidentally observed) datum. A fact, according to Lavoisier's definition, implies the conceptual apparatus that made its production possible. It is implicated in a web of prior epistemological judgments on the "nature of the world" under investigation. Hence every reference to an experimental fact has meaning only in the presence of the epistemological construct that lies behind it.

But then what does one make of the odd statement with which Lavoisier

---

11. Excluded in this argument are physical changes such as changes of state, but this is not because state changes were recognized as being distinct. In fact, the distinction between state changes and chemical changes becomes crucial to the controversy surrounding the decomposition of water, as we shall see in the second half of this chapter, although Lavoisier had begun to elaborate the concept of the three states of matter for himself as early as his April 1773 draft on the nature of the elements. See Gough, "Lavoisier's Theory of the Gaseous State," 33. The text of the draft note is to be found in Guerlac, *Lavoisier—The Crucial Year,* 215–18.

began the "Mémoire sur la nature de l'eau": "Je ne parlerai point de ce qu'ont écrit sur les éléments les philosophes des premiers siècles; ... je passe à ce qui intéresse plus particulièrement les physiciens; je veux parler des faits" (2) [140]. This statement takes on a meaning quite different if it is put in the context of the note which ends the second essay and which is typical of Lavoisier's immediate response to objections to his theories: "J'avoue que cette dernière circonstance [having to do with a reading of the data] formerait une objection assez forte contre ce que j'ai rapporté dans ce mémoire *s'il était possible d'argumenter contre des faits*" (26; my emphasis) [141]. This comment is in line with Lavoisier's constant caveat that one can prove or disprove someone else's experiments only by using demonstrations and facts of the same order:

> Besides, as I have already observed, the difficulties which may present themselves in the explanation of some particular facts, cannot either destroy or shake truths which are solidly established and founded upon decisive experiments. It is a principle, that an opinion cannot be refuted but by proofs of the same kind as those which were used in establishing it. The proofs which we have given of the decomposition and recomposition of water being of the same demonstrative order, it is by experiments of the same order, that is to say by demonstrative experiments, which they ought to be attacked. All the objections hitherto opposed to them, are so far from possessing the slightest character of demonstration, that they barely amount to slight probabilities.[12]

Lavoisier's definition of facts, then, seems to be clearly distinct from the idea of a purely theoretical system, but it is also distinct from the idea of facts as merely empirical data. Not only are facts a middle ground of sorts, relating to the exterior world but implicated in their web of interlocking definitions, but they sound suspiciously like the kind of construct we recognize as being a period commonplace for the structure of language. Language, for Macquer, we recall, was also a construct, namely a complex "table" somewhere in between pure imagining cut off from outside stimuli and pure perception cut off from judgment.

What Lavoisier has generated in the first part of the article concerning the nature of water is hence more important than simply an historical introduction. He has used this historical overview as a vehicle to transmit to his reader (or more precisely, to cultivate in his reader) the rudiments of a new chemical terminology. Moreover, the method by which he evokes the terminology in his reader's judgment itself brings a new perspective on the nature of scientific inquiry and of the epistemological givens that support any terminology. Lavoisier has defined for us the terms he will

12. Lavoisier's notes to Richard Kirwan's *Essay on Phlogiston, and the Constitution of Acids* (London: J. Johnston, 1789), 61.

need in his own experiment. The unsuspected effect of these redefinitions is to align the reader with Lavoisier's perspective so that the reader will recognize in the experiment the facts that Lavoisier wants him to perceive.

The impact of this essay lies not so much in the elegant simplicity with which Lavoisier accomplishes his persuasion of the reader as in the fact that, precisely because the argument is so simple and nonpolemical, and because the process of definition is performed through implication, Lavoisier's reader does not recognize the active emplotting procedure behind the simple history. Rather than arguing openly in favor of his complicated chemical epistemology, Lavoisier induces the reader to generate it for himself. As a result, the reader is not aware of how profound a reorganizing operation has been performed on him or, indeed, that he has been under a persuasive influence at all.

The second essay of the memoir, which recounts Lavoisier's own experiment is simple, clear, and "objective." Well it may present itself as such, dealing as it does in great quantitative detail with the two minimal points remaining to be cleared up; its impact on the reader is nonetheless derived entirely from the care with which the first essay created a receptivity to it. The second essay resolves the two remaining questions. How does one determine that the earth was not already present in the water? (By checking its *purity* using density readings.) Where did the earth come from if the system is closed and the amount of pure water remains constant after the refluxing? (The water dissolved the earth out of the closed glass vessel itself.) But the ability even to conceive of such a simple experiment was dependent on the simplicity and coherence with which all the necessary elements of the proposition were defined (and thus distinguished from each other); the power of the first essay lies in the fact that it is so effective that it makes itself obsolete and hence invisible. It creates the illuson that the second essay is the more important and stands alone, that it itself is a mere historical appendage, just an historical exercise.

It is ironic to note that in the end, the primary assumption that made the memoir "Sur la nature de l'eau" such a masterly performance was proved false by Lavoisier himself in the memoir on the decomposition and recomposition of water. Yet the basic conclusions are not put into question at all, for it seems that the real importance lies in the epistemological shift induced by readings of this type. The fundamental assumptions about the nature of the elements, of the words that denote them, hence of the definitions of the chemical fact, have been irrevocably altered. The concept around which chemical research had been defined, the chemical principle as Macquer saw it, was a bridge between the primary world of ideas and the secondary world of observable qualities. Lavoisier replaces it with the concept of a chemical element whose nature is not merely the sum of observable qualities wherever they may be found, but which has its own enduring material presence. Lavoisier has reversed the Lockean concept of substance, language- and idea-dependent, into something closer to its modern opposite.[13] The Lavoisien principle is purified or isolated, rather than recognized or read. Although his proof of the elemental nature of water may be invalid, the important transformation lies in the changing of the goal of chemical research. This change must be seen in a reformation of the operation of chemical language and in the equally forceful but different emphasis given to chemical terminology as analysis.

Let us turn to the essay written ten years later on the decomposition and recomposition of water. As mentioned at the beginning of this chapter, an ongoing controversy exists to this day about who is to be awarded the credit for having discovered the composition of water. But it is likely that this debate only serves to camouflage the more important question. Much more than appears at first glance was riding on the results not only of Lavoisier and Laplace's experiments, but also of the similar experiments being performed by those who clung to the theory of phlogiston. As Fourcroy asserted, it was primarily with respect to these experiments that the theoretical *prises de position* were being elaborated. "For the 'bons esprits,' for the coolest heads and those most practised in the cultivation of the science, there was a sort of neutrality which resisted not the discoveries, but the total overthrow of the old order of ideas; this sensible party, before adopting a total change, was waiting for a more decisive victory over the march of nature, and it was only to be found in the time of the

---

13. Even more importantly, the very definition of a chemical quality has thus been radically reversed. It no longer is primarily a function of the thinking mind, but is seen as being a function of the material world. Hence it has not only the inverse meaning, but a very different weight inside the language to which it belongs. In effect, the language is seen as secondary to the material entities it names, rather than the principle's being an artificial but useful logical construct whose material reality is not verifiable. Contrast, in this light, the two following quotations.

I mean by elements, as those Chymists that speak plainest do by their Principles, certain Primitive and Simple, or perfectly unmingled bodies; which not being made of any other bodies, or of one another, are the Ingredients of which all those call'd perfectly mixt Bodies are immediately compounded and into which they are ultimately resolved. (Boyle, *The Sceptical Chymist* [London, 1661], quoted in Douglas McKie, *Antoine Lavoisier: Scientist, Economist, Social Reformer* [New York: Schuman, 1952], 41.)

Signalons encore une note du même manuscrit qui nous conduit un peu plus avant dans sa pensée: Elle est intitulée: Idées générales sur les éléments. "Il ne suffit pas qu'une matière soit simple, indivisible ou au moins indécomposée pour qu'elle ait le titre d'élément; il faut encore qu'elle soit abondamment répandue dans la nature et qu'elle entre comme principe essentiel et constituant dans la composition d'un grand nombre de corps. Ainsi, bien que l'or puisse être une substance simple, on ne dira pas que l'or est un élément." Le souvenir des anciens éléments est ici très apparent. Il se manifeste encore chez Lavoisier une façon de penser commune aux chimistes de ce siècle. (Daumas, *Lavoisier*, 170) [142]

decomposition and recomposition of water."[14] However, as C. E. Perrin points out, "when word spread of the alleged synthesis of water, the news came not as a decisive development but as a topic of controversy that lasted for several years ... The experiments on the composition and decomposition of water had resolved to [Lavoisier's] satisfaction the major anomalies confronting his theory. Yet the chemical community at large did not appear eager to adopt his views."[15] To a great extent this can be seen as an inevitable situation, as at least two competing epistemological systems were providing irreconcilable ways of describing the same empirical data. Lavoisier's long paper entitled "Mémoire dans lequel on a pour objet de prouver que l'eau n'est point une substance simple, un élément proprement dit, mais qu'elle est susceptible de décomposition et de recomposition" can be seen as an attempt to resolve these underlying epistemological instabilities that were blocking the acceptance of his more general chemical theory. For, using rhetorical tools similar to those used to induce the shift in his reader's perception that takes place in the memoir "Sur la nature de l'eau," Lavoisier transforms the conceptual field that determines the nature of scientific hypothesis. As a result he redefines the position of the researcher with respect to the object of his study.

As we have come to expect, Lavoisier begins by situating the importance of the discussion in another context: that of the nature of hydrogen. Rather than using a name derived from a phlogiston-related terminology, he will call it "inflammable air".

> Y a-t-il plusieurs espèces d'airs inflammables? ou bien celui que nous obtenons est-il toujours le même, plus ou moins mélangé, plus ou moins altéré par l'union des différentes substances qu'il est susceptible de dissoudre? C'est une question que je n'entreprendrai pas de résoudre dans ce moment; il me suffira de dire que l'air inflammable dont j'entends parler dans ce mémoire est celui qu'on obtient, soit de la décomposition de l'eau par le fer seul, soit de la dissolution du fer et du zinc dans les acides vitriolique et marin; que, comme il paraît prouvé que, dans tous les cas, cet air vient originairement de l'eau, je l'appellerai, lorsqu'il se présentera dans l'état aériforme, *air inflammable aqueux,* et lorsqu'il sera engagé dans quelque combinaison, *principe inflammable aqueux.* ("Décomposition," 334) [143]

Lavoisier's procedure in this memoir is very different from that of his earlier ones. With a certain bravado, he presents his problem directly in terms of a new *name* for an element, asserting that it is specific and distinct, everywhere the same, and that the name will reflect this. And then, concerning a statement that seems to modern eyes to be clear and logical, he says: "La suite de ce mémoire éclaircira ce que ce premier énoncé peut présen-

---

14. Quoted in C. E. Perrin, "The Triumph of the Antiphlogistians," in Woolf, *The Analytic Spirit,* 41.

15. Ibid., 43.

ter d'obscur" (334) [144]. There is a short description of the laboratory procedure used for the synthesis of water, and then we find this justification for the many pages of detailed laboratory-data-based argument that are to follow: "Tel est, en général, le résultat de la combustion de l'air vital [oxygen] et de l'air inflammable [hydrogen]; mais, comme on a voulu élever quelque doute sur l'antériorité de cette découverte, je me crois obligé d'entrer dans quelques détails sur la suite des expériences qui m'y ont conduit" (335) [145].

In essence, this memoir is emplotted using a strategy that reverses that of the memoir on the nature of water. There is no attempt to slowly transform the reader's perception. On the contrary, a definite enthusiasm, an almost martial impatience, betray Lavoisier's confidence that the reader will understand at once the significance of the discovery.[16] He places his argument, in a telling fashion, not in terms of who actually first performed the laboratory procedures. He knows that Watt and Priestley did; however, in order to show that it is not merely the physical event that determines priority, he cites Macquer's recounting of even earlier observations that are recorded in the *Dictionnaire de chymie* of 1778.

> A cette époque, M. Macquer ayant présenté une soucoupe de porcelaine blanche à la flamme de l'air inflammable qui brûlait tranquillement à l'orifice d'une bouteille, il observa que cette flamme n'était accompagnée d'aucune fumée fuligineuse; il trouva seulement la soucoupe mouillée de gouttelettes assez sensibles d'une liqueur blanche comme de l'eau, et qu'il a reconnue, ainsi que M. Sigaud de la Fond, qui assistait à cette expérience, pour de l'eau pure. (Voyez *Dictionnaire de chymie,* seconde édition, article Gaz inflammable). (335) [146]

Lavoisier chooses instead to emphasize the terminology that he will use to describe the results of both his own and his predecessors' experiments. Again we encounter the definitions of the elements and their natures that were developed in the memoir on the nature of elemental water. In the first case, Lavoisier had derived the conceptual vocabulary to prove that if water were an element, it could not be transformed into earth. In this case, he uses it to prove that water is not an element after all. Interestingly enough, his synthesis of water does not invalidate the earlier memoir's conceptual gains. The synthesis of water supports the model of proper theoretical chemical reasoning that Lavoisier is developing and refining, rather than disproving his theory at any one point in its development.

---

16. He was wrong: "The heated reaction to Lavoisier's broadside is evident in the testimony of the Dutch scientist Martinus van Marum, visiting in Paris, who was present at the 13 July [1785] session: 'Then violent objections were made against this [paper], as a result of which the reading was interrupted. This, together with the simultaneous efforts of the reader [Lavoisier] and of his opponents to be heard, led to my understanding very little.' " Perrin, "The Triumph of the Antiphlogistians," 46.

After having presented almost fleetingly the crucial fact that the combustion of oxygen with hydrogen under a bell jar suspended over limewater produces neither carbon dioxide (*air fixe,* as Bucquet would have had it, which would have clouded the limewater) nor any sort of acid at all (as Lavoisier's combustion theory of oxygen as the acid-producer had led him to expect), Lavoisier remarks at length on the observation that *to many eyes, nothing seemed to have been produced,* although there is a *barely discernable dew* on the walls of the glass. And then: "Cependant, rien ne s'anéantit dans les expériences; la seule matière du feu, de la chaleur et de la lumière, a la propriété de passer à travers les pores des vaisseaux; les deux airs, qui sont des corps pesants, ne pouvaient donc avoir disparu, ils ne pouvaient être anéantis: de là la nécessité de faire les expériences avec plus d'exactitude et plus en grand" (337) [147].

The concept of a closed chemical system and of the conservation of matter are obviously crucial to his ability to judge as illusory the lack of results in his predecessors' experiments. It is also crucial to understand that this system is chemically closed, not physically closed. The new distinction between the realm of physics and the realm of chemistry is very important: Lavoisier has ruled out heat as a possible component in chemical compounds. Just as the air, seen mistakenly as a neutral support medium in the transmutation experiments, had not at first been taken into account chemically, so here, also, Lavoisier has made, but much more explicitly, a distinction between the elements that may serve as chemical principles and "elements" that may only serve as physical principles.

Again Lavoisier demonstrates that closure is primarily a question of nonarbitrary epistemological choices. In order to ask a clear chemical question, he needs a closed, hence controlled, chemical environment. But he still needs access to the environment in order to get his answer. The environment must be only selectively closed; ideally, he would like to find an instrument of manipulation and hence a language of observation that will not interfere with the chemical givens. Therefore he chooses to "speak" with the voice of a physicist: heat, fire, and light may cross the glass of the combustion vessel, but they are not recognized as possible components of the products. They may, somewhat like solvents, act on the reagents and the products, but not *in* them. What this implies, of course, is that if there is a "phlogiston," it hasn't anything to do with heat, which is seen here as being a *mechanical* agent, although phlogiston was primarily defined by Stahl as the *chemical* principle of fire.

Lavoisier's language of verification will also be in the domain of the physical: he *weighs* the reagents and the products in a chemical system. Weighing them does not interfere with their chemical natures, but he can retranslate his results back into chemical language to obtain the answer to the question he asked: the methods of physics provide a "natural" and true system for representing chemical events. Complementarily, the crite-rion that Lavoisier uses to define the chemical elements of an experimental system is that they be ponderable. Heat, fire, and light, therefore, are certainly assumed to exist, but as they have no weight, they are not chem-icals. Somewhat like the definition of chemical purity that Lavoisier gauges by measuring density (specific weight) in the memoir on the nature of water, this refinement of the limits of the field of chemistry to what may be weighed may seem at first to be only a practical or technical necessity. However, it can actually be understood as a conceptual necessity in the same way that defining the purity of water was made possible only by the new definition of the nature of an element. The particular identity of water was only subsequently made specific and verifiable by ascertaining its specific weight.

Lavoisier puts the distinction between mechanical and chemical agents to work immediately in the description of his next variation of the ignition of the two gases. This time the hydrogen and oxygen are placed in a vacuum sealed, not by a water-based indicating solution such as limewater, but by a pool of mercury. Lavoisier concludes that the weight of the hydrogen plus the oxygen equals the weight of the miniscule amount of dew produced, which can now be clearly seen as not coming from the liquid used to seal the bell jar. He thus has conclusive proof that water is a compound of hydrogen and oxygen ... on one condition: that heat is not conceded a chemical existence:

> Comme il n'est pas moins vrai en physique qu'en géométrie que le tout est égal à ses parties, de ce que nous n'avions obtenu que de l'eau pure dans cette expérience, sans aucun autre résidu, nous nous sommes crus en droit d'en conclure que le poids de cette eau était égal à celui des deux airs qui avaient servi à la former. On ne pourrait faire qu'une objection raisonnable contre cette conclusion: en admettant que l'eau qui s'était formée était égale en poids aux deux airs, c'était supposer que la matière de la chaleur et de la lumière qui se dégage en grand abondance dans cette opération, et qui passe à travers les pores des vaisseaux, n'avait pas de pesanteur. (339) [148][17]

The experimental closure of the system is intact only if heat has no weight and is not a part of the chemical system, but is understood as being part of the experimental apparatus. What this means is that Lavoisier's need to find an external language for observation that is strictly related to the instruments used to manipulate the chemical components of the system has led him to assume, in practice, although not explicitly, a corresponding

17. For the experiments Lavoisier used to verify this assertion, see "Sur la pesanteur de la matière de la chaleur," *Oeuvres* 5: 292–93. As Daumas says, "Remarquons à ce propos que le calorique devait être une matière bien particulière, à l'encontre des autres substances, aux trois forces fondamentales qu'il énumère dans le premier chapitre du *Traité de chimie:* attraction, répulsion, pression atmosphérique" *Lavoisier*, 167 [149].

theory of state changes. State changes result from the "composition" or "decomposition" of mixtures made up of chemical substances "dissolved" in heat. But as a given volume of liquid water does not become heavier if it becomes gaseous or lighter if it becomes ice, such changes are not defined as chemical changes. This distinction between the realm of the physical and the realm of the chemical is crucial to the interpretation of what otherwise seems to be a pointless experiment yielding no results. For Lavoisier interprets the production of water vapor or dew in such a way as to project as the next step the possibility of the decomposition of water. In order to do this, one must be able, as Watt could not, to distinguish between the production of water vapor (a state change) and the production of two distinct gases, oxygen and hydrogen (a chemical decomposition), under only slightly different conditions of water subjected to extreme heat. The combination of weighing procedures and the concept of the state changes gives Lavoisier this ability.

Lavoisier proceeds to discuss his own experiments on the *decomposition* of water, in which he, typically, first reinterprets many other researchers' prior experiments to show that in his terms, oxygen has more affinity for iron or zinc than for hydrogen. He uses this reading of their work to propose the experiments in which a lump of pure iron is left under pure water to slowly oxidize and then, more efficiently, drops of pure water are passed through a red-hot iron gun-barrel. In both cases, the oxygen from the water combines with the iron, releasing the hydrogen in gaseous form.

The assertion that oxygen has more affinity for iron than for hydrogen is dependent on being able to ascertain whether the hydrogen, once identified as distinct from water vapor, comes from the water or out of combination with a metal. The phlogiston theory defines state changes as chemical changes under certain circumstances; it claims that hydrogen is the long-searched-for fixed fire, and that phlogiston comes from iron as the iron is reduced to its simplest state. It is at this point that the phlogiston theory shows that it cannot provide a conceptual framework in which the experimenter can understand the difference in *kind* between heat changes and compounds.

The results of the decomposition seem clear and simple to us. But this apparent simplicity is dependent on the language Lavoisier uses to describe his experiment rather than on the simplicity of the work itself. Let us look at Lavoisier's transcription of Priestley's experiment. Priestley believed himself to have proven one thing, whereas Lavoisier uses his data to prove the opposite.

> Voici la manière dont opère M. Priestley. Il emplit d'air inflammable, tiré du fer par l'acide vitriolique, une cloche de verre placée sur la tablette de l'appareil pneumato-chimique à l'eau; il s'y introduit, à travers l'eau, du *minium*

qu'il a fait préalablement bien chauffer pour en chasser tout l'air; ce *minium* est placé sur un tesson de creuset, et soutenu par un support; enfin, il fait tomber sur la chaux métallique le foyer d'une lentille de verre: d'abord la chaux se sèche par la chaleur de la lentille; ensuite le plomb se revivifie; en même temps l'air inflammable est absorbé, et on parvient ainsi à en faire disparaître des quantités très-considérables ... Il a conclu de cette expérience que l'air inflammable se combinait avec le plomb pour le revivifier, et que, par conséquent, l'air inflammable et le phlogistique n'étaient qu'une seule et même chose, comme l'avait annoncé M. Kirwan. (344) [150]

In modern terms, a calx is an oxide, hence a compound. In phlogistic terms, it was seen to be the elemental state of a metal, hence an earth. Priestley had thought that by heating the "elemental" lead calx—the *minium*—in the presence of "phlogiston"—the *air inflammable*—he would cause the calx to combine with the phlogiston to form the "compound"—the metal. Therefore, when the hydrogen disappears and the lead oxide changes into metallic lead, Priestley goes on to assume that the experiment proves the long-asserted but never directly proven theory that phlogiston is a chemical principle and that it does have an isolable state. Phlogiston was in fact hydrogen.[18] To be able to interpret the experiment in such a way as to prove both the existence and the chemical identity of phlogiston, Priestley had to confront the data from a particular perspective. This is, of course, the perspective that Lavoisier ridicules in the "Réflexions sur le phlogistique," the perspective solidly anchored in the idealist epistemology that Macquer and Condillac represented.[19] But when read in its own context, Priestley's experiment is perfectly coherent and logical. In fact, *in this context,* it is a singularly simple and elegant proof of the phlogiston theory as a whole. It validates more than a mere observation. By finally isolating phlogiston, Priestley seemed to have validated the very process of reading qualities from compound to compound that had to be theoretically possible if the analytical method of studying

18. See Kirwan, *An Essay on Phlogiston.* Lavoisier says the following in his notes appended to the second English edition: "According to Mr. Kirwan, sulphur is composed of a base or radical, which, when saturated with phlogiston, or, which is the same thing, with inflammable gas or hydrogene . . ." (70). The important thing to notice here is that it is not the same thing at all. Lavoisier divides the properties of phlogiston among oxygen, hydrogen, and caloric. The first two divide among themselves the chemical properties, and the third, caloric, takes on the physical properties.

19. In fact, it is Macquer's version of the phlogistic theory, and not really Priestley's, that Lavoisier is combatting here. Priestley serves more as a straw man; he performed the experiments that were used in France to support a theory that was a successful compromise: "Just as Tycho Brahe's theory offered the advantages of the Copernican system without the inconvenience of a moving earth, Macquer's theory offered the advantages of Lavoisier's theory of combustion without the need to abandon the inflammable principle, phlogiston." Perrin, "The Triumph of the Antiphlogistians," 43.

the world was to be held to be truly "natural." If one accepts Priestley's terms for the experiment, then, one can understand both Macquer's great relief to have finally had his chemical theories vindicated and his inability to see what Lavoisier saw in those of his experiments on the nature of water that came out before Macquer died in 1788. His theory of language, the conceptual field that was formed by the terms *affinity* and *principle* and extended to the status of epistemological groundwork by the third term *analysis,* were at stake in what seemed to be only a simple laboratory procedure: "M. Lavoisier m'effrayait depuis longtemps par une grande découverte qu'il réservait *in petto* et qui n'allait pas moins qu'à renverser de fond en comble toute la théorie du phlogistique ... Où en aurions-nous été avec notre vieille chimie, s'il avait fallu se bâtir un édifice tout différent? Pour moi, je vous avoue que j'aurais abandonné la partie. Heureusement, M. Lavoisier vient de mettre sa découverte au jour; je vous avoue que depuis ce temps j'ai un grand poids de moins sur l'estomac" [151].[20]

However, let us look at Lavoisier's very different reading of Priestley's laboratory procedure:

> J'observai que M. Priestley n'a pas fait attention à une circonstance capitale qui a lieu dans cette expérience, c'est que le plomb, loin d'augmenter de poids, diminue au contraire de près d'un douzième: il s'en dégage donc une substance quelconque; or cette substance est nécessairement de l'air vital, dont le *minium* contient près d'un douzième. Mais d'un autre côté, il ne reste, après cette opération, de fluide élastique d'aucune espèce; non seulement on ne retrouve pas dans la cloche d'air vital, mais l'air inflammable lui-même qui la remplissait disparaît: donc les produits ne sont plus dans l'état aériforme; et puisque, d'un autre côté, il est prouvé que l'eau est un composé d'air inflammable et d'air déphlogistiqué, il est clair que M. Priestley a formé de l'eau *sans s'en douter.* ("Décomposition," 344–45; my emphasis) [152]

The rhetorical strategy of the essay is such that by the time the reader arrives at Lavoisier's description of Priestley's experiment, the chemical context in which the data are presented is foreign to that in which it had been conceptualized by Priestley. The metal/phlogiston/calx complex (a "dry" environment conceptually) has been replaced by a water/oxide/hydrogen complex in which the crucial problem is not the nature of phlogiston (or hydrogen) but the elemental nature of water. This same water was not even seen to be a part of the experimental system by Priestley. The question, as in the first memoir on the nature of water, has again been displaced so as to enable Lavoisier to bring into focus compo-nents of the closed chemical system of the experiment that were "philo-

20. Macquer, quoted in Berthelot, *La Révolution chimique,* 135–36.

sophically invisible" to Priestley. Lavoisier tells us, after all, that "M. Priestley n'a pas fait attention à une circonstance capitale": that the lead calx loses weight in its transformation into the powder. But of course, this circumstance was not at all capital in Priestley's terms as he had set up the experiment. It becomes crucial only as Lavoisier defines the procedure of reading chemical transformations in terms of weight changes rather than in terms of quality transfers, as he had thus defined chemical identities in terms of visible qualities. And in this experiment, Priestley has all of the visible qualities working in his favor. Hydrogen, being extremely inflammable, seems a perfect candidate for the role of phlogiston. Because the different "airs" had not been so successfully analyzable until many of Priestley's own developments in pneumatic laboratory procedures, it was understandable that such a light and reactive gas should have escaped notice. Even more importantly, it was not until pneumatic chemistry that it even became possible to look to the gases as being possibly phlogistic; air had still been considered "elemental," and Stahl, after all, had theorized that phlogiston was an extremely rarified *earth*. But with the opening of the domain of the gases to the field of chemistry, it must have seemed logical, even natural, to look there for the identifying phlogiston qualities of inflammability and lightness (and possibly even for phlogiston's supposed ability to cross glass and other vessels during the process of heating).[21] Hence, according to the qualitative analysis of Priestley—and I use these words to indicate the analytical reading of observable qualities that derives from the classical *épistémè*—there was no reason to look for weight changes. There was even less reason to look for the products in an aeriform or any other state. For Priestley, the product was quite visible: calx plus phlogiston forms metal plus vacuum. It was Lavoisier's problem to explain where the oxygen had gone, since he was the one to have claimed its presence in the calx; it was not for Priestley to have to deal with the fact that the product(s) must be in some other state than aeriform. For him, every component seemed to have been accounted for.

At this point it becomes clear just why Lavoisier had spent so much effort demonstrating the vast difference between the volume of the two gases (or even of hydrogen alone) as compared to the volume of the water from which they are generated or to which they can be reduced, both in his experiments and in those of his many predecessors. For in Priestley's experiment, the volume of water produced was so small as to have been

21. See, for example, Joseph Priestley's letter to Josiah Wedgewood concerning the difficulties experienced in obtaining vessels impervious to gases in Robert Schofield, ed., *A Scientific Autobiography of Joseph Priestley (1733–1804)* (Cambridge: MIT, 1966), 222–23. See also J. B. Gough's discussion of the difficulty even Lavoisier had in distinguishing gases of chemical principles from substances that were only "dissolved" in air or in heat, in his "Lavoisier's Theory of the Gaseous State," 32–34.

negligible. As Lavoisier then remarks, "puisqu'il est prouvé que l'eau est un composé d'air inflammable et d'air déphlogistiqué, il est clair que M. Priestley a formé de l'eau *sans s'en douter*" (345) [153]. Priestley's own procedures misled him, and misled him doubly. First, he would have been incapable of recognizing the product for what it was—that is, a compound of hydrogen and oxygen—because he wasn't expecting a product at all and, more importantly, because water does not have any qualities that are readable in terms of hydrogen: only the metal does. And secondly, because he was sure that *qualities* are the verifying functions of chemical interpretation, he could not even have thought of testing, as Lavoisier did, for the quantitative differences that indicate presence, absence, and transfers of elements from one compound to another. In this case, therefore, Lavoisier—using experimental argument rather than a demonstration of the semantic incoherence of the word *phlogiston* (as he had done in the "Réflexions sur le phlogistique")—has shown the phlogiston theory to be more than merely an incorrect way of thinking. The Priestley-Macquer operational model in the chemical discipline is grounded in the analytic theories of language.[22] Out of this understanding of language are developed the analogical definitions of words and substances, linked by the universal method of analysis. But this chemical *épistémè* has just, for Lavoisier, proven itself to be systematically misleading. Priestley literally cannot see what is before his eyes, because there is effectively nothing to be *seen*. Qualitative analysis à la Macquer or Priestley is dependent on visual perception and on an open field of metaphorical analogues for these qualities. Quantitative Lavoisien analysis is based on closed, indirect methods. One has to know how to look for the results. "Je crois pouvoir répondre de celles qui me sont propres; mais il pourrait arriver que M. Priestley, dans la réduction du minium par l'air inflammable, n'ayant pas pour objet de déterminer les quantités ni les augmentations ou diminutions de poids, n'eût pas cherché à apporter une grande précision dans les résultats" (348) [154]. Priestley's blindness is a function of the nature of his language. Therefore what should have been the most perfect proof of the phlogiston theory for Priestley turns, in Lavoisier's hands, into a most thorough discreditation of both the theory and the language philosophy which supports it.

Whereas in the "Réflexions" Lavoisier gave only a critique of the operation of its language system, in the memoir on the decomposition and recomposition of water, he is able to demonstrate this insufficiency by furnishing his reader with an alternate and more coherent reading of the

22. By "analytic" I mean here the theories derived from the definition of analysis that I have presented using the eighteenth-century philosophers of language. I do not, of course, mean "analytic" in the sense in which modern analytic philosophers use the term.

very same experimental data used by the phlogistonists. But the indirect route that he takes, leading into the problem of phlogiston from the seemingly unrelated problem of the decomposition of water, has served sufficiently to redefine or regenerate the basic concepts of the chemical discipline so that the impact of the new reading, when it comes, is shattering. The reader is forced to see the language itself of Priestley's description as awkward, as dependent on unnecessary philosophical baggage; the criticisms of the "Réflexions" are even more strikingly obvious than is the simple fact that Priestley may be wrong.

If the philosophical critique of phlogiston as an empty concept was made possible by the "Réflexions," the chemical critique was made possible by the kind of reworking of the basic concepts that we saw Lavoisier accomplishing in the memoir on the nature of water. Using these chemical critiques, Lavoisier is developing not only his own specific terminology, but also a new way of functioning inside a scientific language that will counteract the "wrong thinking" of the phlogistonists. This new way of thinking is at stake at the end of the article on the decomposition of water, and Lavoisier demonstrates its effectiveness in two carefully chosen examples. He finally does present laboratory experiments that counter the phlogistonists' critiques of his readings by using substances other than iron or zinc as the metal of the red-hot gun barrel.

> Les phénomènes sont fort différents, si on emploie un métal pour lequel le principe oxygine ait moins d'affinité que pour le principe inflammable aqueux: si, par exemple, on substitue, dans l'expérience précédente, un canon de cuivre rouge à celui de fer, l'eau se réduit bien en vapeur en passant par la partie incandescente du tube, mais elle se condense ensuite par le refroidissement dans le serpentine; il ne s'opère alors qu'une simple distillation sans perte, et il n'y a ni calcination du cuivre, ni production d'air inflammable. (353) [155]

Lavoisier has demonstrated that it is not merely heat that decomposes water (as Watt asserted), nor just any metal (as the phlogiston theory had predicted), but only those metals that have sufficient affinity with oxygen to be able to pull it out of combination with the hydrogen. Much more telling is the (dissimulated) revelation to his reader that his argument has been circular in this article: "D'après cette expérience, on ne pouvait plus douter que la production d'air inflammable obtenue par M. l'abbé Fontana, en éteignant des charbons ardents dans l'eau, et surtout celle obtenue par MM Hassenfratz, Stoultz et d'Hallencourt, dans l'extinction du fer rouge, ne fut une véritable décomposition de l'eau" (354) [156].

At the beginning of his exposition, Lavoisier had used the data from just these experiments to justify his original readings of the affinity of iron for oxygen. Suddenly it becomes clear that the data presented as having been derived from innocent sources that supported his claims had already at that point been translated into Lavoisien terms. Now that Lavoisier has demonstrated to his readers, through his discussion of the Priestley experiment, just how thoroughly predetermined by theory any observation is, he allows his readers to see that the data that were originally given as proof or supporting evidence for his own critique of Priestley's theory were as much in question theoretically as the phlogiston theory. By using interchangeably with their old names terms like *hydrogen* and *oxygen*, whose nature the article is in fact defining, Lavoisier had presented them, from the beginning of the essay, already encoded by the theory he wanted to prove. However—and this point is crucial to understanding Lavoisier's goal—the fact that the argument is presented through a circular proof does not invalidate it at all. Rather than being asked to judge the truth or falsehood of the data, the readers are allowed to see at the same time two different theories to encode it. They are asked to judge the "fit" of the language of observation, its ease, its effectiveness—and it is Priestley who comes out lacking. This effectiveness is defined in terms of the ability to perceive what is important in an experiment (as Priestley was unable to do) and, just as important, in terms of the ability to judge what are new or primary observations and what are secondary ones that may be discounted. As Lavoisier says concerning a supporting experiment, "On obtenait bien, en éteignant ainsi dans l'eau, même le quartz ou le caillou, une très-petite portion d'air; mais *il nous a paru évident* qu'elle provenait de l'eau, qui en tient toujours une portion en dissolution: cet air était dans l'état d'air commun ou à peu près" (355; my emphasis) [157].

Clearly, the simplicity of any description is achieved through the author's conscious selection of what it is necessary to include. The simplest, most elegant description does not include all components of a particular system, only the necessary ones. The ability to perceive and judge *what is relevant*—that is, to determine epistemological and experimental closure—is dependent on the language of description, on the conceptual field that is made up both of terms for observed events and entities in the natural world, and of judgments on how these relate to each other and how perception functions. In other words, experimental perception is dependent on the system of representation. This assertion has been tested by Lavoisier; he has allowed his readers, in fact, to choose between the two conceptual fields.

One way of looking at chemical phenomena has been privileged over the other. The data are less important than the perspective from which they are viewed, and they therefore do not imply that there is an absolute truth that can be reached through unmediated observation. This explains the tone on which Lavoisier ends his article:

> Dans les temps moins éclairés, on aurait présenté cette opération [another experiment—the burning of alcohol] comme une transmutation d'esprit de

vin en eau, et les alchimistes en auraient tiré des inductions favorables à
leurs idées sur les transmutations métalliques. Aujourd'hui que l'esprit d'expérience et d'observation nous apprend à tout apprécier à sa juste valeur,
nous ne verrons autre chose, dans cette expérience, que la preuve qu'il
s'ajoute quelquechose à l'esprit de vin dans sa combustion, et que ce
quelquechose est de l'air. (358) [158]

In effect, Lavoisier has placed us back in the context of his memoir on the
nature of water. Even though the experiments that he has used to demonstrate the elemental nature of water turned out to be wrong in that detail,
the procedure used to think out the problem and to resolve it, and the
much more basic definitions of the fundamental chemical concepts, are
not shaken. Terms like *element, nature, chemical,* and *system* (both experimentally and epistemologically closed) are much less denotative than
connotative. It is less important that their particular referents in the material
world change than that they change in their relationships, their affiliations
to each other, in the way the definition of each term supports the meaning
of the others. These are the basic terms which make up the field that
Lavoisier is using and which form a system of judgments, not on the way
the world is ordered, but on the ways one can perceive it and talk about
it. If the concepts "principle," "affinity," and "analysis" are the poles of
the conceptual field for the philosophical chemistry of Macquer, their very
near neighbors above are those of the newly "material" chemistry of
Lavoisier.

It is important not to lose sight of the fact that although Lavoisier's
chemistry may seem to turn away from the examination of its own analytical
procedures to focus on defining the substances in the material world, the
differences between Macquer and Lavoisier nonetheless lie in a shift of
perspective which is a matter of degree rather than of kind. Lavoisier uses
the same components in his discipline, but he orders them differently
with respect to each other. The results look disarmingly similar to the
earlier philosophical chemistry because of Lavoisier's rhetorical adeptness
in leading the reader to generate the shifts of perspective for himself, but
at the same time they feel disturbingly different because the philosophical
groundwork, the epistemic configuration, no longer presents itself openly.
The philosophical viewpoint is no longer of primary interest, as with the
"analysis" of Macquer; language does not precede experience. On the
contrary, these functions have already been encoded into the new, more
material chemical concepts. They seem, *once acquired,* to derive from the
natural order of the material world. The "philosophical system" that Diderot
spoke of in the *Encyclopédie,* the implicit system to be built by the cross-
references, has been regenerated here, but in an even less visible form.
It is a form which gives itself as artificial in the realm of explicit theory in
order to disguise as natural a much more profoundly constraining encoding of the world. It is built into the perception of the practitioner through

the (conceptual/epistemological) definitions of the (supposedly empirical) chemical terms. In the *Traité élémentaire de chimie,* Lavoisier accomplishes this transformation in his reworking of chemical terminology. The initial striking similarity to Macquer's project in the *Dictionnaire de chymie* serves only to emphasize the effectiveness with which Lavoisier has carried out his own project. This project at once institutes the new rhetoric of the "natural" that will come to characterize the "scientific" for the readers of its texts, at the same time that it hides the rhetorical dimension, the fundamentally unnatural and willed nature of this speaking position.

CHAPTER 7

Nomenclatures and Languages: The Creation of a New Scientific Practice

Il n'y a de science que par une Ecole permanente. C'est cette école que la science doit fonder. Alors les intérêts sociaux seront définitivement inversés: la Société sera faite pour l'Ecole et non pas l'Ecole pour la Société. [159]
Gaston Bachelard

TWO MAJOR TEXTS PROVIDE THE BACKGROUND FOR THE WORK FOR which Lavoisier is best known, his *Traité élémentaire de chimie* of 1789. The first is Guyton de Morveau's "Sur les dénominations chymiques" of 1782,[1] and the second is the much more extensive report on the same subject, the *Méthode de nomenclature chymique* of Lavoisier, Guyton de Morveau, Berthollet, and Fourcroy.[2] In 1782, Guyton de Morveau, of the Dijon Academy of Sciences, published a proposal for a systematic and comprehensive reform of the chemical nomenclature then being used in France. As Macquer had already pointed out, chemical names were often confusing or misleading because they attributed to substances qualities

---

1. Baron Louis-Bernard Guyton de Morveau, "Sur les dénominations chymiques, la nécessité d'en perfectionner le système, & les règles pour y parvenir," *Observations sur la physique, sur l'histoire naturelle & sur les arts & métiers* 19 (1782): 370–82. Hereafter cited as "Dén. chym."

2. Baron Louis-Bernard Guyton de Morveau, Antoine Laurent Lavoisier, Claude Louis Berthollet, and Antoine F. de Foucroy, *Méthode de nomenclature chymique* (Paris: Cuchet, 1787). Hereafter cited as *Méthode*.

that they did not possess (as in liver of antimony or liver of sulfur),[3] moreover, the same substance was given different names according to the procedure used to obtain it. Macquer's *Dictionnaire de chymie* was one attempt to reduce the confusion. But it was Guyton de Morveau's "Sur les dénominations chymiques" that provided the starting point for a much more extensive report on the same subject.

Chemical Nomenclatures

In an argument that sounds like Condillac's formulation of the relationship of science to language, Guyton de Morveau states:

> Je dis qu'aucune langue n'exige plus de clarté; et pour s'en convaincre, il suffit de réfléchir dans combien de différens états elle a à considérer la même substance, tantôt séparée, dans tel ou tel ordre, dans tel ou tel genre de composition, dans tel ou tel degré de combinaison, quelquefois d'une manière abstraite, quoiqu'elle ne soit pas réellement isolée. ("Dén. chym.," 371)

> Demandons maintenant s'il est possible de se reconnaître dans ce chaos; demandons si l'intelligence d'une pareille nomenclature ne coûte pas plus que l'intelligence de la science même; ou plutôt, avouons la nécessité de réformer ce langage, et cherchons à établir les principes qui doivent déterminer le choix dans toutes les circonstances. (373) [160]

According to what requirements should one determine the naming procedure? The answers will be familiar, as Guyton de Morveau grounds his idea of science in the nominalist commonplaces of his era.

> Les dénominations des êtres qui forment l'objet d'une Science ou d'un Art, qui sont ses matériaux, ses instrumens, ses produits, constituent ce que l'on appelle sa langue propre. L'état de perfection de la Langue annonce l'état de perfection de la Science même; ses progrès ne sont sûrs, ils ne peuvent être rapides, qu'autant que les idées sont représentées par des signes précis et déterminées, justes dans leur acception, simples dans leur expression, commodes dans l'usage, faciles à retenir, qui conservent autant qu'il est possible, sans erreur, l'analogie qui les rapproche, le système qui les définit, et jusqu'à l'étymologie qui peut servir à les faire deviner. (371) [161]

We recognize the same givens that Macquer had to work with; language and science are intimately linked. Language is basically a collection of denominations in one-to-one relationships with the ideas named; hence it is structurally a nomenclature. The effectiveness of a language, its "perfec-

---

3. These are the two terms in particular for which Guyton de Morveau will suggest a reform in the article "Hépar" of the 1777 supplements to Diderot's *Encyclopédie*, cited in Maurice Crosland, *Historical Studies in the Language of Chemistry* (Cambridge: Harvard University Press, 1962), 153.

tion," is, as Condillac also would have it, a function of its simplicity, which in turn is a function of two parallel requirements, one concerning that which is represented and the other concerning the terms which represent it. The object under study must be analyzed down to its most basic components, and the signs which represent them, either words or symbols, must be precise: short, easy to remember, each one being used to indicate only one idea. The idea-sign couple is derived not simply from experimental analysis; as the end of the first passage cited above shows, it may also be derived "quelquefois d'une manière abstraite, quoiqu'elle [the substance represented by the idea] ne soit pas réellement isolée." Rather than being conceived of as an empirically derived entity whose name merely marks it or makes it recognizable, Guyton de Morveau's substance is secondary to its name. Like the elements of Macquer's dictionary, a term in this perfected language exists and is operative first and foremost in the language system to which it belongs, among other signs.

In *Le Pluralisme cohérent de la chimie moderne,* Bachelard, talking about early attempts to formalize chemistry, comments that "il est indéniable que le premier facteur de la réduction du divers est l'analogie" (29) [162]. For Guyton de Morveau, this had pertinence, certainly, for the primary reduction of diversity does not take place merely through a lowering of the number of total perceived entities by their separation into groups. What is more important is that, as for Macquer, analogical work in the "sciences" takes place inside the language itself. Reduction through analogy can be operated on language, not on physical objects. The result is a category that includes a large number of objects. There are fewer categories than physical objects, but the categories are not material and cannot be manipulated as though they are. The chemistry of Macquer and Guyton de Morveau rises out of an already-existing theory of language and, unfortunately, through the constant attempts to simplify using analogy, it loses its specificity and falls back into the language theories, to become first and foremost the manipulation of names.

Guyton de Morveau's nomenclature is not intended to solve marginal problems in the operation of the science but to reformulate the central object of chemistry: "Je me suis engagé à traiter la Chymie *dans toutes ses parties*" ("Dén. chym.," 373; my emphasis) [163]. The image used in this quotation shows that he sees chemistry, as did Macquer, as a science of analysis, the goal of analysis being the naming of the components of any compound possible in the real world. And, like Macquer, Guyton de Morveau would like chemical synthesis and logical synthesis to coincide in the same way that the two kinds of analysis did in the *Dictionnaire:* the combinations formed using the terms would reproduce the composition of the compounds being denoted. Hence the *Dictionnaire* and Guyton de Morveau's slightly different sketch of a purified terminology are similar projects, although the focus of Guyton de Morveau's reform is a bit removed from Macquer's. Guyton de Morveau is not intent on clarifying the latent chemical system using the dictionary definitions and the cross-references; he prefers to simplify and organize the names of the substances in order to eliminate the need for a dictionary. The chemical language should be self-explanatory; each name should demonstrate its own definition. Guyton de Morveau sets out two principles to enable him to accomplish this goal:

> PREMIER PRINCIPE. *Une phrase n'est point un nom.* Les êtres et les produits chymiques doivent avoir leurs noms qui les indiquent dans toutes les occasions, sans qu'il soit besoin de recourir à des circonlocutions. Cette proposition fondamentale me paroît d'une vérité évidente, et n'a besoin d'autre preuve que les efforts que nous faisons continuellement pour *ramener les dénominations à cette simplicité d'expression.* ("Dén. chym.," 373; my emphasis) [164]

It is this search for the "simplicité d'expression" that will enable Guyton de Morveau to proceed in elaborating a scalar naming system with more ease than Macquer's first suggestions could have provided. This rule also makes the second principle possible:

> SECOND PRINCIPE. Les dénominations doivent être, autant qu'il est possible, conformes à la nature des choses ... Peu importe quel nom l'on donne à un individu qu'on n'envisage que pour lui-même, qui ne se reproduit pas sous des formes différentes; tout nom qui ne signifiera rien, pourra s'appliquer avantageusement à cet individu, quand l'usage l'aura identifié avec lui, parce que les sons et les mots qui représentent les sons, n'ont réellement par eux-mêmes aucun rapport, aucune conformité avec les choses. Au contraire, quand la convention a une fois attaché une première idée à un mot, c'est induire en erreur que de le transporter à des substances d'un autre genre; et les dérivés, les composés de ce mot sont les seuls noms conformes à la nature des êtres congénères. Ainsi, la dénomination *d'huile de vitriol* est contraire à la règle, en ce qu'elle porte le signe du caractère huileux tout-à-fait étranger à cette substance. Ainsi, le nom *d'acide vitriolique* étant donné, tous les corps formés de ce dissolvant sont des vitriols. (373) [165]

The import of this second principle hearkens back to statements made by Lavoisier: the names must all be of one *kind,* of one *order,* revealing the same kind of information about their substances. The imperative is clear: in general, chemical names will attempt to represent a synthesis. Simple substances may appear in any number of compounds; therefore, rather than giving each compound a trivial name of its own, the chemist will incorporate the names of its components into a single synthetic name. "Ce sont les seules expressions conformes à la nature de ces choses." This nature is therefore the analytic nature, dependent on the analytical method. "Le nom primitif appartient de préférence à l'être le plus simple, à l'être entier, à l'être non altéré. L'expression qui modifie et qui particularise, doit venir par forme d'épithète, ou dans un ordre analogue. *C'est la marche naturelle des idées, qu'il importe toujours de conserver"* (373–74; my emphasis) [166]. What is being reinforced is less the physical reality than a psychological reality. The natural progression of *ideas* leads directly, even inevitably, to the system of chemical nomenclature as a body of scalar combinations of ordered primitive terms: "La dénomination d'un composé chymique n'est clair et exacte qu'autant qu'elle rappelle les parties composantes par les noms conformes à leurs natures" (373) [167].

The table that accompanies Guyton de Morveau's short article is striking in several respects. Rather than being a complete listing of the proposed new names for the chemical compounds, it lists only significant examples: it is subtitled "contenant les principales dénominations analogiques, et des exemples de formation des noms composés" (381–82, reproduced in Appendix A) [168]. Not only does one find the lamentable phlogiston at the top of the column entitled "Bases ou substances qui s'unissent aux acides,"[4] but also, and much more interestingly, there is no small, privileged group of substances that are marked off as elements. What Guyton de Morveau gives is only a partial table: acids crossed with bases generate the salts.[5] Guyton de Morveau does not make any attempt to provide a full listing, as it is not necessary. Once the general principle is understood (and he does explain for about five pages how the names are to be accorded with each other), the reader will be able to proceed on his own. The homology of the new language with its object of study serves as the guarantor for the method.

Rather than breaking out of Macquer's epistemology, Guyton de Morveau's sketch of a reform of the chemical nomenclature serves to reinforce the philosophical cul-de-sac that Lavoisier had already denounced in the "Réflexions sur le phlogistique" and the memoir on the decomposition and the recomposition of water. Ironically, it is this essay that led to the *Méthode de nomenclature chymique.*

The chemical world in general received Guyton de Morveau's initial proposal fairly well.[6] Early in 1787, Lavoisier formed a group, that included Fourcroy and apparently Berthollet (both proponents of the new chemistry) as well as Guyton de Morveau, to refine and extend it. The resulting long report, read to the Académie des Sciences in April 1787, originally comprised essays by each of the four members, a dictionary of synonyms,

4. Guyton de Morveau was still a phlogistonist when he wrote this paper.
5. Here, Guyton de Morveau is clearly following the lead of the Swedish minerologist Torbern Bergman, who had suggested in 1779 a similar procedure specifically for the renaming of salts. See Crosland, *Historical Studies,* 246–47 and 154. Guyton de Morveau was the French translator of Bergman's works.
6. Crosland, *Historical Studies,* 161–63, and Berthelot, *La Révolution chimique: Lavoisier,* 161.

and tables to accompany them. However, it is not Guyton de Morveau's essay that begins the work, but Lavoisier's. As is well known, Lavoisier spent a good deal of time first convincing Guyton de Morveau to discard the phlogiston theory and to adopt in its place his oxygen-hydrogen-caloric chemical system.[7] Given the epistemological harangues that accompany Lavoisier's earlier writings, one would expect to find here also, in justification of Guyton de Morveau's change of allegiance, a full and explicit elaboration of a theory of language to replace the Condillacian analysis system that was so tainted by its relationship to the phlogiston theory. But interestingly enough, Lavoisier spends not only a good half of the polemical introductory essay paraphrasing the *Logique* of Condillac, but even cites verbatim long sections of it. His contribution, at first glance, seems to be limited to more or less trivial comments deriving from or embroidering upon an argument whose real force is attributed to Condillac. Lavoisier's essay appears, then, strangely enough, to be a strident affirmation of precisely the analytic philosophy he seemed to have been challenging in his own earlier papers. But the situation is not so simple. If Lavoisier's goal was merely to disguise his new chemistry in the philosophical trappings of the old in order to impose it on his audience without their being aware of it (a strategy akin to that suggested by Diderot in the article "Encyclopédie"), then no one was taken in. The *Méthode de nomenclature chymique* met with a cool reception from the Academy of Sciences.[8] But it hardly seems possible that a writer of such finesse and subtlety should suddenly resort to the clumsiest and most bald-faced of rhetorical methods, and should underestimate his reading audience so seriously. After all, lest we forget,

7. Crosland, *Historical Studies,* 177; Daumas, *Lavoisier,* 188.

8. For example, in the report made to the academy on the *Méthode,* Baumé said the following:

"Nous n'irons pas plus loin, nous dirons seulement que lorsque nous nous sommes permis ces réflexions nous n'avons pas plus prétendu combattre la théorie nouvelle que défendre l'ancienne. La fonction dont l'Académie nous a chargés, nous impose la loi d'examiner sans passion, de laisser à part toute affection, toute opinion particulière, et de nous mettre en garde autant contre le prestige de la nouveauté, que contre les préjugés qui naissent si naturellement d'un long système d'études et d'une vieille habitude de voir les objets.

"Nous pensons donc qu'il faut soumettre cette théorie nouvelle à l'épreuve du temps, au choc des expériences . . . Alors ce ne sera plus une théorie, cela deviendra un enchaînement de vérités, ou une erreur. Dans le premier cas, elle donnera une base solide de plus aux connoissances humaines; dans le second elle rentrera dans l'oubli avec toutes les théories et les systèmes de physique qui l'auront précédée. Et c'est dans cette vue que nous croyons que le tableau de Nomenclature nouvelle de Chimie, avec les Mémoires qui y sont joints, peuvent être imprimés et rendus public sous le privilège de l'Académie, de manière pourtant qu'on ne puisse pas en inférer qu'elle adopte ou qu'elle rejette la nouvelle théorie; l'Académie doit par cette impartialité qui a toujours fait la base de sa conduite, attendre l'épreuve du temps et le jugement des physiciens." (*Méthode,* 250–51) [169]

Lavoisier "obtint, en 1760, le grand prix de discours français de rhétorique" [170].[9]

Let us start, then, by approaching Lavoisier's essay from an angle that he himself suggests. The introductory essay is, first of all, not a report he wrote himself on his own experiments, but a collectively authored production written explicitly about the philosophical base of the science. "[Guyton de Morveau] a bien senti lui-même, que dans une science qui est, en quelque façon, dans un état de mobilité, qui marche à grand pas vers sa perfection, dans laquelle des théories nouvelles se sont élevées, il étoit d'une extrème difficulté de former une langue qui convînt aux différens systèmes et qui satisfit à toutes les opinions sans en adopter exclusivement aucune" *(Méthode,* 4) [171]. This first note evokes the unstable nature of the science: it is a science in motion, progressing or evolving, but somehow managing to include a multiplicity of theories or systems at once. Lavoisier raises the obvious objections whose validity Macquer had demonstrated: the choice of the language will automatically include a choice of a theoretical chemical system. But he immediately translates this problem into just the terms that one would have expected his adversaries to use against him, and then displaces the question in a most interesting way:

> L'amour de la propriété littéraire a cédé chez [Guyton de Morveau] à l'amour de la science. Dans les conférences qui se sont établies, *nous avons cherché à nous pénétrer tous du même esprit; nous avons oublié ce qui avoit été fait, ce que nous avions fait nous-mêmes, pour ne voir que ce qu'il y avoit à faire;* et ce n'est qu'après avoir passé plusieurs fois en revue toutes les parties de la chimie, après avoir profondément médité sur la métaphysique des langues, et sur le rapport des idées avec les mots, que nous avons hasardé de nous former un plan. (*Méthode,* 5; my emphasis) [172]

The system and theory are put to one side along with the consideration of personal reputation or self-interest while the unselfish (because collective) action is equated with a love of science. Lavoisier has picked up on Guyton de Morveau's statement in his 1782 paper that reform of the language is the necessary starting point for anyone who is "engagé à traiter la Chymie dans toutes ses parties" ("Dén. chym.," 373) [173]. But the modern, "good" chemists that Lavoisier had proposed in the "Réflexions sur le phlogistique" do not set themselves off, alone in their libraries, to meditate upon the secrets of chemistry. They do not follow the pattern described by Macquer in the *Dictionnaire* in his praise of Georg Stahl. The chemist is no longer he who, alone, slowly amassing fact after fact, finally succeeds in dominating the field of chemistry from an elevated plane, whose "coup d'oeil général," in the very act of encompassing his subject, analyzes it and provides it with its own system. For Lavoisier, this mode of operation is

---

9. Berthelot, *La Révolution chimique: Lavoisier,* 10.

such that the resulting plurality of systems becomes a hindrance to communication and to the advancement of the science rather than an impetus for progress.

Now for Macquer, the multitude of *connoissances* that makes up the subject matter of chemistry and the theories that bind them into a science are not equivalent. The *connoissances* are "real"; the theories that make up "la belle science" are not. Like any other author, the scientific writer actively dominates his subject matter in order to create *his* work. But Lavoisier's program eliminates this possibility. A sort of humility is revealed in these lines, and the choice of terms sounds oddly familiar. "L'amour de la propriété littéraire a cédé … à l'amour de la science … nous avons cherché à nous pénétrer tous du même esprit." This is very much the language of religious piety: the individual scientist is dominated by the science, and the science, like a religion, is exterior to and has priority over the desires of the practitioner. In other words, chemistry, rather than the chemist, is the active force. The scientist does not make judgments concerning the functioning of the science; it is accepted as an article of "faith." Lavoisier continues: "Nous avons oublié … ce que nous avions fait nous-mêmes, pour ne voir que ce qu'il y avoit à faire." Clearly, it is this *esprit* which is going to indicate what remains to be done, to the exclusion of or in opposition to individual scholastic interests.

This is a point that one must keep in mind. For, as I shall discuss in greater detail in the following pages, even if the conceptual field of Lavoisier's scientific discipline is almost the same as Macquer's, the fact that the components are the same tends to obscure just how important the differences are.[10] The real difference between the work of Macquer and Lavoisier grows out of this shift of emphasis away from seeing science as an individual operation performed on a language to one in which language sets the parameters for the writers.

10. It is this new perspective, hidden and yet clearly different, that seems to have escaped Daumas. He ends *Lavoisier: Théoricien et expérimentateur* with the following passage: "En ce domaine Lavoisier n'a rien innové; il a adopté les conceptions de son époque sans y rien changer; il pouvait le faire sans inconvénient puisque ces théories n'influençaient en rien son oeuvre personnelle; mais on ne pouvait s'attendre à ce qu'il y provoque des transformations importantes … Si les multiples travaux sur les affinités ont conduit à la théorie atomique, ce sera l'oeuvre des chercheurs du XIXe siècle, de donner naissance à la chimie physique. Malgré son génie, Lavoisier ne pouvait agir et penser qu'en homme du XVIIIe siècle" (177–78) [174]. I would take this passage ironically. It could also be argued, and I shall do this in more detail, that it was the proof of the power of Lavoisier that he took the materials of his eighteenth-century epistemology, applied them to chemistry, and warped the field permanently. So well, in fact, did he operate, that it is Daumas who could not go back and perceive the change, because he recognized only the identity of the materials Lavoisier had had to work with, and not the changes that his use of these very materials had brought about.

To make this opposition a little clearer, consider for a moment the following notation from basic algebra: $f(x) = y$. A function f, when performed on x, gives product y. Assume for the moment that for Macquer, $x =$ the perfectly analyzed chemical language (the best embodiment being a perfected *Dictionnaire de chymie*), and $f =$ the author as operator on the dictionary, who traces his own path through it to generate y, his system. This system is of the order of the x ($=$ language); it is a book. But for Lavoisier, $f(x) = y$ is defined in the opposite way. The symbol f is the language function, which operates upon the scientist, x. The result, y, is no longer on the order of a book; it is no longer a stable, still, concrete product. It is the act of writing, speaking, or thinking a certain way. In this sense, it is a comportment, a specific, rhetorical, epistemological stance that defines, not a system, but a discipline.[11]

With this redefinition in mind, it is interesting to follow Lavoisier through his seemingly conventional evocation of Condillac, in order to see how each all-too-familiar term in the analytic vocabulary takes on a different meaning when read in the context of this shift of priorities.

> Les langues n'ont pas seulement pour objet, comme on le croit communé-ment, d'exprimer par des signes, des idées et des images: ce sont, de plus, de véritables méthodes analytiques, à l'aide desquelles nous procédons du connu à l'inconnu, jusqu'à un certain point à la manière des mathématiciens: essayons de développer cette idée ... l'algèbre est une véritable langue: comme toutes les langues, elle a ses signes représentatifs, sa méthode, sa grammaire, s'il est permis de se servir de cette expression: ainsi une méth-ode analytique est une langue, une langue est une méthode analytique, et ces deux expressions sont, dans un certain sens, synonymes. (*Méthode*, 6–7) [176]

How to proceed becomes a dynamic prescription, not a definition. What is algebra, after all? It can be seen as an analytical system with no referents behind the elements, or as a set of prescriptions for relations between elements. All of algebra's *signes représentatifs* are empty. Once they are "filled in" or given specific numerical content, the researcher leaves the realm of mathematics for the realm of arithmetic. The mathematics is the grammar; it is the list of allowed relations, not really concerned with or

---

11. Something like this transformation is discussed in Michel Foucault's *Surveiller et punir* (Paris: Gallimard, 1975), in terms of military training, pedagogy, and penal confinement. One of the principal groups of theorists to whom he refers is the Idéologues. "Ecoutons encore une fois Servan," he directs us, and then quotes from J. M. Servan, *Discours sur l'adminis-tration de la justice criminelle* (1767), p. 35: "Quand vous aurez ainsi formé la chaîne des idées dans la tête de vos citoyens, vous pourrez alors vous vanter de les conduire et d'être leurs maîtres ... le désespoir et le temps rongent les liens de fer et d'acier, mais ils ne peuvent rien contre l'union habituelle des idées, ils ne font que les resserrer davantage; et sur les molles fibres du cerveau est fondée la base inébranlable des plus fermes Empires" (105) [175].

influenced by the particular content of the signs. Lavoisier, along with Macquer and many others, emphasized the equivalence between an analytical system and a language. But his basic model for an analytical system is not the static, spatial, visual countryside of Condillac's view from the mountain castle, totally content-oriented, in which the process of *relating* is so thoroughly undefined as to be effectively invisible. On the contrary, it is a nonvisual, nonspatial, non–content-oriented series of rules for a grammar; it provides the rules for syntax *without* the words. In effect, what Lavoisier is doing is not setting up a different definition of language, but using the *same* definition of language, now focused on the component that had before been deemphasized, and putting into shadow the structure that his predecessors had emphasized to the exclusion of everything else. He emphasizes the relationships at the expense of the elements being related. What does this inside-out definition of analysis do to our reading of the *Logique?* "L'art de raisonner étoit l'art d'analyser," Lavoisier had pointed out (*Méthode,* 8) [177]. At first, it seems that he is working with the same theory as Macquer. But on the other hand,

> lorsque nous nous livrons, pour la première fois, à l'étude d'une science, nous sommes, par rapport à cette science, dans un état très analogue à celui dans lequel sont les enfans, et la marche que nous avons à suivre est précisément celle que suit la nature dans la formation de leurs idées. De même que pour l'enfant, l'idée est une suite, un effet de la sensation; c'est la sensation qui fait naître l'idée; de même aussi, pour celui qui commence à se livrer à l'étude des sciences physiques, les idées ne doivent être qu'une conséquence immédiate d'une expérience ou d'une observation. (9) [178]

This was the beginning of the argument that Condillac used to prove that analysis was the natural method of reasoning. As he says at the very end of the *Logique,* "Si vous avez quelque peine à vous rendre familière la méthode que j'enseigne, ce n'est pas qu'elle soit difficile: elle ne sauroit l'être, puisqu'elle est *naturelle*" (*Logique,* 191) [179]. What the naturalness of the method means in Lavoisien terms, however, is not that the method reproduces the structure of the object studied, but that analysis is the method of thinking that nature leads the scientist to adopt. For Condillac, nature provides every sensation, whether experienced or observed, with a single *idea* to designate it and recall it. For Lavoisier, it is also important to remember that the child is led to make only very simple links between sensation and idea, and that when he makes a mistake, nature provides an experience to correct him. However, there is no built-in correcting mechanism for the scientist.

> Dans l'étude et dans la pratique des sciences . . . les faux jugemens que nous portons n'intéressent ni notre existence, ni notre bien-être; *aucun intérêt physique ne nous oblige de nous rectifier; l'imagination, au contraire, qui*

tend à nous porter continuellement au-delà du vrai, la confiance en nous-mêmes, qui touche de si près à l'amour propre, nous sollicitent à tirer des conséquences qui ne dérivent pas immédiatement des faits: il n'est donc pas étonnant que, dans des temps très-voisins du berceau de la chimie, on ait supposé au lieu de conclure; que les suppositions transmises d'âge en âge se soient transformées en préjugés; et que ces préjugés ayent été adoptés et regardés comme des vérités fondamentales, même par de très-bons esprits. (*Méthode,* 11; my emphasis) [180]

This argument, which it is easy to skip over as marginal if one is considering analysis from the perspective of Macquer, is essential to the perspective of Lavoisier. Nature is a constraining force: the "reality of things" hurts the child when he judges incorrectly. However, in chemistry the situation, which should be exactly parallel, is not. The budding chemist is like the child, ignorant before a field not yet analyzed. To teach a science in the most efficient way, the ideal pedagogical system would reproduce the system used by nature to educate children, yet no harm will come to the chemist who makes an incorrect judgment. On the contrary, the scientist's tendency is to magnify the importance of his own judgments, leading to an increase of individual deviation from the truths provided by nature. The obvious next step is, then, to somehow mimic "natural analysis," to restore a system of checks and balances to chemistry. But this is not the natural analysis of the *Dictionnaire.* This is the natural analysis of the empirical experimental relationship to the world, whose definition relies on this concept of an outside experience which determines an individual's judgments.

Le seul moyen de prévenir ces écarts consiste à supprimer, ou au moins à simplifier, autant qu'il est possible, le raisonnement qui est de nous, et qui peut seul nous égarer, à le mettre continuellement à l'épreuve de l'expérience; à ne conserver que les faits qui sont des vérités données par la nature, et qui ne peuvent nous tromper; à ne chercher la vérité que dans l'enchaînement des expériences et des observations, surtout dans l'ordre dans lequel elles sont présentées, de la même manière que les mathématiciens parviennent à la solution d'un problème par le simple arrangement des données, et en réduisant le raisonnement à des opérations si simples, à des jugements si courts, qu'ils ne perdent jamais de vue l'évidence qui leur sert de guide. (*Méthode,* 11) [181]

The method proposed to fulfill this requirement is a key one that comes back in the *Traité élémentaire.* Reduce the field of imagination to a minimum, by reducing and restricting the language that the scientist has to work with. If he is constrained to operate with a very limited number of given relationships, if his own reasoning is reduced to a minimum, then there is very little chance for him to wander off into imaginative thinking. It is at this point that Lavoisier refers to the argument that Macquer, Torbern

Bergman, and Guyton de Morveau, especially, had used as the justification for reforming the nomenclature of chemistry. The language of a science is that science; the perfecting of the language is the perfecting of the science. But this same idea looks quite different from Lavoisier's perspective:

> Cette méthode qu'il est si important d'introduire dans l'étude et dans l'enseignement de la chimie, est étroitement liée à la réforme de sa nomenclature: une langue bien faite, une langue dans laquelle on aura saisi l'ordre succéssif et naturel des idées, entrainera une révolution nécessaire et même prompte dans la manière d'enseigner; *elle ne permettra pas à ceux qui professeront la chimie de s'écarter de la marche de la nature; il faudra ou rejetter la nomenclature, ou suivre irrésistiblement la route qu'elle aura marquée. C'est ainsi que la logique des sciences tient essentiellement à leur langue,* et quoique cette vérité ne soit pas neuve, et quoiqu'elle ait été déjà annoncée, comme elle n'est pas suffisamment répandue, nous avons cru nécessaire de la retracer ici. (*Méthode,* 12; my emphasis) [182]

Pedagogy and nomenclature are tightly linked, almost inseparable, as they were for Macquer in the *Dictionnaire de chymie.* But the limits that would result from the choice of a theory, which Macquer had felt to be so misleading and which the dictionary format was intended to avoid, are reinstituted here with vigor. The primary function of Lavoisier's nomenclature is to keep his scientist in line, in both senses of the term. The last lines of the passage quoted above must be taken almost ironically, since the "old truth" that is being repeated here is not an old truth at all, but a new definition of chemical logic hiding behind the terminology that defined the old.

Clearly, it is the strictly limited nature of the discipline that is the constantly repeated criterion. "La perfection de la nomenclature de la chimie, envisagée sous ce rapport, consiste à rendre les idées et les faits dans leur exacte vérité, sans rien supprimer de ce qu'ils présentent, surtout sans y rien ajouter: elle ne doit être qu'un miroir fidèle de ce que la Nature nous présente" (*Méthode,* 14) [183]. It is above all necessary not to add anything that does not come directly from the experiments. The nomenclature should only be, should be nothing more than, a faithful mirror of nature.

It may be helpful to recall for a moment the reasoning process Lavoisier used to present the experiments testing for the mutation of water into earth. The long "historical" preface is actually not interesting in terms of its historical content, but is rhetorically significant. Lavoisier whittles away the question being asked in the experiment to a bare minimum of components. This winnowing-away procedure is consonant with the principles governing chemistry as a discipline that were proposed in the *Méthode.* On the other hand—and this is a crucial point—Lavoisier does not derive his data from some external, objectively perceived nature; instead, Lavoisier himself, through his emplotment of the history, very subtly imposes his simple and elegant translation of the experimental question on his readers.

It is even more telling to recall how the effect on the reader is produced in the memoir on the decomposition and recomposition of water. It is a rhetorical *tour de force* rather than nature that makes the reader keenly aware that he is not observing neutrally what might have been occurring under the bell jar as water was synthesized in Priestley's experiment, but instead is having to make a choice between two equally coherent views of the same minimal experiment. On the other hand, Lavoisier's emplotment of the "Réflexions" leads the reader to a perspective from which he can no longer accept the definition of phlogiston that his predecessors had relied on nor even assign any meaning at all to the term. And the perspective from which the reader views the Priestley experiment on the decomposition and recomposition of water is derived again from redefinitions, this time of the terms *hydrogen* and *oxygen*. Although Lavoisier was not yet performing a full or explicit reform of the nomenclature of chemistry, nonetheless these partial redefinitions served as the starting place from which the reader was taught *how to observe* the experiment and how to proceed to narrow down the experimental question. It is this practice of observation that is important, much more than the specific result obtained, whether chemical substance or chemical theory is in question. This rectification of the experimental perspective is a necessary prelude to the realignment of chemical language with "natural analysis" that takes place in the *Méthode*. "On sent assez, sans que nous soyons obligés d'insister sur les preuves, que la langue de la chimie, telle qu'elle existe aujourd'hui, n'a point été formée d'après ces principes; et comment auroit-elle pu l'être dans des siècles où la marche de la physique expérimentale n'étoit point encore donnée; où l'on donnoit tout à l'imagination, presque rien à l'observation; où l'on ignorait jusqu'à la méthode d'étudier?" *(Méthode, 14) [184]*.

It is with this bias in mind that one can distinguish between Guyton de Morveau's project of creating the purified but passive nomenclature and Lavoisier's project of creating a nomenclature that actively programs its users. "Mais pourvu qu'elle ait été entreprise sur de bons principes; pourvu que ce soit *une méthode de nommer, plutôt qu'une nomenclature,* elle s'adaptera naturellement aux travaux qui seront faits dans la suite; elle marquera d'avance la place et le nom des nouvelles substances qui pourront être découvertes, et elle n'exigera que quelques réformes locales et particulières" *(Méthode,* 16–17; my emphasis) [185].

This is a language which, like Macquer's *Dictionnaire,* will contain within it the potential to predict the field before the work has been performed in the laboratory. But it will avoid the trap of being merely a nomenclature that acts as a depository for a multitude of carefully analyzed but basically unrelated ideas. By being a "méthode de nommer" which prepares the way for the scientist, the nomenclature acts as a body of rules that specifies the constraints to be placed upon the process of naming. Even what has *not yet* been observed is already included, determined, designated, within the nomenclature through the combinatorial rules for naming. Rather than adapting itself as the work is done (as Lavoisier says), it actually defines the work to be done, down to the name that the substance will have once it is isolated.[12] But the working assumption is that the "elements" being related by these rules for naming are derived using the logical constraints imposed by the rules, whereas in the *Dictionnaire* of Macquer, and even in the naming system proposed by Guyton de Morveau in his early paper, the relationships perceived and encoded are assumed to be secondary to the existence of the substances being isolated and named.

There is, of course, a paradox built into Lavoisier's system, the same one that Macquer was attempting to avoid. "Mais notre imagination n'a pas dû en dire plus que la nature ne nous en apprend" (*Méthode,* 18) [188]. Lavoisier is assuming or at least positing that there is something natural or preordained about the forced march of his scientific logic. But any particular set of concrete definitions that makes up the theoretical system is going to be inescapably the result of a scientist's imagination, that is, his creative reasoning. It is not at all difficult to see that the theoretical system in this case is the antiphlogistic caloric/oxygen/hydrogen theory of Lavoisier, who seems, therefore, to be going against the very method that he is proposing.

For the members of the Academy of Sciences, this contradiction was sufficiently obvious to allow them to see the *Méthode* as an attempt to pass off the new theories on the old guard, even if not in as unsophisticated a way as it could have at first appeared. Baumé, writing the report on whether or not the Academy should release the *Méthode* for publication, says the following:

> Cette théorie nouvelle, ce tableau, sont l'ouvrage de quatre hommes juste-
> ment célèbres dans les sciences . . . mais quelle théorie dut jamais sa naiss-

---

12. See Bachelard, *Pluralisme:* "On nommera pour connaître plus que pour reconnaître et la classification des substances élémentaires se révélera elle-même animée par une pensée active qui désigne une place régulière pour un objet avant de trouver cet objet (23) [186]. Lavoisier also extends this reasoning in his essay in support of the system of characters and signs that Hassenfratz and Adet proposed to accompany the new nomenclature (included as Appendix B): "Leur méthode nous paroît avoir encore un avantage; *elle fixera d'avance* les caractères qui devront représenter les substances qui seront découvertes, en sorte qu'il n'y aura plus *d'arbitraire* dans la formation des signes, et qu'une table complette de ces caractères, *présentera en même-temps ce qui est fait en chimie et ce qui reste à faire*" (*Méthode,* 312; my emphasis) [187].

ance à des hommes doués de plus de génie, à un travail plus soutenu, plus opiniâtre? Quelle autre réunit jamais les savans par un concert de plus belles expériences, par une masse de faits plus brillants, que la doctrine du phlogistique? Cet objet mérite donc la plus grande attention, il demande également le concours du temps ... pour être bien discuté, bien apprécié, bien jugé; et ce jugement n'est pas l'affaire d'un jour, parce que ce n'est pas en un jour qu'on renversera les idées reçues dans une science ... qui telle qu'elle est, s'exprime depuis un demi-siècle, avec une merveilleuse clarté. (*Méthode*, 244–45) [189]

But Baumé's recognition of the doctrinaire quality of Lavoisier's theory obscures the fact that Lavoisier makes a clear distinction between the *way* one thinks and *what* one thinks. Macquer made this distinction but tamed its consequences by positing an equivalence between the structure of what is thought with the structure of how one thinks. In fact, for him this homology provided the justification of his view of chemistry, the analytical science, as the most fundamental of all of the sciences. But Lavoisier consistently claims in the "Réflexions" that the way one thinks cannot be directly equated with what one thinks. Method cannot be equated with theory. Therefore one must specify which domain Lavoisier is speaking of when he excludes imagination from science.

In order to make this distinction more acute, we must characterize what Lavoisier means, first, by "theory," and then, by "method." A good formulation to start with is that provided by Jean Starobinski:

La *théorie*, en un sens, est une *hypothèse anticipatrice* sur la nature et les apports internes de l'objet exploré: en ce sens-là, l'on a pu dire avec raison que, dans les sciences physiques, la théorie précédait nécessairement l'invention. Mais en un autre sens, plus lié à l'étymologie, le mot théorie désigne la *contemplation compréhensive* d'un ensemble préalablement exploré, *la vision générale* d'un système régi par un ordre sensé. ...

La *méthode se cache dans le style de la démarche critique*, et ne devient parfaitement évidente qu'une fois le parcours entièrement achevé. ... Elle doit tendre, à travers le savoir du particulier, à la généralisation de ses découvertes: du même coup, elle doit en arriver à se comprendre elle-même ... elle s'achemine vers une théorie (au sens de *theoria*, contemplation compréhensive) ... *Toutefois cette généralisation du savoir critique reste en perpétuel devenir.* [190][13]

13. Jean Starobinski, *L'Oeil vivant II: La relation critique* (Paris: Gallimard, 1970), 9. Starobinski is talking here about the working of a (literary) critical methodology and not about a scientific method. One can argue, however, that the very idea of the structuralist methods (for that is what he is specifically defending in his essay) is derived from an ideal of "scientificity" implicit in the work of founders of the discourses of science like Lavoisier. In that sense, their formalization can be seen as a contemplation of a "science" (as pure method) in itself, and hence as a very appropriate source from which to take such definitions of basic methodological concepts.

The two definitions of theory given here recall the two kinds of theory that Lavoisier uses in his definition of the nomenclature of chemistry. Theory and method are closely related but not equivalent; moreover, there is no stable definition for either one. In fact, theory is necessarily two-sided: it is alternately an anticipatory hypothesis and a comprehensive contemplation (like Condillac's *coup d'oeil général*) of the ground already covered. Because it points out the work remaining to be done and indicates the tools to do it, the anticipatory hypothesis is embodied in the *méthode de nommer* (which therefore is not synonymous, as we shall see further on, with *method* as Starobinski uses the term). The nomenclature as it displays the facts that are already known and their relationships to each other, embodies the comprehensive contemplation that is homologous to the systems of chemistry described by Macquer in the *Dictionnaire* or by Guyton de Morveau in the "Dénominations chymiques." But for Lavoisier, *méthode de nommer* and *nomenclature* work as a couple to provide a theory. Therefore theory is not equivalent to an artificial system or construct as it was for Macquer. It defines an active and evolving field. One can describe the state of chemistry at any one time by producing the nomenclature, but this nomenclature can never be seen as sufficient, exhaustive, or even permanently established knowledge, because it must always be understood in the wider context of the dynamic nature of the anticipatory hypothesis, which gives the field of chemistry an ever-changing configuration. Lavoisier does not speak in terms of absolute truth or error, but in terms of whether the theory is more true or true in a different way from a state of the art that preceded it. One thus understands why Lavoisier's method is not invalidated despite the fact that in 1770 he worked with the assumption that water was an element, whereas ten years later he proved that water was a compound. The chemical method itself is not changed by a transformation in the perception of the object studied, although the theory will certainly be changed.

It is from this point of view that one can read the following comment from Hélène Metzger:

> Cette volonté énergique et constamment en éveil, de jeter désormais un regard frais et jeune sur le monde matériel exploré par la chimie, devait aboutir à une philosophie toute nouvelle de la science et de la matière, en même temps qu'à une modification permanente de l'orientation mentale du savant ... nous allons faire effort pour tenir en contact permanent l'expérience, l'observation précise faite à l'aide d'instruments de mesure, et la systématisation théorique. [191][14]

What interests us here is the "mental orientation" that Metzger mentions

14. Hélène Metzger, *La Philosophie de la matière chez Lavoisier* (Paris: Hermann, 1935), 10.

but does not discuss in detail. It is this new mental orientation that is determined by the change in the definition of method and whose implications are what in the long run form the enduring revolutionary aspects of Lavoisier's work. The method can be directed at specifying the technical means used to emplot the particular argument being developed, as it is in the "Mémoire sur la nature de l'eau," or it can, in a less technical way, be developed to give a wider perspective on the goals of the method itself, as in the memoir on "Décomposition et recomposition." These are the goals that define chemistry's parameters, and for Lavoisier they provide the method with a stability that is not affected by changes in the theory. A concern with what Starobinski calls the "style of the critical procedure" runs throughout Lavoisier's work and constitutes the level on which the real questions are argued. For truth lies in thinking the right way; his opponents' errors are a result not of incorrect experiments but of their "mauvaise manière de philosopher" ("Réflexions," 624). He who follows the proper critical procedure realizes that the theory is in a perpetual state of development that can never be completed. It represents a utopian state of chemical theory that is never *meant* to be reached.

The rhetorical organization of the essay on the decomposition and the recomposition of water is a demonstration of the effect that this critical procedure can have. Lavoisier's method leads to a simultaneous transformation of the nomenclature as a naming method and as a passive embodiment of the state of the art. There, it is devastating to the phlogiston theory both epistemologically and theoretically. For it is in this argument that Lavoisier actually combines the criticism of the logical apparatus of the phlogistonists (as he presented it in the "Réflexions") with the critique of the experimental procedures (as he implied it in the article "Sur la nature de l'eau"). He manages to separate theory from method, to pry apart the two previously superimposable systems, by showing that it was the presumed homology of theory with method, of chemical analysis with philosophical analysis, that caused Priestley and Macquer to be philosophically blind, to be incapable of reading what was happening before them. Lavoisier's reader is shown that the phlogiston theory is not an inadequate theory, but that accepting it implies an incorrect—in fact counterproductive— critical procedure.

The *Traité élémentaire de chimie*

It is not an insurmountable difficulty to give a name to a substance that has just been discovered and to have the chemical establishment adopt the new name in spite of hesitations concerning the theory that proposes the name. However, it is much more problematic to attempt to rename the entire body of chemical substances according to such a theory, although Lavoisier says, near the end of his introductory essay to the *Méthode* that "nous avons observé que l'oreille s'accoutumoit promptement aux mots nouveaux; surtout lorsqu'ils se trouvent liés à un système général et raisonné" (24) [192]. But Lavoisier had to accomplish a total reform in order for his nomenclature to function as the active research tool just outlined. Rather than being a beginning point for the science, such a reform could be characterized as merely one more in the alternating series of mutually modifying theoretical operations that characterize the development of a science. Therefore one understands his enthusiasm for the nomenclature reform initially outlined by Guyton de Morveau in his 1782 paper. But it is also clear why, given the more generalized aim of Lavoisier's revision, he found it necessary to convert his co-workers to his theoretical and methodological points of view before proceeding further and why the relatively modest article of Guyton de Morveau grew to such an all-encompassing undertaking as the *Méthode de nomenclature chymique.*

The rest of the *Méthode* proceeds as an elaboration of the basic rules for the analogical formation of scalar compound names for chemical substances, including tables, charts, and comparisons with the old nomenclature. These sections do not depart substantially from the principles outlined by Guyton de Morveau in 1782, except that the caloric/oxygen/hydrogen theory is used, and that the tables and their explanations attempt to be comprehensive. It has been remarked that Lavoisier's tables show, in fact, just how close his theory was to those of his predecessors, and he himself remarks ironically upon this fact in his reply to Baumé's report on the *Méthode*. "Il est évident que toutes ces théories n'ont de commun entr'elles que le mot de phlogistique qu'elles ont conservé, qui est en quelque façon leur terme de ralliement; que le phlogistique des François n'est point celui des Allemands, moins encore celui des Anglois, que ces différentes théories, loin de pouvoir être appellées *anciennes,* sont au contraire plus modernes même que la doctrine que l'on caractérise sous le nom de *théorie nouvelle*" (*Méthode,* 309) [193]. It is not so much in the substance of the theory itself that Lavoisier's reform lies as in the new definition of what constitutes a scientific theory and in how one defines the parameters of any field. In this sense, one can see the title of this work as being especially significant. The *Méthode de nomenclature chymique* provides, after all, a new definition of method to replace an old. And nomenclature must be seen as having a double theoretical function deriving from the reformulation of the process of scientific reasoning.

From this point of view, it is obvious why in the *Traité élémentaire de chimie* of 1789 Lavoisier begins his project as an attempt to extend the *Méthode* and then, with a complaint reminiscent of Macquer's, tells us that his project got out of hand. Rather than being "merely" an extension of the *Méthode,* his *Traité* has become a reworking of the whole field of chemistry, and a pedagogical treatise at the same time.

> Je n'avais pour objet, lorsque j'ai entrepris cet ouvrage, que de donner plus de développement au Mémoire que j'ai lu à la séance publique de l'Académie des Sciences du mois d'avril 1787, sur la nécessité de réformer et de perfectionner le langage de la chimie, tandis que je croyais ne m'occuper que de la nomenclature, tandis que je n'avais pour objet que de perfectionner le langage de la chimie, mon ouvrage s'est transformé insensiblement entre mes mains, sans qu'il m'ait été possible de m'en défendre, en un traité élémentaire de chimie. [194][15]

Unlike Macquer's, Lavoisier's complaint is not an admission of defeat but an apology for what he sees as a victory. Although in this work he focuses more on the theory than on the method, the method has irrevocably altered the nature of chemical theory.

The *Traité élémentaire de chimie* is divided into four parts. The first is the long, very-well-known epistemological "Discours préliminaire," which is in great part an extended version of Lavoisier's essay in the *Méthode.* Then the body of the work is divided into Part I, on gases, combustion, and the formation of acids (basically his oxygen theories); Part II, on the combination of acids with bases and the formations of simple salts (the theories on the composition of water are in the middle of this section); and Part III, on experimental instruments and procedures.

In the "Discours préliminaire," Lavoisier repeats to a great extent his argument from the *Méthode,* but he quotes Condillac at greater length. He also goes into greater detail to describe just how a theory works to channel the anticipatory hypotheses of the scientific practitioner. As he said in the *Méthode,* for those whose theory is the most to be admired, "imagination" has already been constrained by the structure of the discipline. "Les mathématiciens parviennent à la solution d'un problème par le simple arrangement des données, et en réduisant le raisonnement à des opérations si simples, à des jugements si courts qu'ils ne perdent jamais de vue l'évidence qui leur sert de guide" (*Traité,* 4) [195]. But chemistry still leaves too much leeway for the imagination to wander: the elements are not sufficiently narrowly defined to ensure that the chemists never will "perdre de vue l'évidence qui leur sert de guide." This is the angle from which Lavoisier will attack the problem.

> Ces inconvénients tiennent moins à la nature des choses qu'à la forme de l'enseignement, et c'est ce qui m'a déterminé à donner à la chimie une marche qui me paraît plus conforme à celle de la nature ... mais je crois que [les difficultés] qui restent n'appartiennent point à l'ordre que je me suis

15. *Traité élémentaire de chimie,* vol. 1 of *Oeuvres.* Hereafter cited as *Traité.*

prescrit: qu'elles sont plutôt une suite de l'état d'imperfection où est encore la chimie. Cette science présente des lacunes nombreuses, qui interrompent la série des faits, et qui exigent des raccordements embarrassants et difficiles. Elle n'a pas, comme la géométrie élémentaire, l'avantage d'être une science complète et dont toutes les parties sont étroitement liées entre elles. (5) [196]

His first statement picks up where his discussion leaves off in the *Méthode*. The fault lies not only with chemistry as a comprehensive body of knowledge, but also with chemistry as a method of naming. Therefore Lavoisier extends the *Méthode* to a "forme de l'enseignement" which will fill in the lacunae in the nomenclature in such a manner as to enable the student of chemistry to proceed without deviating from the procedure prescribed, without losing sight of the factual (experimental) evidence which guides him. He will make the nomenclature, a stable repository of both combinatorial rules and definitions, as closely knit as possible. It is in this context that another function of Guyton de Morveau's scalar naming procedure becomes visible, a function that he himself does not utilize, but which is very important for Lavoisier. In *Les Mots et les choses,* Michel Foucault argues that:

> On voit bien comment se partagent à l'époque classique les sciences du langage: d'un côté la Rhétorique, qui traite des figures et des tropes, c'est-à-dire de la manière dont le langage se spatialise dans les signes verbaux; de l'autre la Grammaire, qui traite de l'articulation et de l'ordre, c'est-à-dire de la manière dont l'analyse de la représentation se dispose selon une série successive. La Rhétorique définit la spatialité de la représentation, telle qu'elle naît avec le langage; la Grammaire définit pour chaque langue l'ordre qui répartit dans le temps cette spatialité. C'est pourquoi la Grammaire suppose la nature rhétorique des langages, même des plus primitifs et des plus spontanés. (98) [197]

This spatialization of verbal signs, this elaboration of their relationships to each other, indicates the functioning of tropes, hence the presence of "imagination" at work. It is the figures that produce analogical reasoning (i.e., according to Lavoisier's definition, reasoning that is not constantly checked by experiment), and it is this sort of analogical reasoning that Lavoisier wishes to minimize. And yet, according to Foucault, the Enlightenment believed that this type of imaginative reasoning was inevitably implied by the nature of both rhetoric and grammar. For Macquer, the object of the *Dictionnaire de chymie* was to enable the reader to perform both rhetorical and grammatical operations on well-defined word elements, the highly refined definitions supposedly preventing the grosser abuses of unchecked analogical or metaphorical thinking while maintaining the fecundity that these procedures had demonstrated in other fields less closely related to knowledge about the physical world (for example, literature and philosophy). For Lavoisier, any such operations imply that the researcher has deviated in his thinking from the predetermined "marche naturelle" of the chemical practice.

But how is he to eliminate rhetoric and grammar? First of all, Lavoisier agrees with the general consensus that "la chimie, en soumettant à des expériences les différents corps de la nature, a pour objet de les décomposer et de se mettre en état *d'examiner séparément les différentes substances qui entrent dans leur combinaison*" (*Traité,* 136) [198]. Second, the data of the science to be known are to be presented in an especially simple nomenclature in the way suggested by Guyton de Morveau in the 1782 article; that is, in scalar naming procedures: "La chimie marche donc vers son but et vers sa perfection en divisant, subdivisant, et resubdivisant encore, et nous ignorons quel sera le terme de ses succès" (137) [199]. Therefore, as for Guyton de Morveau, and as Lavoisier reiterated in the *Méthode,* names will mimic the composition of compounds. They will divide, subdivide, and resubdivide again, the final endpoint being potentially infinitely distant. But this does not matter, for the procedure is self-verifying as it continues; in fact, it can even be seen to be self-destructive of its immediate content precisely to the degree to which it is self-verifying as method. If A is found to be BC, and BC then to be DEFG, the procedure maintains itself by destroying successively its old data to replace it with new data of precisely the same order. The new data then designates new experiments to be performed by providing new substances to be decomposed. The method merely extends itself out indefinitely, following the same rules for naming what has been decomposed. In this sense, not only does the method of experimental procedure refine the nomenclature, but the new nomenclature provides a very restricted new number of experiments. Even more radical than might have been expected, then, are the limits placed upon the chemical practitioner, who is reduced to the status of a laboratory technician, totally dominated by his nomenclature. The language of chemistry is, from this point of view, a nomenclature embedded in a natural or already-existing common language. And inside the nomenclature, which is where the actual work takes place, *syntax no longer exists.* Names can be long or short, simple or complex, but they are still merely combinatorial names, not open to either rhetorical or grammatical manipulation. In this way, the syntax is removed from a sentence context and is replaced by synthetic words—words in which the syntax is institutionalized and *de-figured.* Replacing the unpredictable operations of normal verbal constructs are the minimal rules of combination that will order the internal structure of the scientific word. In this way, Lavoisier not only relies on and reaffirms the reasons for the scalar naming procedure that Guyton de Morveau uses, but even more importantly, he has found a structure for his double-edged nomenclature that, in imitation of his ideal mathematicians, reduced "le raisonnement à des opérations si simples, à des jugements si courts, que [les savants] ne perdent jamais de vue l'évidence qui leur sert de guide" (4) [200].

Now, while the "Discours préliminaire" and a few comments interspersed throughout the body of the text refer explicitly to the epistemological problems and positions of the new chemistry, the greater part of the body of the text must by its very nature be limited to presenting the "state of the art" as Lavoisier saw it at that time. The result, of course, is that the explicit chemical theories and data expounded have an antique feeling when compared to the epistemological positions worked out in the "Discours préliminaire." But this hardly seems to be sufficient justification for the generalized attack made upon Lavoisier in the nineteenth century and on into this one by McKie, Partington, and even Daumas, Berthelot and more modern writers like Dagognet, all of whom, in one way or another, assert that Lavoisier did not make any real innovations in the chemical theories of his day. Lavoisier's most important reforms concern not chemical theory *per se,* but the new valorization of method as primary to and productive of theory. Therefore, although reforms in a particular system might be defended tenaciously, once it was shown to be outmoded, the system was dropped without qualms. Each point in the theory should not be seen as territory irrevocably won and to be defended at all cost, but merely as a further step toward a new theoretical position which might well undermine the previous one.[16]

It is in this sense, with this primary caveat, that one should read Lavoisier's heated and sometimes rather personal defenses of his own theories, especially the caloric theory. One might argue that he takes a strong position partly in order to spur equally intense debate and to encourage experimental activities in the scientific community as a whole. For one must remember (and we will return to this question briefly at the end of the chapter) that Lavoisier speaks constantly of real scientific work as being performed *not* by individuals, but by communities of scientists.

Although the theories that Lavoisier proposed are long out of date, some aspects of them are interesting in the light of the definition of chemical practice that he developed, for they mirror many of the particular methodological assumptions he uses and demonstrate just how closely nomenclature and the naming method imply each other.

16. Cf. the following statement of Hélène Metzger: "Le 'connu' dont il part n'est ni un ensemble de postulats métaphysiques posés *a priori* pour l'éternité et dont les conséquences se déroulent ou se déduisent dans l'esprit du chimiste suivant une nécessité implacable et paisible; ni le monde usuel du sens commun avec ses intuitions vagues, ses jugements peu élaborés, ses décrets arbitraires et difficilement conciliables." *Philosophie de la matière,* 10 [201].

His basic construct, as presented in the *Traité,* is a function of the three "elements" we have named before, oxygen, hydrogen, and caloric. But a distinction must be made among the three. Hydrogen and oxygen function somewhat similarly in two ways: they enter chemically into compounds, and they are granted something like an objective reality. The tables that are appended to the *Traité,* especially the one that begins Part II (the "Table of Simple Substances," reproduced in Appendix C), treat oxygen, hydrogen, and caloric as being of the same order (elemental) and as distinguished from other merely presumed simple substances, but it can be misleading to take this categorization at face value. One must distinguish between Lavoisier's description in the *table* of the elemental (i.e., character-determining) substances—light, caloric, oxygen, nitrogen (azote), and hydrogen—and the differences between these substances when he describes them in a *particular chemical context.* Guerlac gives the following analysis of the concept of an element as it is implied in the table:

> Wide distribution, and its presence in a great number of compounds, quali-
> fies a substance to be called an element. Gold, on the other hand, is a
> simple substance, yet it is not an element ... He specifically notes that such a
> substance "enters as an essential and constituent principle" in compound
> bodies. In the older chemistry, from which Lavoisier is unable to free
> himself completely, the elements—the four elements of Aristotle, the *tria
> prima* of Paracelsus, and so on—were thought of as the bearers and the
> causes of the distinctive qualities of bodies into which they enter. As we saw
> in discussing his theory of acids, Lavoisier had strong ties to this "chemistry
> of principles."[17]

This puts us once more in the "chemistry of principles" of Macquer, where the defining characteristic is clearly the quality by which a substance is *read.* But we must here make a distinction, one of degree rather than of kind.

> Cependant, entre l'ancienne conception de l'analyse qui voulait résoudre les
> corps en leurs principes constituants—chacun de ces principes imposant au
> mixte dans lequel il entrait les qualités dont il est porteur—et la conception
> moderne de la décomposition qui veut extraire des corps complexes les
> divers ingrédients qui en se combinant à nouveau formeraient le corps
> primitif, il y a disparate très nette; avec une remarquable pénétration, Chev-
> reul a fait observer que jusqu'à l'oeuvre de Lavoisier, cette opération toute
> logique et grammaticale n'était qu'une analyse mentale, une résolution en
> notions. La véritable analyse chimique ou séparation pratique des éléments
> indécomposables qui par leur combinaison formaient le corps primitif est
> tout autre chose. [202][18]

Hélène Metzger makes the point that the two analyses are of completely

17. Guerlac, *Lavoisier,* 115.
18. Metzger, *Philosophie de la matière,* 13.

different kinds. The first presumes an abstract judgment about not only
the identity but also the philosophical use and the universal nature of the
substances. This use is the one that makes the analysis/affinity/principle
complex function. The second assumes no such thing. Instead, it replaces
the interpretive act with the mere act of decomposition. What is especially
interesting is that both kinds of chemical analysis coexist in the table of
simple substances that Lavoisier proposes. The elements precede the simple
substances, with the result that one has a tendency to read the structure
of the table as privileging the elements, hence as an indication of Lavoisier's
backwardness, of his tendency to revert to the old chemistry of the four
elements. But it is necessary to adjust this opinion in the light of a statement
typical of the kind of scientific position I have been elaborating:

> On ne manquera pas d'être surpris de ne point trouver dans un traité
> élémentaire de chimie un chapitre sur les parties constituantes et élémen-
> taires des corps; . . . Tout ce qu'on peut dire sur le nombre et sur la nature
> des éléments se borne, suivant moi, à des discussions purement métaphy-
> siques: ce sont des problèmes indéterminés qu'on se propose de résoudre,
> qui sont susceptibles d'une infinité de solutions, mais dont il est très-proba-
> ble qu'aucune en particulier n'est d'accord avec la nature. Je me contenterai
> donc de dire que si par le nom d'éléments nous entendons désigner les
> molécules simples et indivisibles qui composent les corps, il est probable
> que nous ne les connaissons pas. (*Traité*, 6–7) [203]

It seems that one must always make a clear distinction between what are
theoretical ("métaphysiques") analyses and what are merely notifications
of the point to which laboratory decompositions have proceeded. The first
group works together to form a chemical theory; the second is a listing
of empirical results. The idea to emphasize, however, is that Lavoisier
assumes that the real "state of the art" is better represented by the *second
group* than by the first. And although the two groups are similar in that
Lavoisier clearly would see them both as provisional descriptions, not to
be taken as true, nonetheless they embody different *kinds* of provisional
statements. As Guerlac suggests, the first group can be characterized as
that group which determines the categories, the family names in effect,
via which the other, empirically derived simple substances will be combined
into words. The names of "oxygène," or "hydrogène," imply just this kind
of generative procedure, as does the attempt, for instance, to call nitrogen
"alkaligène."[19]

19. "Nitrogen, to be sure, is everywhere in the earth's atmosphere and is widely distributed
in animal and vegetable substances. But was this sufficient reason for Lavoisier to elevate it
to the dignity of an 'element' of the first subgroup? Quite possibly he gave it this higher
status because he tended to think, on the basis of Berthollet's analysis of ammonia, that
nitrogen might be the 'principle' of all alkalis, what Fourcroy would have liked to call
'alkaligène.' " Guerlac, *Lavoisier*, 117.

The other two of the five primary elements, however, are much more interesting. Light, especially, seems a peculiar "element" to include. One may guess that it was included more or less as a precaution, for Guerlac says that "Lavoisier never quite satisfied himself about the nature of light, but he knew from the work of IngenHousz and Senebier that light plays an essential part in the gaseous chemistry of vegetation, a matter to which he alluded in a remarkable speculative paper he published in 1788."[20] But the most revealing inclusion is caloric. Hydrogen and oxygen are both isolable, and they combine with the other simple substances in typifiable ways. As I mentioned before, the presence of such substances is deduced for Lavoisier through weight changes, and hence the epistemological axiom underlying all analysis is that of the conservation of mass. But caloric, like phlogiston, is not isolable. It passes through containers. It does form "compounds" with other chemical substances, but of an entirely different kind from those formed by ponderable substances. Caloric has no weight; it only has *effects* of another order, and because they are not characterized by weight measurements, we can posit that these are not chemical effects. Caloric is not really a chemical substance at all in the way Lavoisier has been using the term, even though he is consistent about describing it in combination with other substances.

So what is its nature? We recall that in the "Réflexions sur le phlogistique," Lavoisier describes caloric purely by analogy with water. It is a very tenuous fluid which causes the bodies with which it is combined to behave in accordance with Lavoisier's analogy of a sponge absorbing water. In the *Traité*, the basic argument of the "Réflexions" is repeated almost verbatim and at great length. But Lavoisier's originally confusing assertions that his theory is as coherent as the phlogistonists' takes on new meaning here, with the restrictions on the meaning of *theory* that were the result of the work on nomenclature:

> Nous avons en conséquence désigné la cause de la chaleur, le fluide éminemment élastique qui la produit, par le nom de *calorique*. *Indépendamment de ce que cette expression remplit notre objet dans le système que nous avons adopté,* [i.e., it fits into the structure of the nomenclature] elle a encore un autre avantage, c'est de pouvoir s'adapter à toutes sortes d'opinions; *puisque, rigoureusement parlant, nous ne sommes pas même obligés de supposer que le calorique soit une matière réelle; il suffit,* comme on le sentira mieux par la lecture de ce qui va suivre, *que ce soit une cause répulsive* quelconque qui écarte les molécules de la matière, et on peut ainsi en envisager les effets d'une manière abstraite et mathématique. (*Traité,* 19; my emphasis) [204]

Lavoisier clearly states his position before continuing to re-elaborate the analogy of the sponge that he had used to such advantage in the

20. Ibid., 117.

"Réflexions." Caloric is not "real" in the same way that oxygen and hydrogen are real. However, it is not *unreal* in the way that phlogiston is unreal, for its effects can be measured, and they have a reproducible specificity. Caloric is real for Lavoisier in another way: in the way that gravity was real for Newton. It is a "mentally accomplished materialization" of a measurable entity.[21] It does not matter whether it is materially real or not, as it has certain experimental indices that are always related to it. Temperature is an indication of the relative quantity of caloric present in a particular substance, and this same temperature is related, not to weight, but to indirect measures of *volume* (either using thermometers or the Laplace-Lavoisier ice calorimeter). But caloric is also very selective in its relationship to different chemical substances, and in this sense it behaves like a chemical substance with different saturation points, although Lavoisier describes it just as before, using his very unchemical image of the sponge:

> On entend par cette expression, *calorique spécifique* des corps, la quantité de calorique respectivement nécessaire pour élever d'un même nombre de degrés la température de plusieurs corps égaux en poids. Cette quantité de calorique dépend de la distance des molécules des corps, de leur adhérence plus ou moins grande; et c'est cette distance, ou plutôt l'espace qui en résulte, qu'on a nommé, comme je l'ai déjà observé, *capacité pour contenir le calorique*.(28) [205]

The point to be emphasized here is the way that caloric combines in a distinctive quantity with each particular substance. In a sense, heat capacity reproduces the mysterious specificity that was so crucial to the definition of another term for Macquer and the phlogistonists: affinity. The concept of affinity, like caloric, was a mentally accomplished materialization, a fictional entity that allowed one to read meaning into a series of experiments. The similarity between caloric and affinity is not accidental, either. "Il est probable que l'écartement des molécules des corps par le calorique tient de même à une combinaison de différentes forces attractives, et c'est le résultat de ces forces que nous cherchons à exprimer d'une manière plus concise et plus conforme à l'état d'imperfection de nos connaissances, lorsque nous disons que le calorique communique une force répulsive aux molécules des corps" (31) [206].

In a sense, Lavoisier has used an analogy with affinity to reduce the effects produced by heat to a function of a type of affinity-of-aggregation. Like all affinities, this one shows a selectivity, or is used to posit one cause behind a series of selective effects. But this selectivity is defined in quan-

21. See Ludwik Fleck, *The Genesis and Development of a Scientific Fact* (Chicago: University of Chicago Press, 1979), 133, for a discussion of the role such entities play in modern science. See also my article "Dispensing with the Fixed Point," *History and Theory* 22, no. 3 (1983): 264–77, which develops some of the points that Fleck raises.

titative rather than qualitative terms. It is also the tool (missing in the article on the decomposition and recomposition of water) that provides Lavoisier with the explicit systematic description of the three physical states of matter:

> Tous ces faits particuliers, dont il me serait facile de multiplier les exemples, m'autorisent à faire un principe général de ce que j'ai déjà annoncé plus haut, que presque tous les corps de la nature sont susceptibles d'exister dans trois états différents: dans l'état de solidité, dans l'état de liquidité et dans l'état aériforme, et que ces trois états d'un même corps dépendent de la quantité de calorique qui lui est combinée. Je désignerai dorénavant ces fluides aériformes sous le nom générique de *gaz,* et je dirai en conséquence que, dans toute espéce de gaz, *on doit distinguer le calorique qui fait, en quelque façon, l'office de dissolvant,* et la substance qui est combinée avec lui et qui forme sa base. (25–26; my emphasis) [207]

Heat saturation levels are defined by volume changes: caloric causes *state* changes, not *chemical* changes, in chemical substances. In fact, it is, as phlogiston originally was, a "substance" whose existence is abstracted backwards from a series of absolutely parallel effects, to designate a single cause, rather than a previously existing chemical entity whose characteristic qualities are made explicit in the structure of a simple name. For caloric is not a chemical substance: it is a name for a physical function, and this function is, Lavoisier says, *to be a solvent.*

Now, we have already seen Lavoisier's preference for analysis performed "in the wet way" *(par voie humide)*—in other words, using water as a solvent, which acts as a neutral, nonreactive mechanical base in which to put the reacting substances in contact with each other and to make possible or to speed up reactions. J. B. Gough suggests that Lavoisier's first understanding of the function of elemental air in the formation of "aeriform fluids" was arrived at by analogy with water's action as a solvent: substances were not gases *by themselves,* but only as a result of being evaporated into the air.[22] Caloric clearly was conceptualized to incorporate this same function, especially for this pneumatic chemistry which was so dear to Lavoisier. Although at first glance, the very fact that caloric is found in combination with other substances would seem to define it as a chemical, it enables Lavoisier to read gaseous transformations through an extended analogy with analyses performed in water solutions.[23] As with his original understanding of water solutions, when water was still considered an element,

22. "Lavoisier's Theory of the Gaseous State," 31–32.
23. The creation of water from hydrogen and oxygen would thus be seen as a sort of precipitation, as Lavoisier tries to argue in his discussion of the relationships between lightning and rain (*Méthode,* 302–3). But see also the following passage in the *Traité,* in which he is describing "only" laboratory techniques: "Pour bien saisir ce qui se passe dans la solution des sels, il faut savoir qu'il se complique deux effets dans la plupart de ces opérations:

Lavoisier believes that caloric maintains the identities of the components dissolved in it rather than destroying them. Thus caloric, although defined as a substance, actually acts as a background in which chemical compositions and decompositions can take place and be read. It is not analogous to phlogiston in the old analysis/affinity/principle (phlogiston) paradigm but is much closer to that concept with which Lavoisier himself associates it without ever exploring the connotations: it serves an epistemological function similar to that of *affinity*. Repulsion is that which makes decomposition (and hence analysis), as a *laboratory* rather than as a *logical* exercise, reasonable. Caloric is neutral and mechanical rather than chemical, with the result that the verification of purity through specific density (a weight function) and the utilization of the idea of the conservation of mass as a tool to identify which substances are in compound with others (also a weight function) can proceed without logical or conceptual interference from the caloric—*which has no weight*. Caloric is that which must be both included and excluded for many chemical decompositions to take place: included to make them feasible in the laboratory, but excluded in order to read the results of the experiment in terms of a simple, closed, economical *chemical* system. Even more importantly, caloric resolves the language problem of how to link the world of material substances with the world of dynamic functions. Lavoisier had said that the name *caloric* had been chosen for reasons much more important than the simple fact that it fit into the substance-oriented nomenclature (*Traité,* 19). But rather than being beside the point, the misnaming of the function as a substance is what enables Lavoisier to use caloric in both contexts.

Although many other explanations have been given which fit other facets of the problem very well, it is perhaps relevant to point out that this definition of caloric may provide Lavoisier with one strategic motive, at least, for his famous comment on affinity in the "Discours préliminaire."

Cette loi rigoureuse, dont je n'ai pas dû m'écarter, de ne rien conclure au delà de ce que les expériences présentent, et de ne jamais suppléer au silence des faits, ne m'a pas permis de comprendre dans cet ouvrage la partie de la chimie la plus susceptible, peut-être, de devenir un jour une science exacte: c'est celle qui traite des affinités chimiques ou attractions électives. M. Geoffroy, M. Gellert, M. Bergman, M. Scheele, M. de Morveau, M. Kirwan et beaucoup d'autres ont déjà rassemblé une multitude de faits particuliers qui n'attendent plus que la place qui doit leur être assignée; mais les données principales manquent, ou du moins celles que nous avons ne sont encore ni assez précises ni assez certaines pour devenir la base

---

solution par l'eau, et solution par calorique; et, comme cette distinction donne l'explication de la plupart des phénomènes relatifs à la solution, je vais insister pour la bien faire entendre" (306) [208].

fondamentale sur laquelle doit reposer une partie aussi importante de la chimie. La science des affinités est d'ailleurs à la chimie ordinaire ce que la géométrie transcendante est à la géométrie élémentaire, et je n'ai pas cru devoir compliquer par d'aussi grandes difficultés des éléments simples et faciles, qui seront, à ce que j'espère, à la portée d'un très-grand nombre de lecteurs.

Peut-être un sentiment d'amour propre a-t-il, sans que je m'en rendisse compte à moi-même, donné du poids à ces réflexions. M. de Morveau est au moment de publier l'article *Affinité* de l'Encyclopédie méthodique, et j'avais bien des motifs pour redouter de travailler en concurrence avec lui. (*Traité*, 5–6) [209]

Besides the fact that Lavoisier seems to have worked quite well with Guyton de Morveau and that one would therefore expect him to have happily set forth Guyton de Morveau's ideas on the subject, Lavoisier, interestingly enough, does not even suggest what the affinity theory is. Even though one of his first pedagogical and philosophical principles for the new chemistry was to "accoutumer [les étudiants] de bonne heure à n'admettre aucun mot sans y attacher une idée" (*Traité*, 8) [210], he uses the elective affinities without ever explaining them. One would have expected, given this rule, either that Lavoisier would not use affinity at all in this book, or that he would, after giving all of the reasons for his disapproval of the theories it is related to, go ahead and explain it so that the students would at least have a specific idea to attach to the word *affinity*. One would most likely have expected him not to use affinity theory at all, since in the passage quoted above he has so clearly marked it off as difficult and, although absolutely central to chemistry, not necessary in an elementary work. But he does neither the one nor the other. Instead, he does the one thing we would not have expected: without ever saying what affinity is, he uses the affinities to formalize parts of qualitative analysis, appends charts of relative affinities, and, not content with just using the already-accepted affinities data, also introduces them into the internal operations of his new theory of chemistry. He even includes a table of the relative affinities of caloric with various substances.

In a sense, affinity has been reduced from its previous epistemological role to just an empirical phenomenon. Lavoisier seems to have decided to deal with the language-oriented chemistry of principles that the affinity theory supports—by simply ignoring it. Any attempt at a theoretical explanation of affinity, given the dual nature of affinity as both a chemical and logical construct, would have necessitated a return to the legible library-chemistry of Macquer, whose very mode of operation Lavoisier is eliminating. Therefore, only the nature of affinity as simple or aggregate attraction is still used, although it is used at the most speculative theoretical level, one good example being the attempt to explain the repulsive effect of caloric we mentioned above. On the other hand, chemical affinities, the elective attractions, are demoted to mere observed relations between the simple substances, and they therefore leave the realm of the theoretical and the epistemological to become a laboratory instrument, a means to an end rather than an end (a theoretical goal) in itself.

In this one move, caloric has taken over the epistemological role of affinity, with two very important results. Caloric as a physical agent permitting the interpretation of data through quantitative means undermines the naming process as a logical analytical "metaphysics" and transforms it into an experimental imperative. In this sense, then, one might read the refusal of Lavoisier to become involved in a discussion of the "meaning" or the "nature" of affinity as a reaffirmation of his emphasis on the difference between the new scientific practice and the old. At the same time, caloric, named as though it were a substance, is assumed to be nonproblematical in its chemical combinations, and one tends to forget its epistemological function and to treat it as though it actually were a simple substance. In fact, it is possible to read Lavoisier's division of the simple substances into two groups as a clever rhetorical move. For, as was mentioned before, oxygen and hydrogen are really "elements" as Lavoisier uses the terms only if one chooses to use them to define family groups. There is no necessity for their elevation to the status of elements. The choice is dependent on whether one views the various possible compounds as having been generated by oxygen or hydrogen. In this sense, the distinction between simple substance and element seems at first to be specious. However, it serves the rhetorical function of disguising the fact that the two groups should have been divided between light and caloric on one side and all of the rest as simple substances on the other side. In fact, the naming system used by Lavoisier reduces *element* from its old mystical philosophical meaning to the modern one of a simple substance, for the theoretical distinction between element and simple substance in his table of the elements is disregarded in practice in the text of the *Traité*. Caloric is treated as a simple substance in Lavoisier's practical discussions, despite his periodic statements to the contrary, for the nomenclature forces one to see caloric as an experimentally isolated substance, not as a logically derived principle. It is not subject to the technician's critique of it as a philosophical entity; on the contrary, it takes its place inside the dominating nomenclature. The chemist works within his nomenclature: he learns it and then sees his world through it.

Although the content of the theories themselves has long since been made obsolete, and although the experimental questions Lavoisier asks seem so much closer to the interests of his predecessors than they are to those of modern chemistry, this similarity is an illusion. The basic epistemological construct of chemistry has been changed by Lavoisier's redefinition of chemical theory and its relationship to its critical method. The result is that the same words in this new context have different meanings and different epistemological effects. The "new" chemistry that Lavoisier is proposing in the "old" language is actually, through the operation of the new method which it incorporates, closer to modern chemistry than to the philosophical chemistry of Macquer. For the status of those words has changed; their relationship to the person using them has been reversed. The impersonal language of positivist science directs the ongoing research. It makes meditation on its own epistemological foundations all but impossible to justify as a relevant part of the scientific work.

Yet this situation seems to imply that the effort that Lavoisier had expended to train the critical judgment of his readers was countered by the very effectiveness of the nomenclature he had built to define the discipline. This was surely not the desired result of so many carefully self-displaying rhetorical constructs and the ever-present philosophical polemic. But perhaps the response to this assertion will help explain the difficulty later scientists and historians have faced in trying to recapture the full importance of Lavoisier's founding innovations: he redefined the nature of chemical theory and method.

CHAPTER 8

Science as
Collective Voice

IT TOOK ALMOST TWO HUNDRED YEARS FOR THE LANGUAGE OF chemistry to work out and incorporate the full implications of Descartes' *Discours de la méthode* in terms of the rhetorical positioning of a scientific speaking voice. Descartes had provided a rudimentary but streamlined model of a new, impersonal mode of speaking about the world that is independent of its particular theoretical content at any one time. The chemistry of the phlogistonists was certainly a first step towards this authoritative kind of discourse, in that the affinity theory was one of the first coherent attempts to outline a general definition of the chemical subject matter linked to a methodological comportment. But Macquer's dictionary is a good example of the inherent problem: an authoritative voice (the unchallengeable status of the statements) is possible only if the analytic method is also situated in a nonauthorial and invisibly constraining rhetoric. Macquer's *Dictionnaire de chymie* failed precisely because Macquer insisted on maintaining the theoretical independence of his reader while nonetheless trying to format the book to reflect the epistemological tenets of the analytic method so closely tied to the affinity theory. He thought that in this way the reader might be able to maintain his critical distance from the method and develop his own version of chemical theory, while still being able to take advantage of the findings of earlier chemists as encoded in the articles of the *Dictionnaire*.

Lavoisier attempted a similar division. The paradox of the *Traité* is that it also proposes two mutually exclusive speaking positions that a scientist may occupy. How can the rhetorician who wrote the memoir on the composition and decomposition of water expect his reader to submit to the constraints placed on his critical faculties by the *Méthode de nomenclature chimique?* He must on the one hand be dominated by the theory in order to contribute in the most efficient manner to the elaboration and evolution of his discipline. And yet, implied in the very concept of the evolution of a theory (rather than merely its elaboration or completion) is the possibility that the method may result not merely in cumulative change, but in a radical change in the orientation of the theory. The very existence of the *Traité* is undeniable proof of this possibility. The scientist must somehow then be able both to work inside the theory and to exercise his judgment on it from the external perspective given him by the method. How can this double level of scientific work be maintained? Or, if we translate the question into more modern terms, how can the scientist be at the same time a normal scientist (in Kuhn's terminology) and a paradigm-changing scientist? Both Macquer and Lavoisier address this problem, arriving at different answers, but they both feel that the task is not impossible.

More than simply a treatise aimed at an already-sophisticated audience, the *Traité élémentaire de chimie* is a textbook as well. In fact, it is a textbook aimed more at this sophisticated audience than at real novices. This is nothing new; both for Macquer and for the Enlightenment in general, the pedagogical operation was far from simple or marginal. The *Encyclopédie* was envisioned by both editors as the super-textbook that defined an age: the Enlightenment was a giant undertaking in which generalized access to education would create a "natural" society—a meritocracy whose structure would mirror that of human knowledge. We have seen that the privilege Macquer accorded to chemistry was in part a result of his seeing it as the science whose research procedures most closely reproduce both the natural structure of the material world and the operations of the mind. The structure of the *Dictionnaire* was supposed to transmit this method and encode a natural form of teaching as well. Lavoisier himself recognized the persuasive prescriptive power of pedagogical systems and worked with the Idéologue Condorcet to create a proposal for a new, all-encompassing state educational system for the National Assembly of postrevolutionary France.[1] It is not surprising, therefore, that we find this same concern echoed throughout the *Traité*. "Ces inconvénients tiennent moins à la nature des choses qu'à la forme de l'enseignement, et c'est ce qui m'a déterminé à donner à la chimie une marche qui me paraît plus conforme à celle de la nature" (5) [211]. A "forme de l'enseignement," Lavoisier hopes, will reproduce a *process* of thinking more in harmony with that of nature.

But does Lavoisier mean by this process merely the same nominalist architecture of knowledge that Macquer had used to structure the *Dictionnaire?* It seems not. The "natural education" worked out by Lavoisier and

---

1. See *Oeuvres*, 4: 649–68. See also Roger Hahn, *The Anatomy of a Scientific Institution: The Paris Academy of Sciences, 1666–1803* (Berkeley and Los Angeles: University of California Press, 1971), chap. 8.

Condorcet had proposed to create perfect citizens for the new state by training them to think only according to prescribed patterns, including "the calculus of ethics," and that from the very earliest age. "[Le discours des Idéologues] donnait en effet ... une sorte de recette générale pour l'exercice du pouvoir sur les hommes: l'esprit comme surface d'inscription pour le pouvoir, avec la sémiologie pour instrument; la soumission des corps par le contrôle des idées" [212].[2] The "marche naturelle mentioned in the *Traité* seems to be like this forced march of the Idéologues, imposed by the nomenclature which designates objects to be analyzed. It certainly is a semiology which exercises great power over the mind of the scientist. In this form of teaching, the theory is the teacher and the scientist is forever a student.

It is tempting to posit that Lavoisier (as the one who spelled out the nomenclature) would have preferred to keep the position of the teacher to himself and to leave the position of student to his disciples, the "new chemists" of whom he was so proud. He was hotheaded in defense of his new chemistry; he was touchy about his own international reputation: he chastised Fourcroy, who tried to embezzle credit for the creation of the "French chemistry."[3]

Yet, the effect of the establishment of the new chemistry was so far-reaching as to negate Lavoisier's "authorship" of it. Unfortunately, the Cartesian paradox remains. Either the nomenclature is the work of the genius of one man, in which case he receives the credit for being its author but the system cannot be regarded as "true," or else "nature" has produced "the truth through the person who revealed the system, but he can hardly claim to be the author—in the sense of creator—of the system. Macquer undermined the *Dictionnaire* by trying to leave open the possibility of a multiplicity of systems—each reader was to author the one that best suited his purposes. Lavoisier's "repressive" nomenclature takes the opposite tack. It can allow only scientists and not authors. However, there is a position of authorship left open and even spelled out in the work of Lavoisier: it is that of the rhetorician who wrote the memoir on the decomposition of water. Lavoisier not only showed himself to be a virtuoso rhetorician in this work, but he also forced upon his readers, not the position of a student, but the position of the critic who has to use his own judgment. It is impossible to force someone to be an author, but by demonstrating the working of the ongoing, self-transforming methodological operation, Lavoisier at least potentially prevented the possibility's being eliminated altogether. Whether he liked it or not,[4] Lavoisier's work

---

2. Foucault, *Surveiller et punir*, 105.

3. Daumas, *Lavoisier*, 194.

4. And he didn't: he complained several times that he did not understand why he was not accorded the credit that he felt was his due. See Daumas, *Lavoisier*, 194.

resulted in an epistemological shift rather than in just a new theory or method, and this shift did in fact eliminate the concept of the scientific author in its then-accepted meaning. The *Traité* was supposed to be only a first step, a quick and effective way to transmit the substance of the new chemistry and to introduce the reader to the new thought patterns. Judgmental, original work would come later, once both the chemical and theoretical elements had been mastered. But once you have read the *Traité*, there is no turning back. It is not so easy to think authorially; in fact, this position does not make much sense any more. How could this come about and with what was the scientific author replaced? Let us return one last time to the *Logique* of Condillac, to a passage which Lavoisier does not quote, the very last pages of the book:

> Mais je veux encore prévenir les jeunes gens contre un préjugé qui doit être naturel à ceux qui commencent. Parce qu'une méthode pour raisonner doit nous apprendre à raisonner, nous sommes portés à croire qu'à chaque raisonnement la première chose devroit être de penser aux règles d'après lesquelles il doit se faire, et nous nous trompons. *Ce n'est pas à nous à penser aux règles, c'est à elles à nous conduire sans que nous y pensions. On ne parleroit pas si, avant de commencer chaque phrase, il falloit s'occuper de la grammaire. Or, l'art de raisonner, comme toutes les langues, ne se parle bien qu'autant qu'il se parle naturellement.* Méditez la méthode, et méditez-la beaucoup; mais n'y pensez plus quand vous voudrez penser à autre chose. Quelque jour elle vous viendra familière: alors, toujours avec vous, elle observera vos pensées qui iront seules, et elle veillera sur elles pour empêcher tout écart: c'est tout ce que vous devez attendre de la méthode. . . .
>
> Si, dans les commencemens, vous avez quelque peine à vous rendre familière la méthode que j'enseigne, ce n'est pas qu'elle soit difficile: elle ne sauroit l'être, puisqu'elle est naturelle. (*La Logique,* 189–91; my emphasis) [213]

The problematic term, of course, is the word "naturelle." For the method promoted by Condillac is not the method, but his method: it is not the natural structure of thought revealed, but a theory encoded in a language. Language is the vehicle for thought. Choose a language, and you choose what can be thought. If you choose to embody a theory in a language, then the person using it can only think through the theory. Eliminate figurative thinking from the language structure, and the thinker can no longer innovate inside the language. Last but not least, impose fluency: one day, after much practice, the language will become so familiar that it will seem to be a part of the student himself. In actuality, like the theory of Lavoisier, it is always a construct, always the product of someone else's thinking. This someone remains invisible in order to foster the *illusion* that the theory is natural, although the illusion is produced only by long habit. Invisible, it nonetheless directs the way the student thinks; the language maintains its control by its very *anonymity*. This is the definition of "natural" which Condillac derives and which has its roots in the "natural method" of Descartes. It is a naturalness that depends on a ruse, in which the author who created the method gives up his authorship in exchange for the institutionalization of his practice. There *are* changes that are irreversible; Lavoisier's disciples were not able to understand his complaints. The scientist, dominated by the theory, is responsible for but is no longer recognized (even by himself) as the author of the work he produces inside that theory. It is out of such an illusion that the view of the anonymous practitioners of science emerges; they are practitioners of a scientific discourse who speak with a collective voice in the name of neutral, objective, natural science. And, as Lavoisier's shift of the nature of theory demonstrates, as Condillac's *Logique* assumes, for the person working within such a system, where the teacher is no longer an author, student and teacher become synonymous in the shadow of the real pedagogue. The real author is the new chemical practice: it is now the voice of science that speaks.

It is this reorganization of the relationships between the scientist and his theory that can explain why the *Traité élémentaire de chimie* made it difficult to qualify the nature of the real changes that Lavoisier brought about. Although he is generally recognized as the "father of modern chemistry," such recognition should come for his institutionalization of science as its own speaking voice, not for his chemical "discoveries"—most of which were superseded within a few years of his death. Precisely because science from this point on speaks with an autonomy that guarantees its authority, it becomes difficult to imagine that things could ever have been otherwise, that it could have been necessary to write this state of affairs into existence. For the theoretical work of one scientist may eliminate that of his predecessors, but the discursive practice remains the same.

Guyton de Morveau, *Tableau de nomenclature chymique, contenant les principales dénominations analogiques, et des exemples de formation des noms composés.*

RÈGNES.	ACIDES.	Les Sels formés de ces Acides prennent les noms génériques de	BASES ou substances qui s'unissent aux Acides	EXEMPLES pour la classe des Vitriols	EXEMPLES pris de divers classes.
Des trois Règnes,	Méphitique ou Air fixe.	Méphites,	Phlogistique,	Soufre vitriolique ou soufre commun.	Soufre méphitique ou Plombagine.
	Vitriolique	Vitriols,	Alumine ou Terre de l'argille,	Vitriol alumineux ou Alun.	Nitre alumineux.
	Nitreux	Nitres,	Calce ou Terre calcaire,	Vitriol calcaire ou Sélénite.	Muriate calcaire.
	Muriatique ou du sel marin,	Muriates,	Magnésie,	Vitriol magnésien ou Sel d'epsom.	Acéte de magnésie.
Minéral.	Régalin.	Régales,	Barote ou Terre du Spath pesant,	Vitriol barotique ou Spath pesant.	Tartre barotique.
	Arsenical	Arseniates,	Potasse ou Alkali fixe végétal,	Vitriol de potasse ou Tarre vitriolé.	Arseniate de potasse.
	Boracin ou sel sédatif	Borax,	Soude ou Alkali fixe minéral,	Vitriol de Soude ou Sel de Glauber.	Borax de Soude ou Borax commun.
	Fluorique ou du spath fluor.	Fluors.	Ammoniac ou Alkali volatil	Vitriol ammoniacal.	Fluor ammoniacal.
			Or,	Vitriol d'or.	Régale d'or.
			Argent,	Vitriol d'argent.	Oxalte d'argent.
			Platine,	Vitriol de platine.	Saccharte de platine.
			Mercure,	Vitriol de mercure.	Citrate de mercure.
Végétal.	Acéteux ou Vinaigre,	Acetes,	Cuivre,	Vitriol de cuivre ou Vitriol de Chypre.	Lignite de cuivre.
	Tartareux ou du Tartre,	Tartres,	Plomb,	Vitriol de plomb.	Phosphate de plomb.
	Oxalin ou de l'Oseille,	Oxalates,	Etain,	Vitriol d'étain.	Formiate d'étain.
	Saccharin ou du Sucre,	Saccharates,	Fer,	Vitriol de fer ou Couperose verte.	Sébate martial.
	Citronin ou du Citron,	Citrates,	Antimoine (au lieu de Regule d')	Vitriol de bismuth.	Muriate antimonial ou Beurre d'antimoine.
	Lignique ou du Bois.	Lignates.	Bismuth,	Vitriol de zinc ou Couperose blanche.	Galacte de bismuth.
			Zinc,	Vitriol d'arsenic.	Borax de zinc.
Animal.	Phosphorique,	Phosphates.	Arsenic,	Vitriol de cobalt.	Muriate d'arsenic.
	Formicin ou des Fourmis	Formiates.	Cobalt,	Vitriol de Nickel.	Saccharte de cobalt.
	Sébacé ou du Suif	Sébates.	Nickel,	Vitriol de manganèse.	Formiate de Nickel.
	Galactique ou du Lait.	Galactes.	Manganèse,	Ether vitriolique.	Oxalte de manganèse.
			Esprit-de-vin.		Ether lignique ou Ether de Goetting, &c. &c. &c.

Les soufres & les tidurs deviendront aux mêmes noms de genres, & se distinguent par l'épithète de l'acide.

Les noms de ces bases, ou leurs adjectifs, ajoutés aux substantifs qui indiquent les genres des acides, forment les dénominations exactes, comme on le voit dans les exempla suivans.

Les dix-huit acides, les vingt-quatre bases & les produits de leur union, forment ainsi quatre cents soixante-quatorze dénominations claires & méthodiques, indépendamment des *hépars* ou composés à trois parties, dont les noms viennent encore dans ce systême, comme *hépar de soude*, *hépar ammoniacal*, *pyrite d'argent*, &c. &c,

N. B. Lorsque les acides particuliers déjà entrevus dans la molybdène, l'étain, &c. feront plus connus, on en formera les noms d'acide *molybdique & molybdés*, d'acide *stannique & stannes*, &c. Il en sera de même des nouvelles bases. Le nouveau demi-métal trouvé par M. Bergmann dans les fers cassans, pourra être nommé *fydérotte*, s'il est caché dans le fer.

SOURCE: Guyton de Morveau, "Sur les dénominations chymiques," 1782.

153

Guyton de Morveau and Lavoisier, Tableau de la nomenclature chymique

DÉNOMINATIONS APPROPRIÉES DE DIVERSES SUBSTANCES PLUS COMPOSÉES ET QUI SE COMBINENT SANS DÉCOMPOSITION.

SOURCE: *Méthode de nomenclature chymique*

155

Lavoisier, Tableau des substances simples

	Noms nouveaux.	Noms anciens correspondans.
Substances simples qui appartiennent aux trois règnes & qu'on peut regarder comme les élémens des corps.	Lumiere........	Lumiere.
	Calorique.......	Chaleur. Principe de la chaleur. Fluide igné. Feu. Matière du feu & de la chaleur.
	Oxygène........	Air déphlogistiqué. Air empiréal. Air vital. Base de l'air vital.
	Azote	Gaz phlogistiqué. Mofete. Base de la mofete.
	Hydrogène......	Gaz inflammable. Base du gaz inflammable.
Substances simples non métalliques oxidables & acidifiables.	Soufre..........	Soufre.
	Phosphore.......	Phosphore.
	Carbone	Charbon pur.
	Radical muriatiq.	Inconnu.
	Radical fluorique.	Inconnu.
	Radical boracique.	Inconnu.
Substances simples métalliques oxidables & acidifiables.	Antimoine	Antimoine.
	Argent..........	Argent.
	Arsenic.........	Arsenic.
	Bismuth.........	Bismuth.
	Cobolt..........	Cobolt.
	Cuivre.........	Cuivre.
	Etain..........	Etain.
	Fer	Fer.
	Manganèse.......	Manganèse.
	Mercure........	Mercure.
	Molybdène......	Molybdène.
	Nickel.........	Nickel.
	Or............	Or.
	Platine........	Platine.
	Plomb.........	Plomb.
	Tungstène......	Tungstène.
	Zinc.	Zinc.
Substances simples salifiables terreuses.	Chaux..........	Terre calcaire, chaux.
	Magnésie........	Magnésie, base du sel d'epsom.
	Baryte.........	Barote, terre pesante.
	Alumine........	Argile, terre de l'alun, base de l'alun.
	Silice...	Terre siliceuse, terre vitrifiable.

SOURCE: *Traité élémentaire de chymie*

APPENDIX D

Translations of the French Quotations

1. "But as I propose this text only as a history—or, if you prefer, as a fable in which, among other examples that one may imitate, one may perhaps find as well several others that it would be right not to follow—I hope that it will be useful to some without being harmful to anyone, and that everyone will take my frankness into account."

2. "The reading of good books is like a conversation with the most honest men of past centuries who were their authors, and even a studied conversation, in which they allow us to see only the best of their thoughts."

3. "If my work has seemed worthy enough to me that I show you the model here, I do not by that mean to counsel anyone to imitate it."

4. "Those with the strongest reasoning powers, and who digest (elaborate) their thoughts the best in order to make them clear and intelligible, are always the most able to persuade others of what they are proposing, *even if* they speak only Low Breton, and even if *they have never learned rhetoric.* Those who devise the most pleasant inventions and who know how to present them with the greatest ornament and grace will not fail to be the best poets, *even if the poetic art is unknown to them.*"

5. "Consider that, having only one truth from each thing, whoever finds it then knows as much about it as one can, and that, for example, a child taught mathematics, having performed a sum according to the rules, can be assured of having found, concerning the sum that he is examining, all that the human mind can discover. For finally, the method that teaches one to follow the true order and to enumerate exactly all of the circumstances of what one is looking for, contains all that provides certainty for the rules of arithmetic."

6. *"I took notice that,* while I was thus attempting to think that everything was false, it was necessarily required that I who was thinking this be something; and, noticing that this truth: *I think, therefore I am,* was so firm and so assured that all of the most extravagant suppositions of the skeptics *were not capable of shaking it,* I judged that I could receive this truth without scruple as the first principle."

7. "God has given each of us some light in order for us to distinguish the true from the false."

8. "I believed that I could not keep hidden (several general notions concerning physics), without sinning greatly against the law which obliges us to procure, as much it is within our power, a state of general well-being for all men: for (these notions) made me see that it is possible to attain to knowledge which is very useful to (maintain) life."

9. "The history of the sciences is at the same time the history of the labors, the successes and the deviations of those who have cultivated them. It indicates the obstacles that they had to overcome, and the false routes in which they lost their way. Our object is to put *under (your) eyes* the different states through which this science has passed, the revolutions that it has undergone, the circumstances that have favored or retarded its progress."

10. "The first men in need were, for this very reason, the first artisans."

11. "They seized the principles of the arts through a natural effort, quite different from that perfected reasoning which alone can give birth to the sciences and which was formed only in the space of a long series of centuries."

12. "Before the invention of writing, the apprentice practiced only what he learned from his master through an oral tradition, and he transmitted his bits of knowledge to his successors in the same way; our workers still do it this way, writing nothing, although they live so many centuries after the invention of writing."

13. "It is to this happy epoch that one truly attributes the period of the growth of human knowledge, and the birth of the sciences. (They) harvested with care all the bits of knowledge that could extend and ornament the human mind, made them the object of their research, augmented them by meditating and comparing them, wrote them up, communicated them to each other. In a word, they truly established the first foundations of philosophy. These precious men were the priests and the kings of a people wise enough to accord them their respect."

14. "(the genius to perceive) in one overview the immense multitude of chemical phenomena."

15. "It is certain that what we call *science,* is the study and the knowledge of the relations that a certain number of facts can have with each other."

16. "All who know in detail the phenomena of the operations of chemistry, and who have the genius for this science—that is to say, the faculty to perceive and to compare the relations that these phenomena have with each other."

17. "To analyze is nothing other than to observe, in successive order, the qualities of an object, so as to give them the same order in the mind as the order in which they exist. This is what nature causes us all to do."

18. "It is the same with the vision of the mind. I have present all at the same time a great number of bits of knowledge that have become familiar to me. I see them all, but I do not make them all out equally well. In order to see in a distinct way everything that presents itself at the same time in my mind, it is necessary that I decompose just as I decomposed what presented itself to my eyes. It is necessary that I analyze my thought.

"This analysis is not done any differently than that of those exterior objects. *In the one case as in the other, it is necessary to see everything at the same time.*"

19. "To speak in a way to make oneself understood, it is necessary to conceive of and to express one's ideas according to analytic order, which decomposes and recomposes each thought. This order is the only one that can give them all the clarity and all the precision that they are susceptible of having, and just as we have no other means to instruct ourselves, we have no other way to communicate our knowledge."

20. "Everything confirms, then, that we must consider the languages as so many analytic methods; methods which at first have all the imperfections of beginning languages and which, eventually, make progress as the natural languages themselves make progress."

21. "The exact ideas that one acquires through analysis are not always complete ideas. They can perhaps never even be so, when we are dealing with sense objects. In that case we discover only a few qualities, and we can know them only in part."

22. "For, after all, to figure among the men of knowledge, you do have to write books."

23. "Who would think that an author, moreover a very respectable author, would have wished to renew in our time the taste that the centuries of ignorance had for writing in an obscure manner about the sciences, and in particular about

chemistry? And that to accredit this pretension he praises *Stahl* for an obscurity that one will never find in this author, unless one is indeed a novice in chemistry. And that he has nearly made it a crime to try to dissipate the natural shadows of this science!"

24. "One can imagine the degree of consideration that these characters (the obscurantist chemists) acquired for themselves, these characters who did nothing and from whom one learned nothing!"

25. "A singular mania attacked the heads of all these chemists. It was a sort of generalized epidemic whose symptoms prove just how far human folly can go, when it is engaged in a lively preoccupation with some object. It caused the chemists to make surprising efforts, admirable discoveries, and nonetheless put enormous obstacles in the way of the advancement of chemistry."

26. "By mischance this new object of their research was all too capable of exciting in their souls movements quite opposed to philosophical dispositions."

27. "the price of all goods."

28. "One doubtless sees that I want to talk about the desire to make gold. As soon as this metal had become, through unanimous convention, the price of all goods, it took control of their attention, caused them to lose sight of any other object; they thought that they saw the perfection of chemistry in what was only the solution to one particular problem; the sphere of their science, rather than extending itself, found itself concentrated on a single point."

29. "To keep up their name, they made books like philosophers, they wrote down the principles of their supposed science; but as character never belies itself, they made them in so obscure and unintelligible a manner, that they shed no more light on their pretended art than the laborers, who write nothing, shed on theirs."

30. "Consequently their history is no less obscure and confused than their writings. We don't in fact know the real names of the majority of them. In a word, everything concerning them is a perpetual enigma."

31. "The alchemical mania was (a) leprosy that disfigured chemistry and opposed its progress."

32. "(The madman) is he who is alienated in a state of analogy. He is the Different only to the extent that he does not understand Difference; all signs resemble each other for him, and all similarities have the value of signs. The madman guarantees the function of the *homosemantic*: he brings together all signs, and endows them with a similarity which proliferates endlessly."

33. "obscure, foolish, against all reason, indecipherable, unintelligble, useless, outrageous, inept."

34. "weaknesses, extravagance, mania, blindless, insanity, enthusiasm, foolish vanity, frenzy, exaggeration."

35. "(They) convinced themselves that all of these marvels could be brought about by a single, identical procedure."

36. "It was at this time that a famous alchemist named Paracelsus, a man of *quick, extravagant and impetuous* intellect, added a new folly to those of his predecessors. As he was the son of a doctor, and a doctor himself, he imagined that, using alchemy, one should be able to find the universal medicine, and he died at the age of forty-eight, publishing that he had found the secret of prolonging life to the age of Methuselah. This pretension, as senseless as it was, managed

nevertheless to attract many partisans, and brought about *a violent redoubling in the mania* of the alchemists."

37. "It is true that a stubborn and inveterate malady never disappears suddenly or without leaving a trace."

38. "Universal medicine, although without a doubt the most insane of all the ideas that had entered into the heads of the alchemists, was nevertheless what began to establish rational chemistry, and to lift it out of the ruins of alchemy."

39. "The most essential service that (the alchemists) could render to chemistry was to expose the experiments that failed as clearly as they were obscurantist about the ones that, according to their own lights, were successful."

40. "These true citizens of chemistry were able to furnish excellent remedies, through work worthy of the greatest praise, since the goal was the good of humankind. They were, properly speaking, the inventors of a new chemical art. They wrote their art down *because they were not artisans,* and wrote it clearly, *because they were not alchemists."*

41. "We finally arrive at one of the most brilliant epochs of chemistry: I mean the time at which its different parts began to be collected, examined, compared by men with a sufficiently wide-ranging and deep genius to be able to bring them all together, discover their principles, seize the relations among them, unite them in a rational doctrine, and pose the true foundations of chemistry, considered as a science."

42. "An imagination as quick, as brilliant, and as active as that of his predecessor . . . the inestimable advantage of being controlled by philosophical wisdom and sang-froid."

43. "(who) was worthy of having as a partisan and a commentator the greatest and the most sublime of all the chemical physicists. One should recognize from these glorious and so well-deserved titles the illustrious Stahl, premier doctor of the late king of Prussia."

44. "It is at Stahl's side that we must place the immortal Boerhaave. This powerful genius, the honor of his country, of his profession, and of his century, spread light on all the sciences that he considered. We owe to the overview with which he favored chemistry, the most beautiful and the most methodical analysis of the vegetable kingdom. He seems to leave the human mind impotent to add anything to it."

45. "Since chemistry, brought back to its true object, has been cultivated as a fundamental and essential part of physics, a great number of good treatises have been published on this science. But not one of these treatises is in the form of a dictionary. Several amateurs and men of knowledge, however, seem to wish for a work of this nature, and it was proposed to me that I undertake it. I admit that at first I had some difficulty putting myself to the execution of this project, because it seemed to me that all the parts of chemistry were so linked to each other and so dependent on each other that this science did not lend itself to being treated within an alphabetical order. But as I worked on the opus that I present today to the public, I recognized that the dictionary format was less imperfect, and even much more advantageous than a certain number of men of knowledge and men of letters think it to be.

"In truth, the alphabetical ordering appears to interrupt and disturb any kind of outline or system in a science, but this fault can be remedied by the cross-references that establish the necessary links between all the corresponding articles, as has been done in this work, and in several good scientific dictionaries that are in the public's hands. Moreover, this apparent disorder leaves the reader at liberty to form for himself whatever outline he judges appropriate, and it is quite possible that he may make, in this respect, a better choice than the author himself.

"At any rate, those who take the trouble to read or to consult this work, will recognize easily that it is neither a simple vocabulary nor a dictionary of definitions, but that it is, rather, a series of dissertations, the majority quite extensive, concerning all of the important objects of chemistry, and in which I have tried to fulfill exactly what is announced in the title."

46. "If we then wish to speak about this countryside, it will be noticed that we do not all know it equally well. Some *will construct pictures* that are more or less true.

"(And in order to conceive them *just as they are,* it is necessary that the successive order in which they are observed reassemble them in *the simultaneous order* existing among them.)

"Now, what is this order? Nature indicates it herself; it is the order in which she presents the objects. There are some which call out more particularly to be seen; they are more striking; they dominate; and all the others *seem* to arrange themselves *around* them for them. This is what we observe at first: and when we have taken note of their respective positions, the others place themselves in the intervals, *each one in its place.* We begin, therefore, with the principal objects: we observe them successively, and compare them, in order to judge where the relations exist. When, by this means, we have established their respective positions, we observe successively all those which fill in the intervals, we compare each with the principal object the closest to it, and determine its own position.

"At that point, then, we distinguish all the objects whose form and position we had perceived, and we encompass them all in a single overview. The order that exists among them in our minds is no longer successive; it is simultaneous. It is the very order in which they exist (in the world), and we see them all at once in a distinct manner."

47. "I therefore see that in the sphere of my knowledge there is a system which corresponds to the one that the author of my nature followed when forming me: and this is not surprising, for my needs and my faculties being determined, my research and my knowledge are themselves also determined.

"Everything is linked together in either system. My organs, the sensations that I experience, the judgments that I make, the experience that confirms or corrects them—all form a system for my conservation. This is the system that we must study to learn to reason."

48. "The author of our nature wants us to judge the relations that things have to us, and the relations that they have to each other, *only when the knowledge of these latter can be of some use to us.* We have a means for judging these relations, and it is unique: we observe the sensations that the objects provoke in us. As far as our sensations can extend, just so far can the sphere of our knowledge extend: any further, all discovery is forbidden to us."

49. "Sensations, considered as *representing sensible objects,* are called *ideas:* this is a figurative expression, which properly signifies the same thing as *images.*

"To the extent that we distinguish different sensations, we distinguish species of ideas; and these ideas are either present-time sensations, or they are only the memory of sensations that we have had."

50. "We have just seen that the cause of our errors lies in the habit of judging according to words whose meaning we have not determined: we have seen that words are absolutely necessary to make ideas of all kinds for us; and we will soon see that abstract and general ideas are only delimitations. Everything thus confirms that we think only with the aid of words. This is sufficient to make us understand that the art of reasoning began with the natural languages, that it could make progress only to the extent that they made progress themselves, and that consequently they must contain all the means that we can possess for analyzing well or badly. It is therefore necessary to observe the natural languages."

51. "Analysis is only performed, and can only be performed, using signs."

52. "The natural language of a people determines its vocabulary, and the vocabulary is a fairly faithful table of all the bits of knowledge of this people."

53. "The natural language is a symbol of this multitude of heterogeneous things."

54. "But the knowledge of the natural language is the foundation of all these great hopes; they will remain uncertain, if the language is not fixed and transmitted to posterity in all its perfection; and this object is the foremost of those that it was appropriate for the encyclopedists to occupy themselves with profoundly."

55. "The comparison of phenomena is called philosophy."

56. "the universal science, the assemblage or linking of all the sciences together."

57. "The cross-references of things shed light on the object, indicate its closest ties with the objects that touch it directly, and its more rarified ties to other objects that appear isolated. They call up in our minds common notions and analogous principles, strengthen consequences, interlace branch to trunk, and give to the whole that appearance of unity that is so favorable to the establishment of truth and persuasion. But when necessary, the cross-references also produce an effect that is totally contrary: they oppose notions, they contrast principles, they attack, shake up, and secretly overturn ridiculous opinions that one would not dare to insult openly. *If the author is impartial, (the cross-references) will always serve the double function of confirming and refuting, of troubling and reconciling.* If the cross-references for confirmation or refutation have been thought out well in advance and prepared with address, they will provide an encyclopedia with the characteristic that all good dictionaries should have: this characteristic is *to change the common way of thinking.*"

58. "The cross-references form a tableau whose spaces or intervals *suggest* philosophical speculations."

59. "an ensemble that is tightly pulled together, tightly linked, and highly continuous."

60. "should aim to bring together everything that has been published on each subject, to digest it, to clarify it, to pull it together, to order it and to publish treatises on it in which each thing occupies only the space that it deserves. It is the execution of this extended project—not only the work of the different academies, but all branches of human knowledge—that an *encyclopedia* should supplement. (An encyclopedia is a) work that can be executed only by a society of people of letters and artists, scattered, occupied each with his own section, and linked together only by an interest in the general welfare of humankind, and by a sentiment of reciprocal goodwill."

61. "Philosophy knows only the rules grounded in the nature of beings, which is unchangeable and eternal."

62. "There is a third kind of cross-reference that one must neither abandon oneself to nor reject entirely. These are the ones that juxtapose certain relations in the sciences, analogous qualities in natural substances, and similar procedures in the arts. They lead either to new speculative truths, to the perfection of the known arts, to the invention of new arts, or to the restitution of lost ancient arts."

63. "Revolution is the means of progress in the sciences just as in the arts."

64. "Moreover, this apparent disorder leaves the reader at liberty to form for himself whatever outline he judges appropriate, and it is quite possible that he may make, in this respect, a better choice than the author himself."

65. "The perfection of the arts, the discovery of new objects for manufacture and commerce are, incontestably, what is the most beautiful and interesting in chemistry, and they are what make it truly estimable."

66. "Everyone knows, in effect, that the term 'scholastic' has been imagined only since Descartes, that it dates from the renewal of the sciences, and that it serves to designate, in a scornful manner, what we call the *philosophy of the school*. Now, what was this philosophy of the school? It was that of Aristotle, and of his numerous partisans. All those who have some notions concerning the history of human studies and knowledge, know just how far the peripatetic schools had carried the abuse of what is called the master's authority. A jargon composed of barbaric words, which had no meaning at all, or which served only to express abstract and vague ideas, formed the logic and the metaphysics of the school, and their subtleties were the only foundation of a physics that was as filled with chimeras as it was empty of experiment."

67. "All the essential articles of this work being fairly extensive, they could have formed an ordinary treatise of chemistry, if they had not been subjected to the alphabetical format. (It is necessary) to disturb this order which provides no logical sequence, no linking together, and to indicate *another* which will be free of this inconvenience: (the result is) the following *Table*."

68. "With this simple preparation, I have no doubt that whoever has some taste and disposition for chemistry will be able to read fruitfully the treatises on this science according to whatever order he uses, because he will be in a state such that he will be able to understand them, to seize the relations and the *links that the author will have put between the facts, or else to form for himself another ensemble more like his own way of considering nature:* it may be an ensemble very different from the system of the author whose work he is studying."

69. "One has to admit that they may also produce quite a contrary effect when one uses them with too much confidence, and when one extends their use beyond its limits."

70. "a jargon composed of barbarous words, which have no meaning at all, or which serve only to express abstract or vague ideas."

71. "ANALYSIS, is also used *in chemistry* to dissolve a compound body or to divide its different principles.

"*To analyze* bodies, or to resolve them into their constituent parts, is the principal object of the chemical art."

72. "ANALYSIS. Chemists mean by the word 'analysis,' the decomposition of a body, or the separation of the principles and constituent parts of a compound. We

will say nothing more here on analysis in general; this subject is so extensive, that it would be necessary to pass in review all the objects of chemistry, if we wanted to make clear its specific applications."

73. "Speaking, clarifying and knowing are, in the strict sense of the term, *of the same order."*

74. "Analysis is only performed, and can only be performed, using signs."

75. "To classify, yes; to name, certainly—but we are persuaded that these efforts go beyond genius and suppose gods."

76. "I agree, therefore, that this is not a true dictionary or that, if one wants to consider it as such, it's a bad one, because, in the state that I was able to put it, it has all the faults attached to this format, without having the advantages, which consist principally in a very complete nomenclature, combined with entirely exact cross-references."

77. "the disorder I was unable to avoid."

78. "I therefore beg the reader to consider this work only as a collection of definitions and dissertations concerning the principal objects of chemistry, distributed more or less according to the order of the letters of the alphabet."

79. "In fact, contemporary science instructs itself according to *isolated systems,* according to *parcellized units."*

80. "AFFINITY. One should understand by affinity, the tendency that the parts of a body, whether constituent (heterogeneous) or integrating (homogeneous), have for each other, and the force that causes them to adhere together when they are united."

81. "(Affinity) is, moreover, demonstrated by an infinity of experiments, like, for example, the adherence that two bodies have for each other when applied to each other by highly polished surfaces. Or, the tendency that two drops of water, oil, mercury, or any other fluid have toward each other; they instantly mix together, and unite into a single mass. Or, the convex or spheric form that drops of different fluids take on when they are isolated or supported by a body with which they are not disposed to unite. These are effects that take place even in the void, and which demonstrate the affinity that the integrating parts of bodies have for each other, whether solid or fluid."

82. "(This great effect) is perhaps as essential a property of matter as its extension and its impenetrability, and about which we can say nothing other than that it is so."

83. "The affinity that the principal or constituent parts have is demonstrated by the detail of all the phenomena of chemistry.

"We are not here seeking the cause of this great effect, which is so general that it may be regarded as in itself the cause of all combinations, and (may as well) be used to explain them."

84. "I believe that one can distinguish several sort of affinities. *Not that I think that there really are several different kinds, for it is quite certain that it is ever only a single, identical property of matter that modifies itself in diverse ways, according to circumstances.*

"The second kind of simple affinity produces the union and adherence of heterogeneous parts. It is called the *affinity* of composition. If, for example, the primitive integrating molecules of vitriolic acid unite with those of iron, there results from this union a new body which is neither vitriolic acid, nor iron, but a compound of the two, that is called martial vitriol."

85. "We can call *complex affinity* the one in which there are more than two bodies which act on each other. When two principles are united together, and a third comes along, we see phenomena of composition and decomposition occur, which differ according to the affinities that the three bodies have for each other.

"Third. Sometimes a third principle, which joins itself to a compound of two principles, unites with only one of these principles, and obliges the other to separate itself entirely from the one that it was at first united to. In this case, a total decomposition of the first compound is performed, and a new combination of the remaining principle with the incoming principle is formed. This happens when the incoming principle has little or even no affinity with one of the principles in the compound, and it has a much greater affinity for the other principle than the affinity that the two original principles had for each other."

86. "The affinities of four principles forming two new compounds can, through mutual exchange, bring about two decompositions, two new combinations. This happens every time that *the sum of the affinities that each of the principles of the two compounds has with the principles of the other, surpasses that of the affinities that the principles of the two original compounds had for each other.* This sort of affinity, where a double exchange of principles is operated, can be called *double affinity.*"

87. "The last remark that can be made concerning the simple affinity of composition furnishes a very general, fundamental law of great utility for recognizing, *even without decomposition,* what the principles are of which bodies are composed. Here is that remark: *It is that all compound bodies have properties which participate in those of the principles of which they are compounded.* Thus, for example, the union of two principles, one fixed and the other volatile, forms a compound with a degree of fixity or volatility that is an average of that of its principles.

"It is the same with all the other properties, such as heaviness, opacity, transparence, ductility, hardness, fluidity, etc., and even with the affinities, so that *assuming that we know perfectly the properties of the principles of a compound, we can, by examining the properties of the compound, recognize what its principles are even when its analysis would be impossible.*"

88. "This great effect is so general that it can be regarded as in itself the cause of all combinations, and *be used to explain them.*"

89. "Assuming that we know perfectly the properties of the principles of a compound, we can, by examining the properties of the compound, recognize what its principles are even when its (material) analysis would be impossible."

90. "But no one that I know of, before the late *Mr. Geoffroy* the doctor, ever had the idea of presenting, in a very precise and very short tableau, the effects of the principal combinations and decompositions that are and will always be the foundation and the base of all chemistry."

91. "Mr. Geoffroy's table had two faults: the first was that it was incomplete. The other proves that the author was a man of genius: the table presented some propositions which were not entirely correct, because of their too great generality."

92. "A science which accepts images is, more than any other, the victim of metaphors."

93. "Unmediated knowledge is, in its very principle, subjective."

94. "It can be neither toned down nor disregarded: one has only to look at it, to learn to read it, or to decipher it. *Table of the Law,* or rather, *Law become Table.* There is not a single laboratory where the periodic table of the elements is not hung on the wall. At a time when some swear only by a relativistic science (and hence a fugitive science), it is salutary to point out this fixity: a pure theory has in a way affixed itself in history and the history winds itself around the theory without being able to uproot it."

95. "(He says that) the system of the affinities is a lovely illusion more appropriate for amusing our scholastic chemists than for advancing this science. (He calls them) our reasoners, our makers of tables, etc."

96. "I will only point out here, since the occasion presents itself, that the greater or lesser affinities of the different substances that act on each other, are things of fact and experiment to which one cannot give the name of system, because in physics, this name can be applied only to argument and conjecture, and not at all to facts. Moreover, who can these chemists be that the author intended to designate with the scornful epithet of scholastics?"

97. "the most illustrious and the most estimable that we have had up to the present in physics and in chemistry."

98. "I was unable to perceive any other difference between the old idea of combined fire in bodies and (the phlogiston) of Stahl, unless it is that which is necessarily found between a wild assertion, absolutely gratuitous and lacking any type of proof, and a theory that has been solidly founded on one of the greatest and the most beautiful ensembles of positive facts that it is possible to bring together to serve as its basis. It is doubtless easy to advance, in a vague manner, that fire is one of the principles of bodies, as the ancient philosophers did, long before we had the slightest idea of physics. But to prove it is something else. For that it was necessary that a man of genius appear, as great a chemist as Stahl. He was able to encompass all the proofs with a single general overview into the immense detail of chemical facts that were then known; he increased the number of these proofs through a great quantity of his own experiments, and finally put the cap on the demonstration, by his ever-memorable discovery of the artificial production of sulfur. I must admit that I know no other chemistry than that one."

99. "Stahl demonstrated, in addition, that this igneous principle, similar in this way to other principles of compound bodies, can pass, and indeed does pass, from one combination into another, without becoming free, without reappearing in its state of active fire. And it is by thus following, so to speak, the combined fire through its different mixtures, that this chemist succeeded in making known, in the most satisfactory way, the great effects that this element produces when it is bound with different kinds of substances."

100. "If therefore Lavoisier—I think we can be granted this—did not conceive this project for a systematic and articulated chemical language, neither can we attribute to him the idea that underlies it: the scalar conception of substances. Macquer, in effect, had developed it before him and just as distinctly. The only difference between Macquer and Lavoisier—and even this has to be played down—comes from the fact that the first one held that 'fire, air, water and earth' were fundamental, whereas the other attempted to break them apart."

101. "If everything can be explained in chemistry in a satisfactory manner without recourse to phlogiston, it is for that reason alone infinitely probable that this principle does not exist; that it is an hypothetical being, a gratuitous supposition; and, indeed, it is one of the principles of good logic not to multiply beings without necessity. Perhaps I ought to stick to these negative proofs, and content myself with having proven that we can account for the phenomena better without phlogiston than with it; but it is time for me to explain myself in a more formal and precise manner concerning an opinion that I consider to be a fatal error for chemistry, and which seems to me to have considerably retarded its progress due to the defective manner of philosophizing that it has introduced into chemistry."

102. "The second discovery is that the property of burning, of inflammability, can be transmitted from one body to another: if one mixes, for example, carbon (which is combustible) with vitriolic acid (which is not), the vitriolic acid is converted into sulfur. It acquires the property of burning, whereas the carbon loses it. It works the same way with metallic substances: they lose through calcination their combustible quality. But, if they are put into contact with carbon and, in general, with those bodies that have the property of burning, they revivify, that is, they take back, at the expense of these substances, the property of being combustible. *Stahl concluded from these facts* that phlogiston, the inflammable principle, could pass from one body into another, and that it obeyed certain laws, to which have since been given the name of *affinity*."

103. "I beg my readers, as they begin this memoir, to rid themselves, as much as possible, of all prejudice; to see in the facts only what they present, to banish everything that argument has imagined to be there, and to forget, for a moment, if possible, that his theory ever existed."

104. "the way in which Mr. Macquer presented the doctrine of Stahl in his dictionary of chemistry."

105. "At the period when Stahl was writing, the principal phenomena of combustion were still unknown. He knew concerning this operation only what strikes the senses: the release of heat and light. Nothing was more natural, indeed, than to say that combustible bodies burst into flames because they contain an inflammable principle; but we owe to Stahl two important discoveries, independent of any system, of any hypothesis, and which will be eternal truths: first, that the metals are combustible bodies; (second), that calcination is a true combustion, and that it presents all the phenomena of combustion. This constant fact, which Stahl seems to have been the first to recognize, and which is today generally admitted by everyone, put him in the position of having to admit (the existence of) an inflammable principle in the metals."

106. "But if everything in chemistry can be explained in a satisfactory way without recourse to phlogiston, it is for that reason alone infinitely probable that this principle does not exist. I consider (phlogiston) to be a fatal error for chemistry, and (it) seems to me to have considerably retarded its progress because of the defective manner of philosophizing that it has introduced into chemistry."

107. "Here are, then, two very distinct substances that the disciples of Stahl mix up: a phlogiston without weight and a heavy phlogiston. One is the matter of heat, the other isn't. It is by taking now the properties of one, and then the properties of the other, that they manage to explain everything."

108. "These new facts shook up both the system of Stahl and that of Mr. Baumé. Mr. Macquer felt this to be true, but he believed at the same time that it was not impossible to reconcile the modern experiments with the doctrine of phlogiston. The new theory that he dreamed up to fulfill this object is intelligently set out in the second edition of his *Dictionary of Chemistry*. It is astonishing to see that Mr. Macquer, all the while seeming to defend the doctrine of Stahl by keeping the phlogistic terminology, presents a completely new theory, which is not at all the same as Stahl's. For phlogiston, the inflammable principle, this principle which has weight, compounded of the element of fire and the earthy element, he substitutes the pure matter of light. The result is that Mr. Macquer has kept the word without keeping the thing, and that while appearing to defend Stahl's doctrine, he has dealt it a serious blow."

109. "All these reflections confirm what I had advanced, what it was my object to prove, and what I will repeat again: that chemists have made phlogiston into a vague principle which is not rigorously defined and which, consequently, adapts itself to any explanation in which they want to use it. It is a veritable Proteus that changes form at each instant."

110. "He kept *the word* without keeping *the thing.*"

111. "It is time to bring chemistry back to a more rigorous way of reasoning, to strip the facts—that enrich this science every day—of everything that argument and prejudice have added to them, to distinguish fact and observation from what is systematic and hypothetical; finally, to mark the point to which chemical knowledge has arrived so that those who follow us will be able to take off from this point and proceed with confidence to advance the science."

112. "Although Mr. *Lavoisier* seems tempted to believe that his experiment overturns this theory completely, he is nonetheless too enlightened to assert it positively and in a decisive manner. I was unable to perceive any other difference between the old idea of combined fire in bodies and (the phlogiston) of Stahl, unless it is that which is necessarily found between a wild assertion, absolutely gratuitous and lacking any type of proof, and a theory that has been solidly founded on one of the greatest and the most beautiful *ensembles* of positive facts that it is possible to bring together to serve as its basis. What is so satisfying in Stahl's work on phlogiston for those chemists who truly have the spirit of their science, is this abundance of proof which he was able to muster, and which brings light as well as conviction."

113. "The constant fact, which Stahl appears to have been the first to recognize … Stahl concluded from these facts: that phlogiston, the inflammable principle, could pass from one body to another and that it obeyed certain laws, to which have since been given the name "affinity.""

114. "When we heat a body, solid or fluid, this body augments in dimension in every direction. One can hardly conceive of this phenomenon without admitting the existence of a particular fluid, whose accumulation is the cause of heat and whose absence is the cause of cold; it is without doubt this fluid which gets lodged between the particles of bodies, which separates them and which occupies the space that they leave between each other. In accord with the great number of physicists, I name this fluid, whatever it may be, *igneous fluid, matter of heat and of fire.*"

115. "In order to form distinct ideas about such an abstract matter, let us borrow a comparison from the objects that are the most familiar to us: let us suppose, for a moment, that there is a space, a box, if you like, whose . . ."

116. "The measure of this quantity of the matter of heat has been called *capacity* to contain the matter of heat. A moment of reflection on what happens in water will make all of this much more sensible.

"If we plunge into this fluid pieces of different kinds of wood but all equal, for example, to one cubic foot, the water will introduce itself little by little into their pores; they will swell and increase in weight. But each kind of wood will admit a different quantity of water. We can thus say that each kind of wood has a different capacity for receiving water. The same circumstances can be found in bodies which are immersed in the igneous fluid, in the fluid of heat."

117. "It is clear, *a priori,* independent of hypothesis, that the more that molecules are separated from each other, the more capacity they must leave between themselves to receive the matter of heat, and consequently, their specific heat will be large. Thus the specific heat of a liquid body should be less that that of the same body in a solid state, and this is indeed the result of experiments which have been performed up to this moment on this subject."

118. "I have deduced all these explanations from a simple principle, which is that pure air, vital air, is composed of a particular principle which is proper to it, which forms its basis, and which I have named *the oxygen principle,* combined with the matter of fire and of heat."

119. "If, therefore, vital air only releases the matter of fire that was united to it to the extent that it loses its aeriform state, there should be no release of heat in the combustion of carbon. This circumstance, which seems to contradict the general ideas that I have sought to give concerning combustion, requires a few particular details.

"I first observed that, in the formation of fixed air, the carbon disappeared in its entirety, and that the quantity of this substance thus dissolved in the vital air makes up more than a third of its weight. But, rather than its being the case that the air—which has received such a large quantity of matter and which has lodged it between its constituent molecules—has increased in volume, it turns out, on the contrary, to have diminished by one-nineteenth. It is therefore evident that the particles of vital air have gotten closer together, and that the intervals that they leave have gotten smaller."

120. "But experiment and analogy prove *equally* that the specific heat of air, and of the substance combined with it, is infinitely more abundant that that of any combustible body."

121. "Does this not constitute a new proof that the fluid of heat occupies the interstices of bodies; that, when the interstices get smaller, heat is chased out and becomes free?"

122. *"I would almost say that all bodies in nature are to the matter of heat what a sponge is to water:* press the sponge, and you shrink the little cells that hold the water. Dilate it, and immediately the expanded cells are in a state to hold a greater quantity of water."

123. "I had no other object in this memoir, than to show that Stahl's phlogiston is an imaginary being whose existence he supposed gratuitously, that all the

phenomena of combustion and calcination can be explained in a simpler and much easier way without phlogiston than with phlogiston. I do not expect that my ideas will be adopted right away; the human spirit conforms to one way of thinking, and those who look at nature from one point of view, during a part of their careers, can turn to new ideas only with difficulty. It is therefore up to time to confirm or destroy the opinions that I have presented. Meanwhile, I see with great satisfaction that the young people who are just beginning to study this science without prejudice, and the geometers and physicists who have a new head for chemical truths, no longer believe in phlogiston as Stahl presented it, and that they consider this whole doctrine to be a scaffold more embarrassing than useful for continuing to construct chemical science."

124. Macquer "kept the word without keeping the thing" . . . Lavoisier "kept the thing without keeping the word."

125. "I do not deny that the existence of this fluid is, to a certain point, hypothetical. But, assuming that it is an hypothesis, that it is not rigorously proven, it is the only one that I am obliged to form. The partisans of the phlogiston doctrine are not ahead of me on this article, and, if the existence of the igneous fluid is an hypothesis, we have that in common."

126. "It is easy to see that this doctrine is diametrically opposed to that of Stahl and his disciples."

127. "I beg my readers, as they begin this memoir, to rid themselves, as much as possible, of all prejudice; to see in the facts only what they present, to banish everything that argument has imagined to be there, to transport themselves to the time preceding Stahl, and to forget for a moment, if possible, that his theory ever existed."

128. "However demonstrative the experiments I have used for support may be, we began, following custom, by rejecting facts in doubt. Then, those who seek to persuade a public that everything that is new is not true, or that nothing that is true is new, managed to find, in an ancient author, the first germ of this discovery. Without examining here the authenticity of the work of which they were in such a hurry to provide a new edition, I saw with some pleasure that the impartial public judged that a vague and chance assertion, supported by no experiment, unknown to any men of knowledge, did not prevent my being considered as the *author of the discovery* of the cause of the increase in weight of the metallic calxes."

129. "Till that point it seems as if we are only dealing with Priestley's experiments. But the difference lies in the interpretation, and it is capital. Priestley, I repeat, regarded the two new gases as resulting, one from the union of ordinary air with phlogiston, the other as being this same air deprived of a part of its phlogiston: an opinion which maintained the material unity of air, without concluding anything about its compound nature."

130. "We must recall that Lavoisier and Priestley each worked in a particular state of mind. According to whether one looks at the chronology of the material facts or the order of the interpretation of these facts, we arrive at completely opposing opinions. The wise thing would have been to give to the two sorts of considerations the place that each deserves."

131. "On the nature of water and on the experiments that have been used to claim to prove the possibility of its transformation into earth" . . . "In which the

object is to prove that water is not at all a simple substance, but that it is susceptible of decomposition and recomposition."

132. "Chemists consider fire, just like the other elements, from two very different points of view: that is, as really entering, as a principle or as a constituent part, into the composition of an infinity of bodies; and as being free, pure, forming part of no compound, but as having a very marked and very strong action on all the bodies of nature, and singularly as a very powerful agent in all the operations of chemistry."

133. "I will not speak here about what the philosophers of the first centuries wrote concerning the elements. The exposé that I could present of their opinions would lead me into too extensive detail; it would, moreover, shed little light on the question that I intend to treat. I pass directly to what interests the physicists more particularly; I mean to speak about the facts."

134. "It was therefore 162 pounds of wood, of bark, of roots; in a word, of solid components which owed, according to him, their origin to the water."

135. "Water truly transforms itself into earth through the operation of the vegetation. This is what does not seem to be so thoroughly proven, and what is repugnant to the idea that we customarily have of water and, in general, of all the elements. Plants are compounded not only of water and of earth; they contain oils, resins, saline and odoriferous components, acid and alkaline saps, etc. When, indeed, one combines concentrated vitriolic acid with oil of tartar, there results a concrete mass of vitriolic tartar, although the two beings that entered into the combination were fluid before being mixed. But that a mass of water can, without any addition, without losing any of its substance, transform itself into a mass of earth—this is what is repugnant to common sense, and what it is impossible to accept without being forced to by very demonstrative experiments."

136. "If Boyle had carried out the analysis of this tree, he could have extracted nearly everything in phlegm (fluid). The real quantity of earth that he would have obtained would, without a doubt, have been reduced to a very small quantity."

137. "Air exists in two fashions in nature: sometimes it presents itself in the form of a very rarified fluid, very dilatable, very elastic. This is what we breathe. Sometimes it is fixed in bodies; it combines intimately with them. In this case it loses all the properties that it had before; air in this state is no longer a fluid. *It takes the function of a solid,* and it is only through the very destruction of the bodies of the compounds into which it enters, that it returns to its original state of fluidity."

138. "There are therefore two things in question: the statement of the givens, and the extraction of the unknowns."

"The statement of givens is properly what we mean by the state of the question, and the extraction of unknowns is the argument that resolves it."

"When I proposed that you figure out the number of tokens that I had in each hand, I stated all the givens that you needed. It seemed, consequently, that I, myself, had established the state of the question. But my language did not prepare the solution to the problem. This is why, rather than limiting yourself to repeating my statement word for word, you put it through different *translations,* until you arrived its simplest expression. Then, the argument, in a way, carried itself out by itself, because the unknowns extracted themselves all by themselves. Establishing the state of the question is thus, properly speaking, translating the givens into their simplest expression, because the simplest expression facilitates reasoning, by facilitating the extraction of the unknowns."

139. "It remained to Mr. Boerhaave to appreciate all of these ideas and to reduce them to their just value. We can see, at the end of his treatise on water, the experiments that he performed on this object. It is seen that water does not change its nature through distillation, that it becomes neither acid, nor alkaline, nor more corrosive, nor more penetrating. He reports that one ounce of water produced 6 drachms of earth through two hundred successive distillations, without declaring himself formally on the subject. Mr. Boerhaave presumes that the dust that floats continually in the air could have mixed with the water during its distillation, and could have formed the tiny quantity of earth that was found there by the chemists."

140. "I will not speak here about what the philosophers of the first centuries wrote concerning the elements. I pass directly to what interests the physicists more particularly; I mean to speak about the facts."

141. "I admit that this last circumstance might form a fairly strong objection against what I reported in my memoir *if it were possible to argue against the facts.*"

142. "Let us signal one more note from the same manuscript, which leads us a little farther into his thought. It is entitled: General Ideas concerning the Elements. 'It is not sufficient that a substance be simple, indivisible or at least undecomposed for it to take the title of an element. It must also be abundant in nature and must enter as an essential and constituent principle into the composition of a great number of bodies. Thus, although gold may be a simple substance, one would not say that it is an element.' The memory of the ancient elements is very apparent here. Lavoisier manifests a way of thinking that is common to the chemists of his century."

143. "Are there different kinds of inflammable air? Or rather, is the one we obtain always the same, more or less mixed, more or less altered by its union with the different substances that it has a tendency to dissolve? This is a question that I will not undertake to resolve at this moment. It will suffice to say that the inflammable air that I intend to talk about in this memoir is the one that is obtained, either from the decomposition of water by iron alone, or from the dissolution of iron and zinc in vitriolic and marine acids. Moreover, as it seems to be proved that, in any case, this air comes originally from the water, I will call it, when it is in its aeriform state, *inflammable aqueous air,* and when it is bound in some compound, *the inflammable aqueous principle.*"

144. "The follow-up of this memoir will clarify what in this first statement may seem to be obscure."

145. "Such, in general, is the result of the combustion of vital air (oxygen) and inflammable air (hydrogen); but, as some have wished to raise doubts about my precedence in this discovery, I find myself obliged to enter into some detail concerning the series of experiments that led me to it."

146. "At this period, Mr. Macquer, having presented a white porcelain saucer to the flame of inflammable air which was burning peacefully at the opening of a bottle, observed that this flame was accompanied by no sooty smoke. He only found that the saucer was wet with fairly sizable droplets of a white liquor similar

to water, and he recognized, just as had Mr. Sigaud de la Fond, who was present at this experiment, that it was water. (See the *Dictionary of Chemistry*, second edition, article Inflammable Gas.)"

147. "And yet, nothing is destroyed in experiments. Only the matter of fire, of heat, and of light, has the property of being able to pass through the pores of vessels. The two airs, which are ponderable bodies, therefore cannot have disappeared; they cannot have been destroyed. Whence the necessity of performing the experiments with greater exactitude and on a greater scale."

148. "As it is no less true in physics than in geometry that the whole is equal to the sum of its parts, we believe ourselves well within our rights—given that we obtained nothing but pure water in this experiment, without finding any other residue—to conclude that the weight of the water was equal to that of the two airs that had served to form it. Only one reasonable objection can be offered against this conclusion: asserting that the water that was formed was equal in weight to the two airs, implies that the matter of heat and light—which is released in great abundance in this operation, and which passes through the pores of the vessels—had no weight."

149. "Let us remark at this point that caloric had to be a rather special matter, unlike other substances, with respect to the three fundamental forces that he enumerates in the first chapter of the *Treatise of Chemistry*: attraction, repulsion, atmospheric pressure."

150. "Here is the way that Mr. Priestley proceeded. He filled a bell jar with inflammable air (gotten from iron using vitriolic aid) and placed it on the table of a pneumato-chemical apparatus (isolated by) water. He introduced some *minium*, which he had heated beforehand to expulse all the air, into the bell jar by passing it through the water. The *minium* was placed on an enameled pedestal, and held up by a support. Finally, he focused a glass lens on the metallic calx. First, the calx dried under the heat from the lens. Then, the lead revivified. At the same time, the inflammable air was absorbed, and a great quantity of it can be made to disappear this way. He concluded from this experiment that the inflammable air combined with the lead to revivify it (return it to its metallic state), and that, consequently, inflammable air and phlogiston are the same thing, as Mr. Kirwan had announced."

151. "Mr. Lavoisier had terrified me for a long time with a great discovery that he was keeping under wraps, and that would do no less than upset from top to bottom the whole phlogiston theory. Where would we and our old chemistry have been, if we had had to build an entirely different edifice? For myself, I admit that I would have given up. Happily, Mr. Lavoisier has just brought his discovery out into the open. I assure you that since that moment, a great weight has been lifted from my stomach."

152. "I noticed that Priestley had not paid attention to one capital circumstance that occurs in this experiment. This is that the lead, far from gaining in weight, on the contrary, diminishes by close to a twelfth. Some substance must of necessity, therefore, have been given off. Now, this substance has to be vital air, which makes up about a twelfth of the *minium*. But from another point of view, nothing is left, after this operation, of any elastic fluid of any type. Not only is there no vital air under the bell jar, but the inflammable air itself that had filled it has disappeared.

Hence the products are no longer in an aeriform state. And, given that it has been proven that air is a compound of inflammable air and dephlogisticated air (vital air—oxygen), it is clear that Mr. Priestley formed water *without being aware of it."*

153. "And, given that it has been proven that air is a compound of inflammable air and dephlogisticated air, it is clear that Mr. Priestley formed water *without being aware of it."*

154. "I think I can answer for my own, but it could happen that Mr. Priestley, when reducing the minium using the inflammable air, given that his object was not to determine either the quantities, nor the increase or decrease of weight, would not have sought to use great precision in his results."

155. "The phenomena are very different, if one uses a metal for which the oxygen principle has more affinity than for the inflammable aqueous principle. If, for example, we substitute a gunbarrel of red copper for the iron one in the preceding experiment, the water does indeed turn into vapor when it passes through the incandescent part of the tube. But it condenses back again due to the cooling in the serpentine. We have, therefore, only a simple distillation without loss of substance, and neither is the copper calcined, nor is inflammable air produced."

156. "According to this experiment, we can no longer doubt that the inflammable air that the Abbé Fontana produced when he extinguished glowing coals in water, and above all, that obtained by Hassenfratz, Stoultz and d'Hallencourt, when they plunged red-hot iron into water, were not both true decompositions of water."

157. "We did indeed obtain, by plunging even quartz or a stone into water, a very small portion of air. But *it seemed evident to us* that it came from the water, which always has a little bit of air dissolved in it: this air was in the state of common air, more or less."

158. "In less enlightened ages, one would have explained this operation as a transmutation of wine into water, and the alchemists would have drawn conclusions favorable to their own ideas concerning metallic transmutation. Today, when the spirit of experiment and observation teaches us to appreciate everything at its just value, we see nothing in this experiment other than the proof that something has been added to the spirit of wine during its combustion, and that this something is air."

159. "There is no science except through a permanent school. This is the school that science must found. Then, the social interests will be definitively reversed: society will be formed for the school, and not the school for society."

160. "I say that no language requires more clarity. To be convinced of this, it suffices to think about how many different states (this language) has to consider the same substance in, sometimes separated, in some order or another, in some combination or another, in some degree of combination or another; at other times, (it has to consider it) in an abstract manner, even though (the substance) has not really been isolated.

"Let us now ask if it is possible to orient oneself in this chaos. Let us ask if the comprehension of such a nomenclature doesn't require more intelligence than the science itself. Or, rather, let us admit that it is necessary to reform this language, and let us seek to establish the principles that must determine our choice in all circumstances."

161. "The denominations of beings that make up the object of a science or an art, which are its materials, its instruments, and its products, constitute what we can call its language proper. The state of perfection of the language presents the state of perfection of the science itself. Its progress is not sure, cannot be rapid, as long as its ideas are not represented by precise and determined signs, exact in their attribution, simple in their expression, practical to use, simple to remember, and which maintain—as far as possible, without error—the analogy that links them together, the system that defines them, and even the etymology that can be used to make it possible for people to guess their meaning."

162. "It is undeniable that the first factor for the reduction of the diverse is analogy."

163. "I have undertaken to treat chemistry *in all its parts.*"

164. "FIRST PRINCIPLE. *A sentence is not a name.* The chemical beings and products must have their own names which will indicate them on all occasions, without anyone's having to resort to circumlocutions. This fundamental proposition seems to me to be an evident truth, and to have need of no other proof than the efforts that we continually make to *bring our denominations back to this simplicity of expression.*"

165. "SECOND PRINCIPLE. Denominations must, as much as possible, conform to the nature of things. It matters little what name one gives to an individual object that one considers only for itself, that does not show up in different forms. Any name without a meaning can be advantageously used for this individual, when usage will have identified the name with the individual, because the sounds, and the words that represent the sounds, do not really have any relation to each other by themselves; they have no conformity with the things. On the contrary, when convention has once attached a first idea to a word, it is to induce erroneously to use it for substances of a different type; the derivatives, the compounds of this word, are the only names that conform to the congenerate nature of these beings. Thus, the denomination *oil of vitriol* is contrary to the rule, because it carries the sign of an oily characteristic that is totally foreign to this substance. Thus, the name *vitriolic acid* being given, all the bodies formed with the solvent are vitriols."

166. "The primitive name should preferably go to the simplest being, to the whole being, to the unaltered being. The expression which modifies and particularizes, must be an epithet, or of an analogous form. *This is the natural procedure of ideas, which it is important to maintain.*"

167. "The denomination of a chemical compound is clear and exact only insofar as it recalls the constituent parts using names that are in conformity with their natures."

168. "Containing the major analogical denominations, and some examples of the formation of compound names."

169. "We will go no farther; we will say only that when we allowed ourselves these reflections, we had no more intention of combatting the new theory than we had of defending the old. The function that the Academy charged us with, forces us to examine without passion, to leave all partiality aside, all personal

opinion, and to put ourselves on guard as much against the prestige of the new as against the prejudices that result so naturally from a long system of studies and from an habitual way of looking at things.

"We therefore believe that this new theory will have to submit to the test of time, to the shock of experiment. Then it will no longer be a theory; it will become a sequence of truths, or an error. In the first case, it will provide one more solid base for human knowledge; in the second case, it will join in oblivion all the other physical theories and systems that went before it. It is with this view in mind that we believe that the table of the new chemical nomenclature, with the memoirs that are attached to it, can be printed and made public under the privilege of the Academy; it must be done in such a way, however, that no one can infer that the Academy either adopts or rejects the new theory. The Academy must, through the impartiality that has always been at the foundation of its conduct, wait for the test of time and the physicists."

170. "received, in 1760, the grand prize in French discourse for Rhetoric."

171. "(Guyton de Morveau) himself felt that, in a science which is, in a way, still in a state of mobility, which proceeds by giant steps towards its perfection, in which new theories are presenting themselves, it was extremely difficult to form a language which would be appropriate to the different systems and which would satisfy all opinions without adopting any one in particular."

172. "The love of literary property gave way in (Guyton de Morveau) to the love of science. In the conferences which were set up, *we all attempted to imbue ourselves with the same state of mind. We forgot what had been done, what we ourselves had done, so as to see only what had to be done.* It is only after having passed all the parts of chemistry in review several times, after having profoundly meditated on the metaphysics of languages, and on the relationship of ideas to words, that we dared to form a plan."

173. "committed to treating chemistry in all its parts"

174. "In this domain, Lavoisier innovated nothing. He adopted the concepts of his time without changing them; he could do this without inconvenience, since these theories did not influence his personal work in any way. But one could not expect him to bring about important transformations. If the multiple works on affinity led to the atomic theory, it was the work of the researchers of the 19th century to give birth to physical chemistry. In spite of his genius, Lavoisier could act and think only as a man of the 18th century."

175. "Let us listen one more time to Servan: 'When you will thus have formed the chain of ideas in the heads of your citizens, you will be able to boast that you lead them around and that you are their masters. Despair and time eat away at chains of iron and steel, but they are powerless against the habitual union of ideas; they only pull them tighter. On the soft fibers of the brain is founded the unshakeable base of the strongest empires.' "

176. "Languages do not have as an object (as is commonly believed) only to express ideas and images, using signs. They are, even more, true analytic methods, with whose aid we proceed from the known to the unknown, up to a certain point in the manner of mathematicians. Let us try to develop this idea. Algebra is a veritable language. Like all languages, it has representative signs, its own method, its own grammar—if one can be allowed to use this expression. Hence, an analytic

method is a language, a language is an analytic method, and these two expressions are, in a certain sense, synonymous."

177. "The art of reasoning is the art of analyzing."

178. "When we give ourselves over for the first time to the study of a science, we are, with respect to this science, in a state that is very similar to that of children, and the path that we have to follow is precisely the one that nature follows for the formation of their ideas. Just as for a child, the idea is the result, the effect of a sensation; the sensation causes the idea to be born; in the same way, for whomever is beginning the study of the physical sciences, ideas must be only an immediate consequence of either experiment or observation."

179. "If you have some difficulty in familiarizing yourself with the method that I am teaching, it is not because the method is difficult. It can't be, because it is *natural.*"

180. "In both the study and the practice of the sciences, the false judgments that we draw impinge on neither our existence nor our well-being. *No physical interest obliges us to rectify them. Imagination, on the contrary, which tends to carry us continually beyond the truth, or the confidence that we have in ourselves, which touches our vanity so closely*—both tempt us to draw conclusions that do not derive directly from the facts. It is therefore not surprising that, in the times closest to the cradle of chemistry, people hypothesized rather than concluding; that the suppositions that were transmitted from age to age were transformed into prejudice; and that these prejudices were adopted and considered as fundamental truths, even by very good minds."

181. "The only way to prevent these slips is to suppress, or at least to simplify as much as possible, the reasoning which comes from ourselves, and which alone is capable of causing us to stray. We must put it continually to the test of experience, we must keep only those facts which are truths given by nature, and which cannot mislead us. We must seek truth only in the sequence of experiments and observations, above all in the order in which they are presented, in the same way that mathematicians reach the solution to a problem through the simple arrangement of the givens, and by reducing their reasoning to such simple operations and short judgments, that they never lose sight of the evidence which serves as their guide."

182. "This method, which it is so important to introduce into the study and the teaching of chemistry, is tightly linked to the reform of its nomenclature. A well-formed language, a language in which one will have captured the successive and natural order of ideas, will bring about a necessary and even prompt revolution in the manner of teaching. *It will not allow those who profess chemistry to diverge from the march of nature. They will have either to reject the nomenclature, or else to follow irresistibly the route that it will have marked out. It is in this way that the logic of the sciences is essentially a function of their language,* and although this truth is not new, and although it has already been asserted, as it is not sufficiently widespread, we thought it necessary to retrace it here."

183. "The perfection of the nomenclature of chemistry, considered from this point of view, consists in rendering the ideas and the facts in their exact truth, without suppressing anything that they present; above all, without adding anything: it must be nothing more than a faithful mirror of what nature presents to us."

184. "One should be sufficiently aware, without our having to insist on the

proofs, that the language of chemistry, as it exists today, was not formed according to these principles. How could it have been, in the centuries where the path of experimental physics had not yet been indicated, where imagination counted for all, observation for almost nothing, and where everyone was ignorant even of the method for studying?"

185. "But provided that it has been undertaken using good principles, provided that it is *a method for naming, rather than a nomenclature,* it will naturally adapt itself to the work that will be done later. It will mark in advance the place and the name for the new substances that it will be possible to discover, and will require only a few local and particular reforms."

186. "They will name to know more than to recognize, and the classification of elementary substances will reveal itself to be motivated by an active thought process that designates a regular place for an object before finding the object."

187. "Their method appears to have still another advantage: *it fixes in advance* the characters that will represent substances that will be discovered, such that there will no longer be anything *arbitrary* about the formation of signs, and so that a complete table of these characters *will present at once what has been done in chemistry and what remains to be done."*

188. "But our imagination must not have told us more than what nature teaches us about it."

189. "This new theory, this table, are the work of four men who are justly famous in the sciences. But what theory ever owed its birth to men more endowed with genius, to more sustained and concerted work? What other ever brought together the men of knowledge by a series of more elegant experiments, by a greater mass of brilliant facts, than the doctrine of phlogiston? This object therefore merits the greatest attention; it demands equally the cooperation of time to be discussed well, thoroughly appreciated, well judged. This judgment is not the affair of a single day, because it is not in a single day that one will overturn accepted ideas in a science which, such as it is, has expressed itself with clarity for a half-century."

190. *"Theory,* in one sense, is an *anticipatory hypothesis* concerning the nature and the internal contributions of the explored object: in this sense, it has been said with reason that, in the physical sciences, theory necessarily preceded invention. But in another sense, more tied to the etymology, the word 'theory' means the *comprehensive contemplation* of an ensemble that has been explored beforehand, *the general vision* of a system ruled by a judicious order.

"The method is hidden in the style of the critical operation, and becomes perfectly evident only once the trajectory has been completely traversed. Method, through the knowledge of the particular, should tend toward the generalization of its discoveries. At the same time, it must arrive at a point where it understands itself. It makes its way towards a theory (in the sense of *theoria,* comprehensive contemplation). *Yet this generalization of critical knowledge remains in a state of perpetual becoming."*

191. "This energetic and constantly alert will to (from that point on) always turn a fresh and young eye on the material world explored by chemistry, had to result in a completely new philosophy of science and of matter, at the same time that it brought about a permanent modification in the mental orientation of the man of knowledge. We will try to maintain contact between his experimentation,

his precise observations made using measuring instruments, and the theoretical systematization."

192. "We have observed that the ear accustoms itself promptly to new words, above all when they are linked to a general and reasoned system."

193. "It is obvious that the only thing that all these theories have in common is the word 'phlogiston,' which they have kept, and which is in some ways their rallying point. It is obvious that the phlogiston of the French is not that of the Germans, even less that of the English, and that these different theories, far from being able to be called *old theories,* are, on the contrary, more modern than the doctrine that is characterized by the name of the *new theory.*"

194. "I had no other object, when I undertook this work, than to develop the memoir that I read at the public session of the Academy of Sciences for the month of April 1787, concerning the necessity to reform and perfect the language of chemistry. While I thought that I was dealing only with the nomenclature, while I had no other object than to perfect the language of chemistry, my work transformed itself insensibly in my hands, without my being able to defend myself against it, into an elementary treatise of chemistry."

195. "Mathematicians reach the solution of a problem through the simple arrangement of the givens, by reducing their reasoning to such simple operations, to such short judgments, that they never lose sight of the evidence which serves as their guide."

196. "These inconveniences are tied less to the nature of things than to the form of the teaching, and this is why I determined to give chemistry a procedure that seemed to me to conform better to that of nature. But I think that (the difficulties) that remain do not belong to the order that I prescribed for myself: they are, rather, a result of the state of imperfection that chemistry is still in. This science still shows numerous lacunae, which interrupt the series of facts, and which require embarrassing and difficult adjustments. It does not have elementary geometry's advantage, which is to be a complete science, whose parts are all tightly linked to each other."

197. "It is easy to see how the sciences of language distribute themselves in the classical age: on the one side is Rhetoric, which deals with figures and tropes, that is, the manner in which language spatializes itself inside verbal signs. On the other side is Grammar, which deals with articulation and order, that is, the manner in which the analysis of representation sets itself into a successive series. Rhetoric defines that spatiality of representation, as it is born with language. Grammar defines, for each language, the order which distributes this spatiality in time. This is why Grammar presumes the rhetorical nature of languages, even the most primitive and spontaneous ones."

198. "Chemistry, by subjecting the different bodies in nature to experiment, has as its object to decompose them and to be able to *examine separately the different substances that enter into combination.*"

199. "Chemistry proceeds, therefore, towards its goal and its perfection by dividing, subdividing, and resubdividing again, and we do not know what the end point of its successes will be."

200. "reasoning to such simple operations, to such short judgments, that (the men of knowledge) never lose sight of the evidence which serves as their guide."

201. "The 'known' that he starts from is neither an ensemble of metaphysical

postulates posed *a priori* for all eternity with consequences that unfold or are deduced in the mind of the chemist according to an implacable and peaceful necessity. Nor is it the daily world of common sense with its vague intuitions, its little-elaborated judgments, its arbitrary and difficultly reconcilable decrees."

202. "Meanwhile, between the old concept of analysis, which tried to resolve bodies into their constituting principles—each of these principles imposing on the mixture into which it entered the qualities of which it was the carrier—and the modern concept of decomposition, which tries to extract from the complex bodies the diverse ingredients which, recombined, form again into the primitive body, there is a distinct difference. With remarkable insight, Chevreul pointed out that, until the work of Lavoisier, this completely logical and grammatical operation was only a mental analysis, a resolution into notions. True chemical analysis, or the practical separation of indecomposable elements which in combination form the primitive body, is something else entirely."

203. "You will be surprised not to find, in an elementary treatise of chemistry, a chapter concerning the constituent and elementary parts of bodies. Everything that can be said about the number and the nature of the elements is limited, from my point of view, to purely metaphysical discussions. These are indeterminate problems that people propose to solve, that can have an infinity of solutions, but it is likely that none of these solutions is in accordance with nature. I will therefore content myself with saying that if, by the term 'elements,' one means to designate the simple and indivisible molecules that make up the bodies, it is highly likely that we do not know what they are."

204. "We have consequently designated the cause of heat, the eminently elastic fluid that produces it, by the term *caloric. Besides the fact that this expression fulfills our object in the system that we have adopted* (that is, it fits into the structure of the nomenclature), it has yet another advantage, and that is to be able to adapt itself to all sorts of opinions. *Since, rigorously speaking, we are not even obliged to suppose that caloric is a real substance, it suffices,* as will be seen better by reading what follows, *that it is some kind of a repulsive cause* that separates the molecules of matter, and one can thus envisage its effects in an abstract and mathematical manner."

205. "I mean by this expression—*specific caloric* of bodies—the quantity of caloric respectively necessary to raise the temperature of several bodies of equal weight the same number of degrees. This quantity of caloric depends on the distance between the molecules of bodies, of their greater or lesser adherence to each other, and it is this distance, or rather the space that results from the distance, that has been named, as I have already pointed out, *the capacity to contain caloric."*

206. "It is probable that the separation of the molecules of a body by caloric is itself a result of a combination of different attractive forces, and it is the result of these forces that we seek to express in a more concise manner more adequate to the state of imperfection of our knowledge, when we say that caloric transmits a repulsive force to the molecules of a body."

207. "All these individual facts, of which it would be easy for me to multiply examples, authorize me to make what I asserted above into a general principle: that nearly all bodies in nature are capable of existing in three different states— in a state of solidity, of liquidity, and aeriform—and that these three states of the

same body depend on the quantity of caloric which is combined with it. I will, from now on, designate these aeriform fluids using the generic name of *gas,* and I will consequently say that, in every kind of gas, *one must distinguish between the caloric which functions, in some way, as a solvent,* and the substance that is combined with it and forms its base."

208. "To truly grasp what takes place in salt solutions, one must know that two effects complicate each other in most of these operations: solution by water, and solution by caloric. As the distinction provides the explanation for most of the phenomena which have to do with solution, I will insist on this so that it will be understood thoroughly."

209. "This rigorous law, which I had to stick to, that I would never reach conclusions beyond what the experiments present, and that I would never supplement the silence of the facts, did not allow me to include in this work the part of chemistry most likely, perhaps, to become one day an exact science: this is the part that deals with the chemical affinities or elective attractions. Geoffroy, Gellert, Bergman, Scheele, de Morveau, Kirwan, and many others have already assembled a multitude of individual facts that only await the place that is to be assigned to them. But the principal givens are lacking; or at least, the ones that we do have are not yet sufficiently precise nor sufficiently certain to become the fundamental basis on which such an important part of chemistry must rest. The science of affinities is, moreover, to ordinary chemistry what transcendental geometry is to elementary geometry, and I didn't think that I should complicate these simple and easy elements (that are meant to be within reach of a very large number of readers) with such great difficulties.

"Perhaps a sentiment of pride has, without my acknowledging it to myself, given some weight to these reflections. Mr. de Morveau is about to publish the article 'Affinity' in the *Methodical Encyclopedia,* and I had many reasons to fear working in competition with him."

210. "to accustom (the students) early on to not accept any word without attaching an idea to it."

211. "These inconveniences are linked less to the nature of things than to pedagogical form, and this is what determined me to provide chemistry with a process which seemed to me to be more in conformity with that of nature."

212. "(The discourse of the Ideologues) provided, in effect, a kind of general recipe for the exercise of power over men: the mind, as surface for the inscription of power, with semiology as the instrument; the subjection of bodies through the control of ideas."

213. "But I wish to warn young people against a prejudice which must be natural in beginners. Because a method of reasoning is supposed to teach us to reason, we are led to believe that at each occasion for reasoning, the first thing to do is to think of the rules according to which it is supposed to be done, but we are mistaken. *It is not up to us to think about the rules; it is up to them to lead us without our thinking about them. One would never speak if, before beginning each sentence, it were necessary to deal with the grammar. Now, the art of reasoning, like all languages, is spoken well only insofar as it is spoken naturally.* Meditate on the method, and meditate on it well. But do not think about it any more when you want to think of something else. One day it will become familiar to you: then,

always with you, it will observe your thoughts, which will proceed by themselves; it will watch over them to prevent them from straying. This is all that you must expect from the method.

"If, in the beginning, you have some difficulty becoming familiar with the method that I teach, it is not because it is difficult. It cannot be, since it is natural."

BIBLIOGRAPHY

Abrahams, Harold J. "Lavoisier's Proposals for French Education." *Journal of Chemical Education* 31 (1954): 413-16.

Abrahams, Harold J. "A Summary of Lavoisier's Proposals for Training in Science and Medicine." *Bulletin of the History of Medicine* 32, no. 5 (1958): 389-407.

Acton, H. B. "The Philosophy of Language in Revolutionary France." In *Studies in Philosophy*, ed. J. N. Findlay, 156ff. London: Oxford University Press, 1966.

Albury, William Randall. "The Logic of Condillac and the Structure of French Chemical and Biological Theory, 1780-1801." Ph.D. diss., Johns Hopkins University, 1972.

Anderson, Wilda. "Diderot's Laboratory of Sensibility." *Yale French Studies* 67 (1984).

Anderson, Wilda. "Dispensing with the Fixed Point." *History and Theory* 22, no. 3 (1983): 264-77.

Auroux, Sylvain. *L'Encyclopédie: "Grammaire" et "langue" au XVIIIe siècle*. Paris: Mame, 1973.

Auroux, Sylvain. *La Sémiotique des encyclopédistes*. Paris: Payot, 1979.

Bachelard, Gaston. *La Formation de l'esprit scientifique*. Paris: Vrin, 1926; rpt. 1975.

Bachelard, Gaston. *Le Pluralisme cohérent de la chimie moderne*. Paris: Vrin, 1973.

Barthes, Roland. *Le Degré zéro de l'écriture: Suivi de nouveaux essais critiques*. Paris: Seuil, 1972.

Barthes, Roland. "Les Planches de *l'Encyclopédie*." In *Degré zéro de l'écriture*, 89-105.

Barthes, Roland. *Sade, Fourier, Loyola*. Paris: Seuil, 1971.

Bergman, Torbern. *Physical and Chemical Essays*. Tr. Edmund Cullen. London: J. Murray and Wm. Creech, 1788.

Berkenhout, John. *First Lines of the Theory and Practice of Philosophical Chemistry*. London: n.p., 1788.

Berthelot, Marcellin. *La Révolution chimique: Lavoisier*. Paris: Alcan, 1890.

Boas, Marie. *The Scientific Renaissance, 1450-1630*. New York: Harper, 1962.

Boyle, Robert. *The Sceptical Chymist*. London: n.p., 1661.

Cajori, Florian. "On the History of Caloric," *Isis* 4 (1922): 483-92.

Carlid, Göte, and Johan Nordstrom, eds. *Torbern Bergman's Foreign Correspondence*. Stockholm: Almqvist and Wiksell, 1972.

Carter, Richard B. *Descartes' Medical Philosophy: The Organic Solution to the Mind-Body Problem*. Baltimore: Johns Hopkins University Press, 1983.

Cassirer, Ernst. "Influence of Language upon the Development of Scientific Thought." *Journal of Philosophy* 39, no. 12 (1942): 309-27.

Clagett, Marshall, ed. *Critical Problems in the History of Science*. Madison: University of Wisconsin Press, 1969.

Coleby, Leslie J.-M. *The Chemical Studies of P. J. Macquer*. London: n.p., 1938.

Conant, J. B. *The Overthrow of the Phlogiston Theory*. Cambridge: Harvard University Press, 1950.

Condillac, Etienne Bonnot l'Abbé de. " 'De l'analyse du discours,' extrait du *Cours d'étude pour l'instruction du prince de Parme"* (1775). In Porset, *Varia Linguistica,* 145-211.

Condillac, Etienne Bonnot l'Abbé de. *Essai sur l'origine des connaissances humaines.* Preceded by "L'Archéologie des frivoles," by Jacques Derrida. Paris: Galilée, 1973.

Condillac, Etienne Bonnot l'Abbé de. *La Logique; ou, Les premiers développemens de l'Art de Penser, ouvrage élémentaire, que le Conseil préposé aux Ecoles palatines avoit demandé et qu'il a honoré de son approbation.* Geneva: n.p., 1785.

Condillac, Etienne Bonnot l'Abbé de. *Oeuvres de Condillac, revues, corrigées par l'Auteur, imprimées sur ses manuscrits autographes, et augmentées de La Langue des Calculs, ouvrage posthume. Cours d'études pour l'Instruction du Prince de Parme.* Vol. 3. *Traité des sensations.* Vol. 8. *L'Art de raisonner.* Vol. 23. *La Langue des calculs.* Paris: Houel, 1798.

Contant, Jean-Paul. *L'Enseignement de la chimie au Jardin royal des plantes de Paris.* Cahors: Coneslant, 1952.

Crosland, Maurice. *Historical Studies in the Language of Chemistry.* Cambridge: Harvard University Press, 1962.

Dagognet, François. "Présentation du 'Discours préliminaire.'" *Cahiers pour l'analyse* 9 (1968): 194ff.

Dagognet, François. "Sur Lavoisier." *Cahiers pour l'analyse* 9 (1968): 178-94.

Dagognet, François. *Tableaux et langages de la chimie.* Paris: Seuil, 1969.

Darnton, Robert. *The Business of the Enlightenment: A Publishing History of the Encyclopédie, 1775-1800.* Cambridge: Harvard University Press/Belknap, 1979.

Daumas, Maurice. "La Chimie dans l'Encyclopédie et dans l'Encyclopédie méthodique." *Revue d'histoire des sciences* 4 (1951): 334-43.

Daumas, Maurice. *Lavoisier: Théoricien et expérimentateur.* Paris: Presses universitaires de France, 1955.

Degérando, Joseph. *Des Signes et de l'art de penser.* Paris: n.p., 1799.

Derrida, Jacques. *De la grammatologie.* Paris: Minuit, 1967.

Descartes, René. *Discours de la méthode pour bien conduire sa raison et chercher la vérité dans les sciences* (1637). Ed. Etienne Gilson. Paris: Vrin, 1925; rpt. 1976.

Descartes, René. *Oeuvres philosophiques.* Ed. Charles Adam and Paul Tannery. Paris: Léopold Cerf, 1905.

Diderot, Denis. "Eloge de Richardson." In *Oeuvres esthétiques,* ed. Paul Vernière, 23-50. Paris: Garnier, 1965.

Diderot, Denis. *Introduction à la chimie.* Ed. Charles Henry. Paris: Dentu, 1887.

Diderot, Denis. *Le Neveu de Rameau.* In *Oeuvres romanesques,* ed. Paul Vernière, 395-492. Paris: Garnier, 1962.

Diderot, Denis. *Oeuvres complètes.* Ed. Jacques Proust, Henri Varloot, and Herbert Dieckmann. Paris: Hermann, 1976–.

Diderot, Denis. "Pensées sur l'interprétation de la nature." In *Oeuvres philosophiques,* ed. Paul Vernière, 175-245. Paris: Garnier, 1965.

Diderot, Denis. "Le Rêve de d'Alembert." Ibid., 249-388.

Diderot, Denis; Jean le Rond D'Alembert, et al. *L'Encyclopédie; ou, Dictionnaire raisonné des sciences, des arts, et des métiers.* 2d ed. Berne and Lausanne: Sociétés Typographiques, 1781.

Duchet, Michèle, and Michèle Jalley, eds. *Langue et langages de Leibnitz à l'Encyclopédie.* Paris: 10/18, 1977.

Ehrard, Jean. *L'Idée de nature en France à l'aube des Lumières.* Paris: Flammarion, 1970.

Fleck, Ludwik. *The Genesis and Development of a Scientific Fact* (1935). Ed. Thaddeus J. Trenn and Robert K. Merton. Tr. Fred Bradley and Thaddeus J. Trenn. Chicago: University of Chicago Press, 1979.

Foucault, Michel. *L'Archéologie des sciences.* Paris: Gallimard, 1969.

Foucault, Michel. *Les Mots et les choses.* Paris: Gallimard, 1966.

Foucault, Michel. "Qu'est-ce qu'un auteur?" *Bulletin de la Société française de philosophie,* July-September 1969, 73-104. Tr. in *Textual Strategies,* ed. Josué Harari, 141-60. Ithaca: Cornell University Press, 1979.

Foucault, Michel. *Surveiller et punir.* Paris: Gallimard, 1975.

Geoffroy, Etienne-François. "Tables des affinités." *Mémoires de l'Académie Royale des Sciences,* 1718, 202-12.

Gillispie, Charles Coulton. "The *Encyclopédie* and the Jacobin Philosophy of Science: A Study in Ideas and Consequences." In Clagett, *Critical Problems in the History of Science,* 255-89.

Gough, J. B. "Lavoisier's Theory of the Gaseous State." In Woolf, *The Analytic Spirit,* 15-39.

Guédon, Jean-Claude. "Chimie et matérialisme: La Stratégie anti-Newtonienne de Diderot." *Dix-huitième siècle* 11 (1979): 185-200.

Guédon, Jean-Claude. "Le Status épistémologique de la réaction chimique de *l'Encyclopédie* à Gay-Lussac" In *Colloque Gay-Lussac,* 103-31. Paris: Ecole Polytechnique, 1980.

Guerlac, Henry. *Antoine-Laurent Lavoisier: Chemist and Revolutionary.* New York: Scribners, 1968; American Council of Learned Societies, 1975.

Guerlac, Henry. "Joseph Priestley's First Papers on Gases and Their Reception in France." *Journal of the History of Medicine and Allied Sciences* 12, no. 1 (1957): 1-12.

Guerlac, Henry. *Lavoisier—The Crucial Year: The Background and Origin of His First Experiments on Combustion in 1772.* Ithaca: Cornell University Press, 1961.

Guyton de Morveau, Baron Louis-Bernard. "Sur les dénominations chymiques, la nécessité d'en perfectionner le système, & les règles pour y parvenir." *Observations sur la physique, sur l'histoire naturelle & sur les arts & métiers* 19 (1782): 370-82.

Guyton de Morveau, Baron Louis-Bernard; Antoine-Laurent Lavoisier; Claude Louis Berthollet; and Antoine F. de Fourcroy. *Méthode de nomenclature chymique.* Paris: Cuchet, 1787.

Hahn, Roger. *The Anatomy of a Scientific Institution: The Paris Academy of Sciences, 1666-1803.* Berkeley and Los Angeles: University of California Press, 1971.

Hahn, Roger. "Scientific Research as an Occupation in Eighteenth-Century Paris." *Minerva* 13, no. 4 (1975): 501-13.

Hall, A. R. *The Scientific Revolution, 1500-1800. The Formation of the Modern Scientific Attitude.* Boston: Beacon, 1962.

Hall, Marie Boas. "The History of the Concept of Element." In *John Dalton and the Progress of Science,* 21-39. New York: Barnes & Noble, 1968.

Hannaway, Owen. *The Chemist and the Word.* Baltimore: Johns Hopkins University Press, 1975.

Hempel, Carl G. *Aspects of Scientific Explanation and Other Essays in the Philosophy of Science.* New York: Free Press, 1965.

Holton, Gerald. *Thematic Origins of Scientific Thought.* Boston: Harvard University Press, 1973.

Kirwan, Richard. *Essay on Phlogiston, and the Constitution of Acids.* London: J. Johnston, 1789.

Kuhn, Thomas S. *The Essential Tension: Selected Studies in Scientific Tradition and Change.* Chicago: University of Chicago Press, 1977.

Kuhn, Thomas S. *The Structure of Scientific Revolutions.* Chicago: University of Chicago Press, 1972.

Lavoisier, Antoine-Laurent. "Dans lequel on a pour objet de prouver que l'eau n'est point une substance simple, un élément proprement dit, mais qu'elle est susceptible de décomposition et de recomposition." *Mémoires de l'Académie Royale des sciences,* 1781.

Lavoisier, Antoine-Laurent. *Mémoire sur la chaleur. Lu à l'Académie Royale des Sciences le 28 juin 1783. Par Mm. Lavoisier et de la Place, de la même Académie.* Paris: Imprimerie Royale, 1783.

Lavoisier, Antoine-Laurent. "Mémoire sur l'existence de l'air dans l'acide nitreux, et sur les moyens de décomposer et de recomposer cet acide." *Recueil de Mémoires et d'observations sur la formation et sur la fabrication du salpêtre.* Paris: Lacombe, 1776.

Lavoisier, Antoine-Laurent. *Oeuvres de Lavoisier.* Paris: Imprimerie Impériale, 1862.

Lavoisier, Antoine-Laurent. *Opuscules physiques et chymiques.* Paris: Durand et Didot le jeune, 1774.

Lavoisier, Antoine-Laurent. "Réflexions sur le phlogistique, pour servir de suite à la théorie de la combustion et de la calcination, publiée en 1777." *Mémoires de l'Académie Royale des sciences,* 1783.

Lavoisier, Antoine-Laurent. *Traité élémentaire de chimie. Présenté dans un ordre nouveau et d'après les découvertes modernes, avec figures.* Paris: Cuchet, 1789.

Leicester, H. R. *The Historical Background of Chemistry.* New York: Dover, 1936.

Locke, John. *An Essay Concerning Human Understanding* (1690). 4th ed. (1699 dated 1700). Ed. Alexander Campbell Frazer. London: Clarendon, 1894; New York: Dover, 1959.

Lovejoy, A. O. *The Great Chain of Being.* Cambridge: Harvard University Press, 1936.

McKie, Douglas. *Antoine Lavoisier: Scientist, Economist, Social Reformer.* New York: Schuman, 1952.

McKie, Douglas. "The Eighteenth-Century Revolution in Chemistry." *Nature* 167: 460-62.

McKie, Douglas. "Macquer, The First Lexicographer of Chemistry," *Endeavour* 16, no. 63 (1957): 133-36.

Macquer, Pierre Joseph. *Dictionnaire de chymie.* Paris: Lacombe, 1766; 2d ed., 1778.

Macquer, Pierre Joseph. *Eléméns de chymie-pratique.* Paris: Jean-Thomas Hérissant, 1756.

Macquer, Pierre Joseph. *Elémens de chymie-théorique.* Paris: Didot le jeune, 1756.

Macquer, P. J.; J. P. Cadet; and A.-L. Lavoisier. *Expériences sur le diamant.* Paris: n.p., 1772."

Mayer, Jean. *Diderot, homme de science.* Rennes: Imprimerie Bretonne, 1959.

Meldrum, A. N. *The Eighteenth-Century Revolution in Science: the First Phase.* Calcutta: n.p., 1930.

Meldrum, A. N. "Lavoisier's Work on the Nature of Water and the Supposed Transformation of Water into Earth (1768-1773)." *Archeion* 14 (1932): 246-47.

Metzger, Hélène. *Les Doctrines chimiques en France du début du XVIIe à la fin du XVIIIe siècle.* Paris: Presses universitaires de France, 1923.

Metzger, Hélène. "L'évolution de l'esprit scientifique en chimie de Leméry à Lavoisier." *Thales* 3 (1936): 107-13.

Metzger, Hélène. "La Littérature chimique française aux 17e et 18e siècles." *Thales* 2 (1935): 162-66.

Metzger, Hélène. *Newton, Stahl, Boerhaave.* Paris: Blanchard, 1930.

Metzger, Hélène. *La Philosophie de la matière chez Lavoisier.* Paris: n.p., 1953.

Morris, R. J. "Lavoisier on Air and Fire: The Memoir of July 1772." *Isis* 60 (1969): 374-82.

Mosconi, Jean. "Analyse et Genèse: Regards sur la théorie du devenir de l'entendement au XVIIIe siècle." *Cahiers pour l'analyse* 4 (1966): 53-88.

Newton, Sir Isaac. *Opticks: or, A Treatise of the Reflections, Refractions, Inflections, and Colours of Light* (1704). London: Innys, 1718.

Neville, R. G. "Macquer and the First Chemical Dictionary, 1766." *Journal of Chemical Education* 43 (1966): 486-90.

Partington, J. R. *The Composition of Water.* London: Bell, 1928.

Partington, J. R. *A History of Chemistry.* London: n.p., 1962.

Partington, J. R., and Douglas McKie. "Historical Studies on the Phlogiston Theory, IV: Last Phases of the Theory." *Annals of Science* 4 (1939): 113-49.

Paty, Michel. "La Matière dérobée: Sur les lieux et modes d'intervention réciproque de la physique et de la philosophie." *La Pensée* 202 (1978): 16-37.

Perrin, C. E. "The Triumph ᶜᶠ the Antiphlogistians." In Woolf, *The Analytic Spirit,* 40-63.

Porset, Charles, ed. *Varia Linguistica.* Bordeaux: Ducros, 1970.

Prigogine, Ilya, and Isabelle Stengers. *La Nouvelle Alliance: Métamorphose de la science.* Paris: Gallimard, 1979.

Roger, Jacques. *Les Sciences de la vie dans la pensée française du XVIIIe siècle.* Paris: Colin, 1963.

Scheler, Lucien. *Lavoisier et le principe chimique.* Paris: n.p., 1964.

Schofield, Robert, ed. *A Scientific Autobiography of Joseph Priestley (1733-1804).* Cambridge: MIT, 1966.

Screech, M. A. *Montaigne and Melancholy.* Susquehanna: Susquehanna University Press, 1984.

Serres, Michel. "L'Histoire des sciences." In *Hermès V: Le Passage du Nord-Ouest,* 131-64. Paris: Minuit, 1980.

Servan, J. M. *Discours sur l'administration de la justice criminelle.* Paris: n.p., 1767.

Shaftesbury, Anthony Ashley Cooper, Third Earl of. *Characteristics of Men, Manners, Opinions, Times.* 3d ed. London: John Darly, 1723.

Smeaton, W. A. "Macquer." In *Dictionary of Scientific Biography,* ed. Charles Gillis-pie, 8: 618-24. New York: Scribner's, 1973.

Starobinski, Jean. *L'Oeil vivant II: La relation critique.* Paris: Gallimard, 1970.

Starobinski, Jean. "Remarques sur *l'Encyclopédie.*" *Revue de métaphysique et de morale* 75 (1970): 284-91.

Venel, Gabriel François. "Chymie." *Encyclopédie,* 8:12-62.

Voltaire, Jean-Marie Arouet, dit de. *Lettres écrites de Londres sur les anglais et autres sujets.* Basle (London): n.p., 1734.

White, Hayden. *Metahistory: The Historical Imagination in Nineteenth-Century Europe.* Baltimore: Johns Hopkins University Press, 1973.

White, Hayden. *Tropics of Discourse: Essays in Cultural Criticism.* Baltimore: Johns Hopkins University Press, 1978.

Williams, L. Pearce. "The Politics of Science in the French Revolution." In Clagett, *Critical Problems in the History of Science,* 291-308.

Williams, L. Pearce. "Science, Education, and the French Revolution." *Isis* 44 (1953): 311-30.

Woolf, Harry, ed. *The Analytic Spirit: Essays in the History of Science.* Ithaca: Cornell University Press, 1981.

INDEX

The Johns Hopkins University Press

BETWEEN THE LIBRARY AND THE LABORATORY

*This book was set in ITC Garamond type by EPS Group,
Inc., from a design by Susan P. Fillion. It was printed
on 50-lb. Glatfelter offset paper and bound in Holliston
Roxite A cloth by Thomson-Shore, Inc.*

33-34 :   effect on reader (rhetorical)
              to what extent can this rhetoric /
u*   reader-response be thought
              historically

67-68 !